TURKEY and EUROPE
in
HISTORY

Published by EREN Press, İstanbul, Turkey

İstanbul, April 2006

ISBN 975-6372-24-9

Printed in the Republic of Turkey

For information, address:

EREN Yayıncılık
Kitap-Dağıtım Tic. ve San. Ltd. Şti.
Tünel, İstiklâl Cad. Sofyalı Sokak No. 34
80050 BEYOĞLU – İSTANBUL
Tel.: (212) 251 28 58 – (212) 252 05 60
Fax: (212) 243 30 16
e-mail: eren@eren.com.tr
www.eren.com.tr

Production by Muhittin Salih Eren

Halil İnalcık

TURKEY and EUROPE

in

HISTORY

Sevgili Ergun,
Tarihimize yeni bir açıdan bakmamızı
sağlayacak güzel bir kitap.
Severek okuyacağını sanıyorum.

26. 03. 07

⊆ EREN

to Nur Bilge Criss

Transliteration

j, **dj** = in Turkish pronounced **c** as **j** in jungle

Arabic letter of ʿayn ع is rendered ʿ and hemze ʾ as in *tāʾife*.

Persian Izâfe always as **i** (not ı) *Bāb-i Ālī* ı as in *kapı*.

CONTENTS

B
Turkey and Europe

Preface

From the midst of the fifteenth century on the Ottoman-Turkish Empire played a crucial role in shaping European history. This factor has not been weaved into Western historiography to its detriment, because explaining concepts such as raison d'etat, realpolitik, balance of power or even European identity remain somewhat shortchanged without according the Ottoman-Turkish Empire a role in the evolution as well as functioning of these concepts. Mutual systemic influences are a foregone conclusion however overlooked. This volume comprises nine research articles on the basic characteristics of the Ottoman Empire and its political/economic relations with Europe, published previously, but updated with further evidence.

The first article is an evaluation of Max Weber's theory, which depicts the Ottoman state system as an "arbitrary patrimonialism" in comparison to the patrimonial states of Europe. Weber's categorization reflects the overwhelming European biases concerning the Ottoman state.

The second article is an attempt at periodization in synchrony with European history, which amalgamates current research. Reciprocity with "the outside" is focused upon as the major basis of Ottoman culture.

The third article analyzes an 18th century socio-political phenomenon, the rise of the provincial gentry, its evolution and attempts at imposing their privileges on the central government in the form of a covenant. This process ended in dismal failure.

The fourth article addresses the issue of duality in the state and social institutions, which emerged as Western and Islamic types emanating from the Westernization reform movements of the 19th century.

The fifth article discusses the Westernization-modernization concepts of the Atatürk era.

The sixth article is a tour of the horizon from 1500 to 1815 on interactions beween Anatolia and Europe as well as on the effects of the Ottoman Empire on the European state systems and their evolution.

The seventh article is a general evaluation of the impact of the Ottoman Empire as a great power in the formation of modern Europe. (See article 9 for details).

The eight article scrutinizes the rise of Russia in Eastern Europe and the struggles against this parvenu by the Crimean Khanate and the Ottoman Empire.

Article nine discusses culture and acculturation and places the role of the Ottoman Empire in this context and in the European balance of power during the internecine Italian wars between 1494 and 1559. The essay follows with an evaluation of cultural exchanges between Europe and Ottoman Turkey from the 16th century until the beginning of the 18th century.

The Ottoman Empire is generally depicted and perceived as the adversary and antithesis of Europe and Europeanness in Western historiography because of certain historic reasons such as the Christian crusading tradition, public hostility due to long lasting warfare, cultural estrangement and perhaps because the Ottomans remained outside the Enlightenment process. However, there is much more to it than confrontation. Our research findings presented in this compilation point to the impact of the Ottoman-Turkish Empire in shaping modern Europe, specifically as of the 16th century and socio-cultural exchanges between the two realms through five hundred years of encounter.

These articles were first published in:

I.   "Comments on Sultanism: Max Weber's Typification of Ottoman Polity", in *Occasional Papers,* I, eds.Ch. Issavi and B. Lewis, Princeton 1992, 49-72.

II.   "The Ottoman Empire", *History of Humanity: Scientific and Cultural Development, From the Sixteenth to the Eighteenth Century.* Volume V, Edited by Peter Burke and Halil Inalcik. UNESCO, London: Routledge, 1999, 216-225.

III.   "The Nature of Traditional Society: Turkey", in *Political Modernization in Japan and Turkey,* eds. R.E. Ward and D.A. Rustow, Princeton: PUP, 1968, 49-56.

IV.   "Change in Ottoman Turkish Society", Published for the first time in this volume.

V.   "The Caliphate and Atatürk's *İnkilâb",* in *Belleten* (vol. 46, Ankara 1982), 353-365.

VI.   "Turkey and Europe: A Historical Perspective", *Perceptions, Journal of International Affairs,* II-1 (Ankara, March-May 1997), 76-92.

VII. "The Turkish Impact on the Development of Modern Europe", in *TheOttoman State and its Place in World History,* ed. K.H. Karpat, Leiden: E.J. Brill 1974, 51-58.

VIII. "Struggle for East European Empire, 1400-1700: The Crimean Khanate, Ottomans and the Rise of the Russian Empire", *Turkish Yearbook of International Relations,* vol. XXI (Ankara, 1995), 1-16.

IX.   "Mutual Political and Cultural Influences Between Europe and the Ottomans". *Ottoman Civilization,* eds., Halil İnalcik and Günsel Renda; English Translation and Editing: Ellen Yazar, Mary Işın, İstanbul: Ministry of Culture and Tourism, 2002, 1049-1089.

A

Ottoman-Turkish Empire
and
Modernization

1

Comments on "Sultanism": Max Weber's Typification of the Ottoman Polity

In his analysis of the patrimonial state, Max Weber often refers to the special character of the Ottoman state *as an extreme case of patrimonialism.*[1] In general, he says, the patrimonial state makes administrative and military organization "a purely personal instrument of the master to broaden his arbitrary power."[2] Patrimonial authority, "where it indeed operates primarily on the basis of discretion will be called sultanism, which is distinct from every form of rational authority.[3] "It is also totally different *from estate-type domination (ständische Herrschaft)"* that existed in the medieval west.[4] Patrimonialism, and in the extreme case sultanism, tends to arise whenever traditional domination develops an administration and a military force that are purely personal instruments of the master. "Appropriation by the master personally is a phenomenon of patrimonialism."[5] Then the pre-eminence "turns into personal right." Patrimonial power is something of personal possession. "Where domination is primarily traditional... It will be called *patrimonial authority;* where it indeed operates primarily on the basis of discretion, it will be called sultanism."[6]

"The classic location of sultanism," Weber underlines, "is the Near East."[7] Sultanism is characterized by complete reliance on *military force and arbitrary power, or despotism.* There occurs a complete "differentiation between military and civil subjects," and increasing professionalization of the army. The

---

[1] Max Weber, *Economy and Society: An Outline of Interpretive Sociology,* trans. G. Roth and C. Wittich (Berkeley: UCP, 1978), 1: 231-232; 2:1031.

[2] Ibid.

[3] Ibid.

[4] Cf. N. Machiavelli, *The Prince,* trans. T. G. Bergin (Arlington Heights, 1986 reprint of 1947), pp. 10-11.

[5] In Weber's sociology, the concept of *patrimonialism* is often used synonymously with *power,* or *authority* as "one of the most important elements of communal action" (Weber *Eonomy and Society:* I, 322-324, 336).

[6] Ibid., I; 232.

[7] Ibid., I; 231-232; 2:1017.

Janissary and Mamluk armies, consisting of slaves, were typical examples of such professional armies. They were made part and parcel of the ruler's household and served him with absolute loyalty. Their later transformation is explained by Weber in terms of their having become a "traditional status group" enjoying relative independence from the sultan's patrimonial control. Let us add that in their new function they sided with other traditional groups, such as the ulema and religious orders. The Janissary corps identified itself with Bektashism, one of the independent religious-traditional groups in the empire. It is to be noted that the abolition of the corps and Bektashism occurred at the same time, when Mahmud II embarked upon the restoration of his central patrimonial power in the period from 1812 to 1826.

As one of the most fundamental principles of patrimonial power, the Ottoman ruler in all situations jealously reserved the judicial authority for himself which was administered personally in the central imperial council or, by delegation, through the qadis whom he appointed.[8] In the sultan's law codes it is repeatedly stated that no subject *(ra'iyyet)*, in particular peasants, shall incur any obligation, taxes, services, or fines without a decision rendered in due process of law by his qadi. In striking contrast to the feudal lord's judicial right in the West, no local authority, even in the age of *a'yāns* in the eighteenth century, was allowed to exercise judical power. This was a distinctive characteristic of the centralist and absolutist Ottoman regime.

What made the Ottoman imperial system a "sultanism" in Weber's sense may also be the Ottoman sultan's arrogating political as well as spiritual power in his person. "Domination," Weber stresses, may be based on either physical force or "psychic coercion by distributing or denying religious benefits."[9] The former type, represented by a military monarchy, is the "typical natural form of domination." The latter type, called by Weber "hierocratic organization," is represented by the church. But the Ottoman sultan's simultaneous monopoly of political and spititual powers produced a perfect type of absolute patrimonial rulership. In fact, his dual titulature, sultan-caliph and padishah-khan, signifying the divine and temporal origins of his power, was an expression of his two capacities; however, there was never any real unity between the two.[10] In the classical period, when the patrimonial state (with its dual monopoly) seemed paramount, the ulema were actually prevented from exercising power, and the padishah enacted *'urfī* (state) laws independently from the *sharī'a*

---

[8] Ibid., I: 237.
[9] Ibid., I: 54.
[10] See note 11.

(Islamic religious law).[11] Yet, when the sultan's power began to decline at the turn of the seventeenth century, the ulema, in alliance with other traditional forces, assumed an increasingly dominant place in state affairs. It can be said that this dichotomy actually constituted the underlying conflict in all Islamic states. It was particularly true in the sultanates founded by Turkish dynasties, which were jealous of their absolute patrimonial domination. Still following Weber's course of interpretation, we can suggest that the Ottoman sultans, particularly in the period of "decline," were attempting to compensate for their loss of power by emphasizing their spiritual domination as caliphs and integrating the ulema into their bureaucratic apparatus.

That state power was indeed regarded as the collective property of the ruler's household is quite apparent in early Ottoman history. In line with a Central Asiatic tradition that survived with the Ottomans, the realm was divided among the sons of the reigning ruler.[12] Despite the begotten tradition of disastrous civil wars it remained strong until the time when the notion of state power came to be conceived as an impersonal authority, absolute and indivisible, embodied in the ruler to serve "Islam and (the Islamic) state"*(Dīn u Dawla)*. This development coincided with the transformation of the bureaucracy into a relatively autonomous group and the ulema's assertion of its paramount position within the polity. These groups, supported by public opinion, actually became responsible for the establishment of a new protocol for succession to the throne based on the principle of seniority. Thus, new traditions emerged and became prevalent in the Ottoman polity and modified the "Sultanism" of the Ottoman ruler as the political and social structure evolved (see below "Sultanism, Status Groups" p. 16-25).

Finally, recognizing no legal limits or traditional checks, sultanism can be interpreted as "the pure form of patriarchal domination," or patrimonialism.[13] Realized in its near perfect form in Ottoman sultanism, as the logic of the system required, Ottoman absolutism was taken as the typical form of absolutism by the theoreticians of the sixteenth century. Obviously Weber, living in an age of liberal idealism, could not see the Ottoman regime through the eyes of a Jean Bodin.[14]

---

[11] H. İnalcık, "State, Sovereignty and Law During the Reign of Süleyman I," *Proceedings of the Conference on Süleyman the Magnificent* (Chicago and Princeton, June 1987).

[12] H. İnalcık, "Osmanlılar'da Saltanat Verâset Usûlü ve Türk Hakimiyet Telâkkisiyle İlgisi," *Siyasal Bilgiler Fakültesi Dergisi,* XIV (1959):575-610.

[13] Weber, *Economy and Society,* 2:1009.

[14] L. Valensi, *Venise et la Sublime Porte, la naissance du despote* (Paris, Hachette 1987), pp. 78-86.

Sultanism, Status Groups, and Estate-Type Patrimonialism

As a conduit of regulatory power, Weber affirms,[15] patrimonial domination, whether of the head of the family, a feudal lord, or a patrimonial ruler, is a decisive determinant of social and economic relationships.[16] "Social positions may be established by an autocratic ruler which, in relation to other free strata, are privileged through freedom from taxation and special land rights."[17] The patrimonial state may also appropriate direct control over the economy through "managerial powers."

Weber defines status order as follows:

> The way in which social honor is distributed in a community between typical groups participating in this distribution we call the status order.[18] The market and its processes knows no personal distinctions: "functional" interests dominate it. It knows nothing of honor. The status order means precisely the reverse: stratification in terms of honor and styles of life peculiar to status groups as such.

In this order status groups are stratified according to the principles of their *consumption* of goods as represented by special life styles.[19] In a patrimonial system it is not the legal order but the ruler's favor that conditions honor,[20] and social honor sometimes becomes the basis of domination within a group, as seen with the notables.[21] Honor as social estimation depends on the ruler's distribution of power. Stratification by status is based on honorific and material monopolies. But status honor need not be linked with economic conditions. *Status order is the opposite of class order.* Whereas class is determined exclusively by economic interests conditioned by the commodity of labor markets, status groups are created by power or domination. While property or lack of property are the basic categories of market conditions, property is not always recognized as a status qualification in status order.[22]

---

[15] Weber, *Economy and Society,* 1:131-132; 2:1006-1015.
[16] Ibid., 2: 1071.
[17] Ibid., 2: 927.
[18] Ibid., 2: 936.
[19] Ibid., 2: 937.
[20] Ibid., 2: 1068.
[21] Ibid., 2: 1009.
[22] Ibid., 2: 927, 93.

It is possible, however, that status groups can evolve into a closed caste,[23] and that status can be bound to a class group. But both status and estate-type societies in essence can be viewed as politically stratified. The ruler's will in creating status groups is seen specifically in establishing social positions for a military group which, "in relation to other 'free' strata, are privileged through freedom from taxation and special land rights *(Bodenrecht)*. In return, the incumbents are obliged to undergo military training and to be at the lord's arbitrary or limited disposal for military or administrative purposes."[24] As will be seen, "the military" is the main or exclusive status group in the Middle Eastern patrimonial state.

Although sometimes no distinction is made between estates and status groups in current literature, in Weber these two are clearly distinct concepts. "Feudalism is estate-type patrimonialism,"[25] or estate-type domination involving hereditary fiefs and established siegneurial powers that put limitations on the lord's discretion. In estate-type domination, an individual or an organized group appropriates positions along with the economic advantages associated with them. The contractual allegiance of the feudatory relations, the established rights limiting the lord's discretion, makes an essential difference in estate-teype patrimonialism. There the estate is under the guarantee of a bilateral contract involving the appropriated rights, whereas in pure patrimonialism the ruler's arbitrariness and discretion are the norm.[26]

> In the case of pure patrimonialism, there is complete separation of the functionary from the means of carrying out his function. But exactly the opposite is true of the estate-type of patrimonialism. The person exercising governing powers has personal control of the means of administration.[27]

The difference between the two is best seen in comparing the western fief with the Ottoman *tīmār* and the western landed military aristocracy with the sultan's *kuls,* which included the tīmār-holding *sipāhīs*. A status group can evolve into an estate-type under certain conditions. Also, estate-type patrimonialism may prove to be an evolution toward a bureaucratic state or an obstacle to it.[28]

---

[23] Ibid., 2: 932-33.
[24] Ibid., 2: 1070-71.
[25] Ibid., 1: 232; 2:1036.
[26] Ibid., 2: 1032.
[27] Ibid., 1: 234.
[28] Ibid., 2: 1035, 1037.

In the Ottoman Empire, status groups were organized and legitimized exclusively through the sultan's favor. Such favor was rendered in an elaborate ritual that included the grant of a magnificently decorated imperial *berāt* (diploma). No exercise of power, no rank, and to title deed was legitimate without the possesson of a berāt, which, with the ruler's seal, showed his favor. The sultan's retrieval of the berāt, or his death, annulled all kinds of authority and disposition in the society. The ritual was often coupled with the grant of royal symbols, a standard, a robe of honor *(khil'at)* prepared in the ruler's palace by imperial tailors, and a richly harnessed horse; the grantee recognized the favor by a present *(pīshkesh)* symbolizing his loyalty.[29] Bearing the sultan's emblems as the external marks of authority and rank had an awe-inspiring, almost sacred, character, overshadowing all other social and economic distinctions. The status of social groups, immunities, and privileges existed only through the regulations or *fermāns* accorded directly by the ruler.[30]

Theoretically, the whole social organization was based on estates, groups created or formalized by an act from the patrimonial ruler. Such status groups were stratified in the social pyramid so often described in the mirror-for-princes literature of the Middle East. What Weber meant by *sultanism* was originally derived not from Islamic precepts but from the caliphal state organization, which owed its basic philosophy and structure to the Byzantine and Sassanian heritage. This Iranian state tradition was transmitted to the Ottomans through native Iranian bureaucrats and the literary activity of the Iranian converts who translated Sassanian advice literature into Arabic.[31]

According to the letter of Tansar,[32] a royal advice letter from Sassanian times,

> men are divided into four estates... and at their head is the king. The first estate is that of the clergy... the second estate is that of the military,... the third estate is that of the scribes... the fourth estate is known as that of the artisans, and comprises tillers of land and herders

---

[29] The tradition of offering presents as a token of allegiance at the New Year *(Nowrūz)* ceremonies at the Ottoman court goes back to ancient Iran; the Achaemenian reliefs depicting the ceremony on the staircase of the outher palace at Persepolis illustrates such a ceremony, see "Maṭbakh" (H. İnalcık) *Encyclopaedia of Islam,* 2d ed. (*EI²* hereafter), p. 810.

[30] A striking examples is Meḥmed II's law-code on state organization: *Kānūnnāme-i Āl-i 'Osmān,* ed. M. Ârif, *Tārīkh-i Osmānī Encümeni Mecmū'ası,* Supplement (İstanbul 1330?1914).

[31] See A. von Kremer, *Kulturgeschichte des Orients unter den Chalifen* (Vienna, 1875 and 1877); see also the articles '*adab, Ibn Kutayba, Ibn al-Muḳaffa'* and *Djāḥiz* in *EI².*

[32] *The Letter of Tansar,* trans. M. Boyce (Rome, 1968), pp. 1-3.

of cattle and merchants and others who earn their living by trade.... Assuredly there shall be no passing from one to another unless in the character of one of us outstanding capacity is found.... The King of kings... kept each man in his own station and forbade any to meddle with a calling other than that for which it had pleased God... to create him. He laid commands moreover on the heads of the four estates.... All were concerned with their means of livelihood and their own affairs, and did not constrain kings to this by evil devices and acts of rebellion.... The commands given by the King of kings for occupying people with their own tasks and restraining them from those of others are for the stability of the world and the order of the affairs of men.... He has set a chief over each [estate] and after him a trusty inspector to investigate their revenues.[33] The King of kings has issued a decree to exalt and ennoble their (noble families) rank.... By it he has established a visible and general distinction between men of noble birth and common people with regard to horses and clothes, houses and gardens, women and servants....[34]

In the advice-to-king literature, the clergy (the ulema in the Islamic system) is sometimes placed after that of the men of the sword, who represented the sultan's authority. But in any case the ruler is the head and source of legitimacy for all ranks and status groups. From the foundation of the Arab empire under the Umayyads, and particularly under the Abbasids, this Iranian estate system appears to have determined the whole social structure of the Islamic state.

The use of the titles *shāhānshāh*, king of kings, and *pādishāh*, great king, originally the titles of the Sassanian emperors, was banned in Islam until the tenth century, when they were assumed by the newly rising non-Arab rulers in order to assert their image as omnipotent rulers within caliphal universalism.[35] The favorite title of the Ottoman sultans was *pādishāh-i 'ālempenāh*, "the universal ruler in whom the whole world finds protection."[36] While designating the ruler's supreme power for the purpose of protection, the title in particular emphasized the Iranian notion of omnipotent ruler.

---

[33] Ibid., p. 33.

[34] Ibid., p. 36; R. Frye, *The Heritage of Persia* (Cleveland and New York, 1963), pp. 51-52, raises the question to what extent this ideal "organised division of society" is the continuation of an Aryan or Mesopotamian herritage.

[35] W. Madelung, "The Assumption of the Title Shāhānshāh by the Buyids and The Reign of the Daylam," *Middle Eastern Studies,* pp. 28, 84-108, 169-83.

[36] "Pâdişâh" (H. İnalcık), *İslâm Ansiklopedisi,* IX: 491-95; B. Lewis, *The Political Language of Islam* (Chicago and London, 1988), pp. 13-70.

A complete description of the ranks and hierarchy of the ruling elite is to be found in the formulary manuals designed for the education of the state bureaucrats.[37] The elite *(mu'tabarān),* says al-Khōyī,[38] consists of two groups *(ṭā'ifa);* the first includes the ruler and high dignitaries and the second the leading ulema *(a'yān-i Dīn).* Among the members of each group there is a hierarchical subdivision *(ṭabaḳa)* for which specific titles and styles of address must be used. The members of the central government are ranked over provincial dignitaries. The second *ṭā'ifa* consists of two layers *(ṭabaḳa):* the first of which includes qadis, *muftīs,* and *mudarris*es, legal experts, teachers, and others; and the second, physicians, astronomers, and men of letters. In the introductory part to his compilation of state papers, the Ottoman chancery chief Ferīdūn gives the same ranking system, placing men of the sword and men of the pen above the ulema.[39] During public gatherings, the rank and seat of dignitaries was predetermined by the marshal of ceremonies *(teshrīfātjı),* and occasionally serious disputes arose over ranking, particularly among religious officials.

Whereas the Iranian notion of omnipotent ruler and estate society prevailed in the Islamic state, a parallel theory, apparently of Greek origin, emphasizing division of labor and social solidarity, could be found in the Islamic literature on ethics. According to the anthropomorphic interpretation of society found in this literature,[40] there are four groups *(ṭā'ifa),* like the four elements in the human body: first, men of the pen *(ahl-i ḳalem);* second, men of the sword *(ahl-i shimshīr);* third, traders and artisans *(tüjjār wa arbāb-i ḥiraf wa ṣanāyi');* and fourth, the agriculturalists *(ṭā'ifa-i zirā'at).* Separation and equilibrium between these groups is seen as essential for the health and good functioning of the body politic. If traders or agriculturalists become soldiers or soldiers become traders or artisans, society begins to fail and deteriorate.[41] Whereas the Iranian tradition maintained that the whole society was organized by, and geared to, the ruler's demands, the anthropomorphic theory emphasized

---

[37] Hasan al-Khoyī, *Gunyet'ul-Kātib ve Munyeu't-Ṭālib,* ed. A. Erzi (Ankara, 1963); the work was written in 690/1291, the MS published was copied in 879/1474.

[38] Ibid., p.3.

[39] A. Ferīdūn, *Munsha'āt al-Salāṭīn* (İstanbul, 1274/1857) pp. 2-13.

[40] Kınalı-zāde 'Alā al-Dīn 'Alī, *Akhlāḳ-i 'Alā'ī* (Bulak, 1248/1832), written in 1564, II:5; III:7; Hajjī Khalīfe, *Destūr al-'Amel li-İslāḥ al-Khalel* (İstanbul 1280/1863), 119-140. C. Fleischer, "Royal Authority, Dynastic Cyclism, and Ibn Khaldunism in sixteenth Century Ottoman Letters," *Journal of Asian and African Studies* (1983), pp. 198-220.

[41] Kınalı-zāde, p. 7-8.

solidarity. Expounded in detail in al-Fārābī's *Ideal State*,[42] the anthropomorphic theory was popularized in Naṣīr al- Dīn Ṭūsī's *Ethics*.[43]

As formulated by Naṣīr al- Dīn Ṭūsī or by Dawānī,[44] the prevailing theory of society and "social classes" regarded society purely as a political entity, focusing mainly on the ruling elite, which was composed of *ṭā'ifa*s, "communities," or status groups.[45] In this system the productive classes were considered necessary merely for the support of the state, and the state, in essence, consisted of the ruler and those who represented royal authority. We have purposely avoided the discussion of the place or claims of the sharī'a (Islamic law) and the ulema in order to focus on the definition of sultanism as a Weberian type of patrimonial state.

In any event, in the Islamic state extra economic criteria are taken as the basis for material life and for stratifying men in society. The economy is a communal economy.[46] Society is conceived essentially as a political and moral entity and the social classes as *ṭā'ifa*s, status groups. In this society the social relations are based, in Weber's terms, on patriarchal domination, dependency, rank, and loyalty. It is the ruler's duty, "for the good order of the world" *(nizām-i 'ālem)* or for the good of "Islam and [the Islamic] state" *(Dīn u Dawla)*, to ensure that this order is preserved and each man is kept in his own *ṭā'ifa*. The same Naṣīr al- Dīn Ṭūsī reportedly[47] advised the Mongol khan

---

[42] *Al Fārābī's Abhandlung der Musterstaat,* ed. F. Dieterici (Leiden, 1964), pp. 55, 187.

[43] *The Nasirean Ethics,* trans. G. Wickens (London, 1964), p. 193.

[44] Kınalı-zāde, II, pp. 105-12.

[45] The term commonly used for groups thus distinguished is *ṭā'ifa,* meaning community. The term is also used for a nation, a religious group, or a professional group such as a guild. The term *ṭabaḳa,* emphasizing more explicitly the hierarchiacal order, is also used for status groups (see R. Mottahedeh, *Loyalty and Leadership in an Early Islamic Society* (Princeton, 1980), p. 104-7; Kınalı-zāde, 2:7-9. As noted before, the term *ṭabaḳa* is sometimes used only for a sub-group in a *ṭā'ifa* (Al-khoyī, *Gunyet,* pp. 14-16). Summarizing Naṣīr al-Dīn al-Tūsī and Djalāl al-Dīn Dawānī, Kınalı-zāde points out that along with trade, craftsmanship, and agriculture, political power *(amāra)* is a legitimate means of acquiring wealth. This attitude in Islamic culture is found more strikingly expressed in the concept of *ghanīma,* i.e., booty gained in "legitimate" war and the most welcome and legitimate type of property. Yet Muslim thinkers have argued that goods acquired throigh torture and injustice are not morally acceptable, although in practice they are necessary to maintain public order (Kınalı-zāde, 2:9). Kınalı-zāde argues that moral satisfaction should not be forgotten while endeavoring for excellence and success in a profession.

[46] Weber, *Economy and Society,* II: 1014.

[47] Ibn al-Fuwāṭī, *Al-Ḥawādith al-Jāmi'a,* ed. M. Jawād (Baghdad, 1951), p. 343, cited by A. Yaşar Ocak, "XIV-XVI, Yüzyıllarda Kalenderi Dervişleri ve Osmanlı Yönetimi" (paper submitted to the Colloquium on "Saints and Sainthood in Islam," Berkeley, April 1987).

Hulagu that, since the wandering Ḳalandarī dervishes could not be placed in any of these ṭā'ifas, they should be eliminated.

The Ottoman patrimonial system, particularly in its classical age (1300-1600), can be viewed as resting on an emphatically regulated polity. The *ḳul ṭā'ifesi,* the palace and the army, constituting the ever-expanding household of the ruler, can be traced back to the initial warband of *nöker*s or *yoldash*, comrades, who assembled around Osman Ghāzī, the founder of the Ottoman state.[48] Weber's theory of charismatic leadership and patron-client solidarity furnishes an illuminating concept for the emergence of the typical Turco-Mongol state.[49] In the Eurasian steppe, every conqueror started his career with a warband of *nöker*s, usually personally bound to him by *anda*, an oath of loyalty unto death. The core group maintained itself through solidarity of interest in booty and conquest. Recruited from among the allies or captured enemies, *nöker*s or *yoldash*, to whom the early Ottoman traditions make frequent reference, formed the original household of Osman Ghāzī, and their descendants monopolized all the key positions in the Osmanlı state for more than a century and Osmanlı signified those who were affiliated with the person of Osman and represented the leader's power or the "Ottoman" state, which meant the same thing. As organizers of the conquests and of central bureaucracy, the ulema maintained a parallel position of control within the power group. Later on, when the state became increasingly dependent on their bureaucratic skills, the ulema families, in particular the Çandarlıs, assumed both military and bureauucratic control and became supreme at the center of government, whereas several old families of *nöker* origin maintained their original status in the distant frontier zones of the Balkans. The radical change came under Mehmed II the Conqueror, who dismissed the Çandarlıs from power and made the slaves from his seraglio, with no hereditary rights, the only group entrusted with authority. The change signified the replacement of the personal *nöker*s by an impersonal body of servants whose ranks were determined by a set of rules *(ḳānūn)* and whose loyalty to the ruler was the exclusive criterion for being entrusted with authority. The ruler's household was reorganized to maintain his omnipotence in a state now transformed into an empire in which the direct personal control of the ruler was no longer possible. Or in Weber's terms, personal household patriarchalism simply evolved into a centralist and formalized patrimonialism—a change only in degree in the dependency relationship of the household.

---

[48] See H. İnalcık, "The Question of the Emergence of the Ottoman State," *International Journal of Turkish Studies,* 2/2 (1981-1982), pp. 72-79; id., "The Khan and Tribal Aristocracy: The Crimean Khanate under Sahib Giray I", *Harvard Ukrainian Studies,* 3-4 (1979-80): 445-66.

[49] Weber, *Economy and Society,* 1:241-54, 2:1070-93.

Meḥmed the Conqueror, the ultimate founder of the Ottoman centralist empire, emphatically upheld the Iranian tradition, as reflected in his law code[50] and government as well as in the "palace" culture, including its architecture and literature. It was not a coincidence that his favorite son, Jem, bore the name of a legendary king of ancient Iran. Mehmed's law code governing state organization reserved to the highest dignitaries the privilege of eating at his table and is symbolic of the change;as Weber indicates "Originally the patrimonial officials are typically maintained at the ruler's table and from his supplies, as is every other household member.[51] Patrimonial officials, especially their highest ranks, retained for a long time the right to be fed at the lord's table when they were present at court..." "In a relatively larger apparatus," Weber adds, "a further evolution was the maintenance... by the granting of benefices or fiefs to patrimonial officials."[52] Whereas in the orient patrimonial officialdom, Weber asserts, never transcended its basically household character, in the West it evolved into a bureaucratic officialdom whose jurisdictions derived from impersonal interests.[53]

The traditional status order did not remain mere theory; state papers and regulations show that it was applied by a bureaucracy that was imbued with it and considered it the foundation of the state and society. The candid narrator of Ottoman life and society, Evliyā Çelebi,[54] describes urban populations in the second half of the seventeenth century in terms of traditional status ranking. Groups representing the ruler's authority always came first. These were followed by men of religion, who were stratified among themselves as descendants of the Prophet and ulema, including muftis and qadis. Last were the civil notables of the town. Separated from these groups, which together comprised the elite *(a'yān ve eshrāf)*, ordinary subjects *(re'āyā)* were also differentiated according to their status as members of mercantile or artisan associations.

We have seen that the only status groups created by the Ottoman ruler consisted of the "military" groups, which constituted part of his household, primarily the palace—the troops of his "Porte" *(ḳapı-kulları)*, the *tīmār*-holding cavalry in the provinces, and the bureaucratic apparatus that managed the sources of revenues in his land.[55] As for the rest of society, consisting of the

---

[50] "Kānūnnāme-i Āl-i 'Osmān," edited by M. 'Ârif, *TOEM,* Supplement (İstanbul, 1330/1914), p. 27.

[51] Weber, *Economy and Society,* 2: 1031.

[52] Ibid.

[53] Ibid.

[54] *Seyāḥatnāme* (İstanbul, 1314-1898), 2: 90-91, 213.

[55] See H. İnalcık, *The Ottoman Empire: The Classical Age, 1300-1600* (London, 1973), pp. 76-118.

re'āyā, the tax-paying productive groups, the ruler's role was limited to reorganizing or formalizing under state regulations, to serve his patrimonial system, the social classes of the preconquest period.[56] In the sultan's orders or state papers, the *re'āyā,* or any group of *re'āyā,* were addressed only indirectly through state officials in the provinces, primarily through qadis, who at the same time represented the local community. The conquered productive masses, the Ottoman *re'āyā,* were systematically excluded from the "military household" *(ḳuls).* Instead, they were, in Weber's terminology, "extra-patrimonial subjects" or "political subjects" whose function was to supply the ruler's needs.[57] Forced into compulsory associations to serve the ruler's demands, they were subordinated to the political structure machien that he had created. In Weber's analysis of the patrimonial state, the ruler's use of "non-privileged masses and especially the rural masses" in military service is emphasized.[58] These were elevated to a privileged position relative to the majority of ordinary subjects, but were never given *'askerī* (elite) status. This group of subjects, well known in the Ottoman case under the status designation of "exempt" *(mu'āf ve müsellem) re'āyā,*[59] was integrated into the "military" class only under exceptional conditions. Although these *re'āyā* soldiers lost their privileged status in the second half of the sixteenth century, the Ottoman state continued to use *re'āyā* as mercenaries. They, too, however, were denied the full privileges of the sultan's "military" *ḳuls.* Fierce struggles between the *ḳuls* and the mercenaries *(sekbān* and *sarıdja* companies) —called *jelālīs* when they turned rebellious— fill the annals of seventeenth-century Ottoman historians.[60] In the eighteenth century, as professional soldiers less costly than regular *ḳuls,* they came to form the main body of the sultan's army and of the "private" armies of provincial notables. The poorest rural elements thus obtained employment in the imperial army without ever acquiring the privileges of the household *ḳuls.* In the Balkans such local organizations of Christian soldiery, created by the Porte, became the nucleus for troops supporting the cause of nationalistic rebellious minorities like the Serbs, Greeks, Bulgarians, and Albanians in the nineteenth century.

---

[56] Weber, *Economy and Society,* 2:1013: "Originally, patrimonial administration was adapted to the satisfaction of purely personal, primarily private household needs of the master."

[57] Ibid., 2:1020-1021, distinguishes them clearly from status groups.

[58] Ibid., 2:1015, 1018.

[59] H. İnalcık, "Osmanlılarda Raiyyet Rüsûmu," *Belleten,* 23, 195, 575-616.

[60] H. İnalcık, "Military and Fiscal Transformation in the Ottoman Empire, 1600-1700," *Archivum Ottomanicum,* 6 (1980): 283-337.

In Weber's scheme such changes can be interpreted as clues to the weakening of central patrimonial control.[61] In fact, the Janissaries and other divisions at the Porte were transformed into semi-autonomous traditional status groups possessing their own special regulations with consolidated privileges. Increasingly conscious of their own corporate interests, they became an important force in the struggle for power. As for the mercenaries, they, too, being organized into permanent companies in the provinces, challenged the sultan's centralist authority. The seventeenth century witnessed a violent struggle, with temporary compromises, between these "autonomous" groups.[62] The Köprülü revival of centralist patrimonial-bureaucratic power in the second half of the century collapsed under the disastrous impact of the long war in the period between 1683 and 1699.

An important feature of the Ottoman patrimonial system, often confused in the literature, has to do with the fundamental difference in the ruler's attitude toward his *ḳul*s and toward the *re'āyā*. If confiscation of property or capital punishment was carried out against the *re'āyā* without due process of law in the religious court, the act was regarded as religiously wrong and a flagrant injustice *(ẓulm)*, injurious to the reputation of the ruler. In the classical mirror-for–princes literature, the ruler was admonished to avoid such acts and to prevent his subordinates from exercising injustices. The ruler's discretionary punishment *(siyāset)* was legitimate in principle only against his *ḳul*s.[63]

As Weber notes, the ruler's exercise of power in the interest of maintaining a balance of power between rival status groups was a fundamental principle of the Ottoman political system.[64] The Sultan's *ḳul*s versus the *re'āyā*, ulema versus *ḳul*s and bureaucrats, Janissaries versus *sipāhī*s, or salaried army versus timariot army, low rank qadis against high ulema—all were status groups traditionally in conflict. The ruler was conscious of the necessity of employing his regulative power to keep them in equilibrium, since this guaranteed his "domination" of the polity. However, there were times in Ottoman history when this equilibrium was upset. Threatened by his *ḳul*s in the capital, Süleyman I is reported to have said that he might use against the *ḳul*s the large group of unskilled workers from the tanneries available in the capital city.

---

[61] Weber, *Economy and Society,* 1:255-71; 2:1038-44, 1051-64, 1092-94.

[62] H. İnalcık, "Military and Fiscal Transformation," mentioned in note 60.

[63] U. Heyd, *Studies in Old Ottoman Criminal Law,* ed. V. L. Ménage (Oxford, 1973), pp. 259-71.

[64] Weber, *Economy and Society,* 1:161.

The Sultans of the troubled seventeenth century organized peasants into military companies to fight against rebellious mercenaries in the countryside.

A final note on patrimonial status order and socio-economic structure. We know that through innumerable regulations, monopolies, immutinies, and market inspections, characteristics for which the Byzantine and Ottoman empires are known, patrimonial power shaped the economy exclusively for the ruler's demands and thereby influenced to a great extent the formation of social classes.[65] However, specific developments in demographic and socio-economic conditions —for example, the emergence of the metropolis of Istanbul— brought about situations with which the regulatory power and wisdom of the patrimonial state was not capable of coping. So there existed a constant conflict between the imperial regulations and the realities of the market or of rural developments occurring under the pressure of changing demographic and economic conditions.

Extensive bureaucratic documentation witnesses this constant struggle between the state and the market. For example, in the guild system, which was always vigorously supported by the state, the latter had sometimes to yield to the pressure of increased demand for goods; this yielding caused neglect of certain strict provisions of antiquated regulations. The state agreed to the formation of new guilds and tolerated the activities of extra guild artisans. Perhaps more spectacular escapes from patrimonial control are found in the agrarian sector under changing economic and demographic conditions. Weber discusses these phenomena while dealing with the dissolution processes of patrimonial empires.[66] Economic and social forces would be fully released to bypass the regulations and shape the social classes when centralist power was weakened and lost control of market forces. In fact, conflict was always present in patrimonial states, and thus it can be argued that in reality a ruler could never succeed in creating pure patrimonialism and a perfect status society.

"Sultanism", Tradition, and Traditional Groups

It can be argued that the concept of "tradition" in Weber's sociology approaches what Emile Durkheim and the structuralists in general mean by collective representations, institutions, and structures. Tradition in Weber's sense is both the origin and validating principle of patrimonial domination. "What is customary and has always been so" had a sacred character and demanded obedience to the particular person who represented it. The "ruler's

---

[65] Ibid., 1: 238-41.
[66] Ibid.

powers are legitimate insofar as they are traditional."[67] Upon succession to the throne, the Ottoman sultan, after mentioning all his royal ancestors, asserted that he became ruler "by inheritance and by being entitled to it *(bi'l-irs wa'l-istiḥḳāḳ)*." In Weber, tradition and custom are dealt with as closely related concepts. In fact, custom, "a collective way of acting" *(Massenhandeln)*, a uniform activity, which is a matter of custom and persists by unreflective imitation,[68] appears to be a factor modifying the patrimonial ruler's discretionary power. Mere habituation, Weber points out, is the first factor that stereotypes the patrimonial relationship. From there the sanctifying power of tradition evolves: "the master is restrained from introducing innovations."[69] He is also restrained from using his discretionary power by the possibility that his economic interests would be hurt by innovations[70] (the Ottoman policy of preserving the preconquest practices in taxation may be remembered here). The sultan's agents are ordered to follow in their decisions, first, sultanic law and the sultan's written orders; and then, if there is no clear reference to the matter in either of these, to do "what had long been practiced." Thus, a stable order diminishes the area of the master's discretion in favor of traditional prescription. The master may formalize this traditional order by regulations. In fact, most of the Ottoman sultanic laws were formalized versions of indigenous customs, *'urf u 'ādāt.* But the enactment, Weber believes,[71] never committed the ruler legally:

> Sometimes it appears that sultanism is completely unrestrained by tradition, but this is never in fact the case. The nontraditional element is not, however, rationalized in impersonal terms, but consists only in an extreme development of the ruler's discretion.

Law in the Ottoman Empire was theoretically, if we use Weber's terminology, "the ruler's personal will" or "ultimately nothing but purely subjective rights and privileges of individuals deriving from the ruler's grant of favor."[72] However, the *ḳānūn* codes of the founding sultans, Meḥmed the Conqueror and Süleyman the Lawgiver, which were actually formulated by the bureaucrats themselves, were claimed to be unalterable fundamental rules, or "restrictive traditions" in Weber's terms.

---

[67] Ibid., 1: 336.
[68] Ibid., 1: 319.
[69] Ibid., 2: 1011.
[70] Ibid., 2: 1012.
[71] Ibid.
[72] Ibid., 1: 232.

As for the traditional groups, we have discussed above how the Janissary corps was transformed from a purely patrimonial army in the personal service of the sultan into a traditional group through a typification process similar to what took place in western patrimonial states.[73] But from the beginning this process was most visible with the ulema.[74] As far as the Ottoman imperial system is concerned, the Islamic tradition was in fact the most effective check on the limitless arbitrary power of the sultan. As the custodians of Islamic tradition, the ulema, though stratified and often in conflict within its own ranks, played a major role throughout Ottoman history as a traditional and legitimate center of resistance. Other groups often took sanctuary with the ulema to protect their traditionally established rights against the discretionary power of the sultan.

When it comes to productive groups, a different concern and motivation on the part of the ruler can be discerned. The preconquest "classes" made up traditional groups, differing from the ruler's personal retainers "by virtue of the right of mobility... by owing traditional and therefore fixed services and taxes and by freely disposing of property and land. The disposition of property and land are arranged under customs or customary laws."[75] The obligations of this class are bound by tradition. This description of traditional or "political subjects" perfectly fits that of Ottoman *re'āyā*.

In addition to the restrictive power of tradition, Weber stresses that it was the ruler's concern to maintain the subjects' compliance and economic capacity to support him.[76] That concern limited arbitrary acts and "personal sanctions" of the ruler and his officials.[77] Patrimonialism has an inherent tendency to regulate economic activity in terms of utilitarian welfare or absolute values. This tendency stems from the character of the claim to legitimacy and interest in the contentment of the subjects.[78]

It is commonplace knowledge that the Ottoman ruler regulated the economy in general as part of his patrimonial goals, but in some sectors, such as rice cultivation and mining, his bureaucracy directly managed the production process itself because of immediate need for the products.[79] The ruler's

---

[73] Ibid., 2: 1036-42; however, he, 2:1028, finds a fundamental difference between the West and the East in "the typification and monopolistic appropriation of the powers of office."

[74] Ibid., 2: 1028.

[75] Ibid., 2: 1020-22.

[76] Ibid., 2: 1030.

[77] Ibid., 2: 227.

[78] Ibid., 2: 243.

[79] "Managerial" role of the total state is analyzed in detail in K. A. Wittfogel, *Oriental Despotism: A Comparative Study of Total Power* (New Haven, 1957); Ottoman bureaucracy's managerial capacity is best revealed in a special sector of agriculture: see

regulatory power manifested itself most strikingly in the agrarian economy. We shall see that the Ottoman government restored and systemically controlled a specific agrarian system based on peasant family farm units, or the *çift-khāne* system in the conquered lands.

As an incisive agrarian historian, Weber was able to see that patrimonial empires had a systematic policy of protecting and maintaining small peasant farms from exploitations. "The prince," he says,[80]

> had primarily a fiscal and military interest in the "mediatized" subjects: an interest in maintaining their number, that is, the number of small holdings sufficient to support one peasant family; in preventing their exploitation by the local patrimonial authorities beyond a point at which their capacity to satisfy his own demands would suffer; in retaining the power to tax them and call them up for military service directly without any mediation.

Weber clearly defined the basic economic principle underlying the regime of peasant family farms.[81]

> The appropriation of the means of production and personal control, however formal, of the process of work constitutes one of the strongest incentives to unlimited willingness to work. This is the fundamental basis of the extraordinary importance of small units in agriculture, whether in the form of small-scale proprietorship or small tenants who hope to rise to the status of owner.... It is very important in all parts of Asia and also in Europe in the Middle Ages.... The existence of the small peasant in a sense depends directly on the absence of capital accounting and on retaining the units of household and enterprise.

H. İnalcık, "Rice Cultivation and the çeltükci-Re'âyâ System in the Ottoman Empire," *Turcia* 14 (1982): 69-141.

[80] Weber, *Economy and Society,* 1058.

[81] Ibid., 1: 131. On family farm and the marginalist school, see A. V. Chayanov, *The Theory of Peasant Economy,* eds. D. Thorner, Basile Kerblay, and R. E. F. Smith, with a foreword by Teodor Shanin (Madison, 1986). On the problems of labor intensity and labor absorption in developing Asian countries, see A. Booth and R. M. Sundrum, *Labor Absorption in Agriculture* (London, 1985); for structures and problems of Turkish agriculture, see Korkut Boratav, *Tarımsal Yapılar ve Kapitalizm* (Ankara, 1980); Burhan Oğuz, *Türkiye Halkının Kültür Kökenleri,* II-2: *Tarım Hayvancılık-Meteoroloji* (İstanbul, 1988); H. İnalcık, "State, Land, and Peasant," in H. İnalcık et al., *An Economic and Social History of the Ottoman Empire,* Cambridge: CUP, 1994, 143-154.

In Weber's time, protection of the small farmer and the small-scale farm in agriculture had become a hotly debated political issue, and the economic advantages of both were frequently stressed.

As for the traditional groups in towns and cities, guilds with well-established traditions constituted the backbone of urban society. The patrimonial system, according to Weber,[82] evolved into sultanism when the ruler was able to turn his "extra-patrimonial subjects" (tax-paying producers) and "collective responsibility associations" (guilds and village communities) into patrimonial groups completely dependent upon himself. Under different conditions, such associations in the west had evolved more into self-governing municipal associations. In the Ottoman case, the key question is to what extent the Ottoman ruler really controlled the guilds. Although Gabriel Baer held that, under the Ottomans, guilds came under the direct control of the state, documentary evidence does not confirm this.[83] A trend toward dependency can be detected, but in general the guilds preserved their autonomy. State control was confined to formally legitimizing guild officers after their election by the members of the guild from among their fellow guildsmen. As a rule, it was the local qadi who performed the validation. The real character of the Ottoman guild system and its position vis-à-vis the state has only recently begun to come to light through the examination of qadi court records.[84]

We believe that it is necessary to revise the view made popular by Orientalists influenced by Weber that the Islamic city in general was unorganized, unstructured, and completely dependent upon the state. Every Ottoman guild possessed its own warden (kethudā), and all guilds in a city formed a group under the town kethudā. It is true that all guilds achieved and maintained a formal and legitimate existence through the ruler's grant of a diploma. The guilds were also validated spiritually through the system of professional ethics and brotherhood called akhī-ism and through their affiliation with one or another religious order. The ruler's efforts to incorporate the akhīs and the religious orders into the system of status groups through grants of wakf and donations were not always successful. The malāmatī and widespread

---

[82] Weber, Economy and Society, 1:231-41; 2:1009-45.

[83] G. Bear, Egyptian Guilds in Modern Times (Jerusalem, 1964); see my review in Archivum Ottomanicum, 1(1969), p. 319; and H. İnalcık, "The Appointment Procedure of a Guild Warden (Ketkhudā)," WZKM, 76 (1986), Festschrift Andreas Tietze: 135-142; C. Cahen, "Y a-t il eu des Corporations professionnelles dans le monde musulman classique," The Islamic City, ed. A. H. Hourani and S. H. Stern (Philadelphia), pp. 51-63.

[84] For a useful bibliography on the subject, see S. Faroqhi, Towns and Townsmen of Ottoman Anatolia (Cambridge, 1984), pp. 125-70; H. İnalcık, "Bursa," Belleten, 24 (1960): 45-102.

kalander-abdāl orders in the Ottoman Empire constantly fought against such attempts. Sometimes, in alliance with discontented segmentary social groups, such as nomads, their resistance took the form of mass insurrections, such as those of Shaykh Badr al-Dīn (Bedreddin) in 1416, Shāh-Ḳūlū in 1511, and Ḳalender-oghlu in 1527.

In brief, although the Ottoman state was known as one of the most accomplished status societies in Islamic history, it still appears to have fallen short of achieving pure patrimonialism in this respect. Incidentally, the institution of *ketkhudā* had a broad significance in the Ottoman social setting. In fact, the *ketkhudā* or *ḳahyā* (from Persian *ketkhudā,* household steward) was a basic element in the establishment of a "solidarity group" in general. In Ottoman society virtually every group, from the guilds to the Janissary corps, was organized around *ketkhudā*-ship. Elected by his peers, a *ketkhudā* was supposed to represent the interests of the group before the outside world, particularly the state. Although the *ketkhudā* acquired his legitimacy and authority vis-à-vis the group only upon receipt of a diploma or certificate from the ruler's local agent, the qadi, the procedure was no more than a formality. The real decision always rested with the group and a *ketkhudā* was removed from office usually upon the demand of the group. Through the *ketkhudā*-ship a variety of social groups possessed a considerable degree of autonomy with respect to their intirnal affairs.

"Sultanism" and the Ottoman Bureaucracy

Patrimonial domination, according to Weber, "establishes itself through an administrative apparatus."[85] Either by virtue of a constellation of interests or by virtue of authority, domination expresses itself and functions through law and administration."[86] The creation of an administrative apparatus marks the development from patriarchal to patrimonial domination *(Herrschaft).*[87]

Under a patrimonial ruler, the army and the bureaucrats are selected and organized as in a patrimonial household, to respond exclusively to the ruler's demands. Government offices are organized and maintained along purely personal lines. In the choice of officials, loyalty to the ruler supersedes all other concerns. Officials are therefore selected from among the ruler's personal attendants, and professional training and specialization are not always

---

[85] *Max Weber on Law in Economy and Society,* trans. E. Shils and M. Rheinstein, ed. M. Rheinstein (New York: Clarion, 1954), p. 330.

[86] Weber, *Economy and Society,* I: 334-36.

[87] Ibid., 1: 220-25; 2: 1025.

considered necessary prerequisites.[88] Promotions depend not on objective rules
but on the ruler's favor and arbitrary choice. The ruler makes his officials'
economic compensation completely subject to his discretion with no provision
for hereditary service. Officials never constitute a corporate group or a legally
autonomous monopolistic sodality.[89] In brief, the basic features of patrimonial
bureaucracy stem from its personal patrimonial character. According to
Weber,[90] the household characteristics of the patrimonial state were maintained
"in a grotesque degree ... at the Turkish court" up to the nineteenth century.

In its developed form in the sixteenth century, however, the Ottoman
bureaucratic apparatus displayed a number of features that do not permit us to
subscribe completely to Weber's description. Under Süleyman the Lawgiver
(1520-66) the Ottoman bureaucracy cannot be viewed purely as part of the
ruler's household, nor were its offices based purely upon personal relations and
absolute subordination to the ruler. Empirical research suggests that the
Ottoman bureaucracy evolved from a pure "patrimonial" structure to an
increasingly self-conscious and autonomous organization that functioned in a
relatively "rational" system of fixed rules and training. Weber himself observes
that, in the course of financial rationalization, the patrimonial state
imperceptibly moves toward a rational bureaucratic administration.[91] Although
their autonomy was not consolidated with hereditary rights as in the West,
Ottoman bureaucrats could scarcely be immune to group solidarity as they
acquired specialized training through long years in guild-like bureaus.[92] The
rationale and legitimation of their activities were based not so much on the
ruler's pleasure and tradition as on their expertise and, ultimately, on the
interests of the Islamic "religion and state" *(Dīn u Dawla)*. They became
critical of the arbitrary acts of the later sultans who behaved, in their judgment,
contrary to the established Ottoman state tradition instituted by Meḥmed the
Conqueror and Süleyman I.[93] Despite the patrimonial rule which made all the
legal dispositions of a dead sultan null and void, the bureaucracy was
concerned about maintaining established tradition. As the custodians of
institutions, which they believed formed the underpinning of "Religion and

---

[88] See "Ghulām" (H. İnalcık), *EI²*, 2: 1085-91.

[89] Weber, *Economy and Society,* 2: 1031.

[90] Ibid., 2: 1025.

[91] Ibid., 2: 1014.

[92] See H. İnalcık, "Reîs-ul-Küttâb," *IA,* 9: 671-83.

[93] In one of the most important of such memorials, dated 1620, *Kitāb-i Müstetab,* ed. Y.
Yücel, *Osmanlı Devlet Teşkilâtına Dair Kaynaklar* (Ankara, 1988), Text: 4, 9, 18, 29,
44, the neglect of the state regulations and the subsequent deterioration in state affairs
are traced back to Murad III's reign (1595-1603).

State," they came into conflict with palace favorites and other powerful traditional groups such as the ulema.

Traditional group solidarity and autonomy were particularly apparent in the finance department, which had always recruited specialized experts. No sultan, not even Selim I, the most autocratic of the Ottoman sultans, could dispense with their services. Having been inherited from the old Middle Eastern bureaucratic tradition, state revenues and expenditures were under the strict control of the finance department, which operated according to extremely complex bureaucratic and bookkeeping techniques.[94] Every state undertaking was entrusted to a finance agent *(emīn)* who delivered a report on completion of the job to the head of the finance department. Though formally dependent on the grand vizier, the absolute deputy of the sultan, the head of the finance department was acutally independent in his decisions; conflicts between these two often called for the personal intervention of the sultan himself. Arbitrary demands on public funds by the sultan's favorites met with bitter criticism from authors with financial experience.[95] The transformation of military prebends *(tīmārs)* into sinecures, for example, was denounced as ruinous to "the Religion and the State." In the classical period, bureaucrats were recruited not from among the ulema but from a professional group of experts who tried to maintain their monopoly through nepotism and clientship. Even bureaucrats who owed their origin to the ruler's household and the ulema adopted the professional ethics and rules of the career group.

In the classical period, the central bureaucracy consistently worked to eliminate or restrict arbitrary exactions and practies through regulations and the rulers' edicts or rescripts of justice *('adāletnāme),*[96] which were actually formulated and issued by the bureaucrats themselves. They constantly endeavored to define and keep close control over the acts and jurisdictions of provincial agents. Inspectors *(mufettish)* with extraordinary powers were sent to the provinces wherever there was a need. The declared motive was always to promote the interests of "the Religion and the State" and to protect "the poor,

---

[94] I. M. D'Ohsson, *Tableau Général d'Empire Ottoman,* 7 vols. (Paris, 1783-1824); İ. H. Uzunçarşılı, *Osmanlı Devletinin Merkez ve Bahriye Teşkilâtı* (Ankara: TTK, 1948); J. Shinder, "Ottoman Bureaucracy in the Second Half of the Seventeenth Century: The Central and Naval Administration," Ph.D. diss., Princeton, 1971; C. H. Fleischer, *Bureaucrat and Intellectual in the Ottoman Empire: The Historian Muṣṭafā ʿĀlī (1541-1600)* (Princeton: Princeton University Press, 1986); L. Darling, "The Ottoman Finance Department and the Assessment and Collection of the Cizye and Avariz Taxes, 1560-1660," Ph.D. diss., University of Chicago, 1989.

[95] Most of the memorialists and historians belonged to the group of bureaucrats, in particular to the finance department.

[96] H. İnalcık, "Adâletnâmeler," *Belgeler,* II (1965): 49-145.

powerless *re'āyā*" against injustices. When they believed the interests of "the Religion and the State" were at stake, the same bureaucrats tried hard to convince the sultan to take radical measures regardless of resistance, and became responsible for genuine reforms. It is not by chance that nearly all of the great Ottoman reformer-statesmen emerged from among the bureaucrats *(küttāb)*. It was through their actions that such innovations as Western technology in methods of warfare, the printing press, and even Western legal and administrative institutions found their way into the Ottoman Empire in later centuries. However, it must be admitted that since all political actions had to have the sultan's approval in order to be valid, the success of the bureaucrats depended on their position of power. Once in office, they themselves insisted on the absolute and indivisible character of the sultan's power, using it then to introduce necessary reforms that aimed ultimately at consolidating the bureaucracy's own centralized control.

Having identified themselves with the state and its interests, the bureaucrats tried to consolidate the basis of their power and legitimacy. No wonder that during the sweeping reforms known as *Tanzīmāt* (1839—76) the bureaucrats were denounced as despots by the newly emerging westernized intelligentsia. But in the end, military and civil bureaucrats, in alliance with the intelligentsia, would seek to base legitimacy on the national will through new bureaucratic instruments and notions borrowed from the West. Throughout this long history it was largely the development of a de facto autonomous bureaucracy that appears to have been responsible for change in the patrimonial Middle Eastern state. In some of the more traditional Islamic countries, it was not the bureaucrats but other traditionally autonomous groups, such as the ulema who were mainly responsible for change. Briefly speaking, in the Islamic patrimonial empire it was these two groups, the civil and military bureaucrats and the *ulema,* evolving into increasingly autonomous groups that finally replaced the sultans' patrimonial state.

Oriental Feudalism: Prebendalism

In general, Weber believes, the manner by which military service was remunerated determined the type of feudalism.[97] Allowances in kind from the ruler's storehouse, the mark of a primitive state in the remuneration of officials, depended on the specific economic conditions in the original patrimonial state.[98] In fact, in the Ottoman Empire the allowances in kind *(ta'yīnāt)*, which favored groups directly attached to the sultan's household, persisted for a long

---

[97] Weber, *Economy and Society,* 2: 1032.
[98] Ibid., 2: 1031.

time. From the benefice system, which was the next stage in remuneration, "fee benefices" *(sportelpfründe)* developed first. In this system the ruler assigned the collection of certain fees to the direct remuneration of the official. This system, was also widely used in the Ottoman system from the earliest times; for example, the service charge of the sultan's agent *(ghulāmiyye)* in the collection of the poll tax, or the qadis receiving fees for judicial court service. Finally, Weber observes, "the remuneration could take the form of a landed benefice or service land *(Amts- oder Dienstland)* for the incumbent's own use."[99] The prebend is a particular form of nonhereditary benefice patrimonially granted by the ruler to his retainers. "When an administrative staff is supported in this form, we shall speak of prebendalism. In such a situation there may be a system of promotion on a basis of seniority."[100] Weber categorized the Ottoman *sipāhī (tīmār)* system as a typical example of prebendalism:

> The income sources of the Turkish sipahis, of the Japanese samurai, and various similar types of oriental retainers are benefices, not fiefs. In some cases, they have been derived from the rents of certain lands; in others, from the tax income of certain districts. In the latter case, they have generally been combined with the appropriation of governmental powers in the same district.[101]

Weber finds one of the most developed forms of prebendalism in the arbitrary patrimonial power enjoyed by the ruler and benefice-holder in the Ottoman Empire. Because of the patrimonial nature of the benefice, powers and economic rights generally included "privately appropriated economic advantages." In Ottoman documents these are called *tekālīf-i shakka,* exactions. Under sultanism arbitrariness "in determining fees, newly imposed obligations and monopolies" is claimed as a right. Bribery and corruption are logical consequences of the system. In all of this, Weber has in mind the Ottoman Empire. But "typification" also took other directions, as in Western Europe, where "estate type hereditary division of powers" developed. There,

> patrimonial rights are checked under the obligation of the ruler to compromise with the ruling elite. Benefices are called fief if they are appropriated as hereditary and granted by contract. Thus, legal and

---

[99] Ibid., 2: 1032.
[100] Ibid., 1: 235.
[101] Ibid., 1: 236.

restrictive characters distinguish western fief feudalism *(Lehen Feudalismus)* from Asiatic types.[102]

The central bureaucracy systematically attempted to prevent the spread of hereditary benefices *(mālikāne* and *mülk tīmārs)* and to maintain a kind of check and balance system in the provincial administration; these efforts were all designed to preserve the ruler's absolute control and monopoly over the "benefices." In the Ottoman Empire, it is true, the appropriation of benefices, which occurred to some extent in all periods but particularly in the period when the classical system began to disintegrate, never developed into a western-style hereditary aristocracy. For Weber, while prebendalism such as that of the Ottoman Empire developed into an extreme type of patrimonialism, its evolution in Western Europe led to the rise of a rational bureaucracy.

One can easily recognize in Weber's theory the well-known hypothesis of a contrary evolution of the western and the Asiatic empires. In this extremely schematic reductionism, the specific characteristics of the Ottoman system are overlooked, or rather obscured in favor of a popularized theory of the despotic Asiatic empire. Perhaps one can also detect the impact of the intense anti-Ottoman propaganda during the nineteenth century.

At the same time, Weber asserts that there were certain fundamental features common to the eastern and western benefice systems. First, prebendalism, like western feudalism, is the outcome of certain socio-economic conditions. "It originates in the reversion from monetary financing to financing in kind."[103] The patrimonial retainer receives his support either in the form of allowances from the lord's maganize or treasury or "by rights of land use in return for services."[104] It is important to stress that while an ordinary cash salary *('ulūfe)* involves the ruler's treasury and thus makes the soldiery directly dependent, the prebend affords the recipient greater independence through indirect, albeit limited and reversible control over land and peasants. As a further development, the appropriation of land and peasant labor by a group of hereditary landowners means, in Weber's terms, "an extreme marginal case of patrimonialism," which is shaped purely by patrimonial loyalty.[105] The last case in the Ottoman Empire can perhaps be seen in the *a'yān* regime. But his came about rather as an outgrowth of the tax farming system and decentralization, and the hereditary principle was never complete.

---

[102] Ibid., 1: 239.

[103] Ibid., 1: 260, 2: 1071.

[104] Ibid., 1: 235.

[105] Ibid., 2: 1069-70.

Following the observation made by western thinkers since Machiavelli, Weber underlines the lack of a "homogeneous manorial aristocracy" in Islamic countries due to the absence of a common interest in safeguarding "the ownership of serfs."[106] Instead, he says, there was constant competition among benefice holders for peasant labor. In the *çift-khāne* system, both land and labor came under the strict control of the state in order to maintain a definite agrarian organization whose aim was to eliminate consolidated, hereditary estates. Even during the eighteenth century the *a'yān* control over land and labor was precarious, because any legitimation of such control depended on the sultan's favor, as manifested by a diploma and an official title. The attempt in 1808 to give a kind of constitutional foundation to the *a'yān*'s actual control failed totally in the face of the sultan's patrimonial power and of resistance by traditional forces.[107]

In the West, as well as in the Ottoman state, the candidate for remuneration had first to prove his qualifications for providing the service assigned. In the Ottoman case the immediate superior (usually the *alay-beyi*) had to testify to the candidate's fitness, which was the crucial factor in acquiring a *tīmār*. The recommendation process, at the same time, established a kind of clientship between the candidate and his superior. This patrimonial relationship can be seen at every level of the Ottoman ruling elite. In the classical period a new sultan coming from his provincial seat to the capital felt obliged to promote his retainers to imperial posts. Thus, every succession brought with it a power struggle and political crisis of greater or lesser intensity depending upon the prevailing issues and circumstances. It was against law and tradition to deprive a *sipāhī* of his *tīmār* without cause. Although *tīmār*-holders could not transfer their actual *tīmār*s to their sons through inheritance, the latter nevertheless had the right under law to obtain other *tīmār*s whose size, albeit smaller, was determined by the size of their father's *tīmār*s. Also, in the *tīmār* system, under bureaucratic supervision, there was a tendency to isolate the service obligations from personal household loyalties, and thus to reduce the ruler's discretionary control over *tīmār* holders.

---

[106] Ibid., 2: 1067.
[107] H. İnalcık, "Sened-i Ittifak ve Gülhâne Hatt-i Humâyunu," *Belleten,* 28 (1964): 603-22.

2

The Ottoman - Turkish Empire

Political Development

The Ottoman state first appeared on the map of world history as a small emirate which straddled the uneasy border between the Seljukid and the Byzantine Empires in north-western Anatolia. It expanded rapidly and during the period 1389-1402 achieved status as a major imperial power, reaching as far as the Danube in the north and Euphrates in the east. The first imperial experiment was brought to a sudden halt when the Ottomans, failing to use the strategic advantage gained by their defeat of a crusader army led by the Hungarian King Sigismund in 1396 at the battle of Nigbolu (Nicopolis), turned their military energies instead to the ill-timed annexation of Muslim emirates in Anatolia. In the ensuing mêlée, which was concluded by a major Ottoman defeat at the hands of Timur in 1402 at the battle of Ankara, the Ottomans' empire in Europe and Asia lost its cohesion. In the subsequent period between 1402 and 1413, the empire was wrecked by inveterate civil war as rival claimants to the throne sought to rebuild patrimonial hegemony. During the period of civil war the scope of Ottoman sovereignty in Anatolia was severely restricted, and the centre of political power in the state shifted to the European province. It was during this period that Edirne came into its own as the empire's chief political capital. While the era of the civil war is usually considered to be confined to the period of 1402-13, unstable political conditions persisted until 1425-threatening at times to restart the process of imperial disintegration. After 1430 when the Ottomans succeeded in capturing Salonica from the Venetians, the state entered into a renewed period of imperial expansion in Europe and they defeated a succession of crusader armies mobilized from the West. The Ottomans, by their victory over the Polish-Hungarian King Ladislas at the battle of Varna in 1444, firmly restored the empire's dominance over the Balkan lands and brought the final fall of the Byzantine empire within the realm of possibility.

The Ottoman sovereign derived his imperial authority from three separate sources of legitimacy: from his adoption of the Islamic title *sultan*, from the Turco-Mongol designation *khakān*, and from the rank of *kayser* inherited from the rulers of the Eastern Roman Empire. Following the capture of Constantinople in 1453, the Ottoman sovereign felt himself a legitimate successor to the Roman imperial tradition. Indeed, the claim of the Ottoman Empire to universal rule dates from the period after the fall of Constantinople.

Within the short span of sixty-four years after the fall of Constantinople the Ottomans had added the Arab capitals of Damascus, Cairo, Mecca and Medina to their imperial patrimony and were catapulted into a position as the premier Islamic power in the world.

The Ottoman Empire, 1453-1600

The Ottoman state developed into a Western Asiatic empire whose lands in the Middle East and in the Balkan peninsula bridged the continents of Europe and Asia, remaining intact for more than five centuries between 1400 and 1922 (see Map 19). Since it was Ottoman society within the constellation of Asian societies that maintained the closest and most continuous political, economic, and cultural relations with Europe, it is natural that the history of the Ottoman Empire should have developed along lines that closely paralleled the major trends of European history. At the same time, the Ottoman Empire pursued close political, cultural and economic relations —especially during the sixteenth century— with its eastern neighbours in Iran, the Arab lands and India.

In the fifteenth and sixteenth centuries the idea of a unified Europe on the basis of Christian ideology and a holy war against the Ottomans was either a myth or an effort to exploit public opinion in Europe in order to legitimize the policies of individual states. During the fourteenth and fifteenth centuries, a crusade was possible only when Venice and Hungary agreed and supported such an enterprise in view of their own political interests (Inalcik, 1969-89).

In actual fact, Ottoman military power provided an element of balance against whatever ambitions the Habsburgs and the Papacy may have had for dominating Europe. In fact, the spread of Protestantism benefitted greatly from Ottoman pressure on the Habsburgs (Fischer-Galati, 1959; Kortepeter, 1972). Furthermore, documentary evidence suggests that in 1494, when Charles VIII of France was preparing to invade Italy, even the Papal States hoped to receive asistance from the Ottomans. In short, at the threshold of modern times, instead of the unity of Europe under the Pope and the emperor, *Realpolitik* and a new political order, based on independent national monarchies, called for a system based on a balance of power and the Ottoman state became an important component of the new European state system.

In the following centuries Ottoman power often proved a necessary component of this new order.

As for the Arab world, without the Ottomans the map of the Islamic world would have been drastically different today. By the end of the fifteenth century Spain had brought her *reconquista* into the Maghrib and began to capture coastal cities. If the Maghrib has remained Muslim, it was because of the Ottoman presence and struggle against the *reconquista*. Also, in 1517 when the Portuguese fleet attacked Jidda to capture the Holy Cities of Islam, it was the Ottoman admiral, Selman Reīs, who repulsed them (Bacqué-Grammont and Kroell, 1988). Within twenty years, the Ottomans built a defence line from Aden to Abyssinia which foiled the repeated Portuguese attempts to enter the Red Sea. Through the Persian Gulf and the Red Sea, under Ottoman protection, the Arab lands began to receive Indian goods and there was a full revival of the spice trade in the Middle East in the mid-sixteenth century. Syrian and Egyptian cities recovered their prosperity and expanded. Aleppo, in particular, became the centre of the caravan roads from Hejaz, Basra-Baghdad and Iran and soon was noted as the principal trade centre of the entire region.

It is true, however, that the Arab lands had to share the reverses and heavy financial burden of the Ottoman imperial presence. The concentration of power and wealth in the Ottoman capital overshadowed such old Arab metropolises as Cairo, Baghdad and Damascus which once enjoyed universal significance in power and wealth.

The reasons for the Ottoman achievements can be summarized under several headings. Above all else it was the Ottomans' mastery of the technology of modern warfare, including new weaponry and shipbuilding techniques, and their active recruitment of foreign engineers and technicians that ensured their success in countering the threat posed by the contemporary European powers. The second factor in their success was their geographical position which gave them the possibility of controlling the rich trade routes between the East (Iran and India) and the West (the European states), and secured them financial and material plenty. Finally, the centralized bureaucratic system of rule adopted by the Ottomans was developed to a point of perfection so striking as to attract the notice of the sixteenth-century political theorist of absolute monarchy in the West, Jean Bodin. The Ottoman sovereign possessed absolute control over all revenues and financial resources of the realm and could allocate them to whatever purposes he saw fit. Thus, as the European states gained wealth and power, the Ottoman sultan was in a position effectively to channel the resources of his state to meet the challenge. It is an unquestionable fact that by the mid-sixteenth century the Ottoman state had emerged as a superpower claiming universal rule. There was no aspect of world affairs from the developments in Germany, England and Holland to the political situation of Sumatra in which the Ottomans did not take an avid and direct interest (Allen, 1963). Particularly during the sixteenth century the Ottoman Empire assiduously sought to capitalize on every development in the realm of international affairs so as to turn it to its own advantage within the context of its own plan for world domination. In the sixteenth century the empire was actively involved on a number of different fronts. In the Mediterranean it confronted the oftentimes combined power of Venice, the Papacy and Spain. In the Ukraine and the lower Volga, it fought to contain Russian imperial expansion. It was poised ready in the Indian Ocean to forestall the threat posed by the deployment of Portuguese fleets seeking to extend Portugal's dominance as a sea power into the Red Sea and Persian Gulf. And last but not least it was in a state of continuous confrontation with the Holy Roman emperors throughout their extensive holdings which stretched from Central Europe to the Mediterranean. In 1571 the Ottoman defeat at Lepanto constitutes a turning point in the history both of the Ottoman Empire and Europe (Braudel, 1949). At Lepanto the Ottomans learned that there were limits to the empire's resources for international conflicts, and they brought to a definitive end their grand undertakings aimed at establishing domination over Europe on the one hand and the Indian Ocean on the other. They subsequently concentrated their strength and resources on the spheres of more immediate imperial concern in the Mediterranean, in Central Europe and in their own backyards in the Islamic East. The Ottomans recognized that the Europeans whom they once confronted successfully had now acquired a preponderant status in world affairs. The Ottomans acknowledged that European advances in a number of different spheres from control over economic resources and world trade routes to mastery of the technology of modern warfare and military science made further attempts to compete with them futile. In this regard it is noteworthy already in the seventeenth century that the Ottomans found it necessary to import their top grade steel and gunpowder from England. Traditional Ottoman methods in mining, engineering, and in many other branches of industrial output had become obsolete, leaving Ottoman producers hopelessly incapable of competing with Western-produced goods which now began to dominate world markets. Around this time, European products began to earn a reputation for being both high quality and inexpensively produced. Thanks to the additional advantage secured by the favorable trading concessions granted by the Ottomans, mercantilistic Europe began to flood Ottoman markets with its manufactured goods. This process was to reach its culmination in the second half of the eighteenth century at which time the Ottoman Empire assumed its place as a peripheral economic power subordinated to the capitalist world economy.

The Ottomans were also crippled as a world power by their surrender of sea power in the Mediterranean to the Western states. From the 1590s upon the entry into the Mediterranean arena of the superior English and Dutch vessels, the end was spelled for both the Venetian and the Ottoman hegemony in that sea, and brought about their mutual capitulation to the rising economies of the North Atlantic. Even the interregional traffic within the empire on the sea routes that linked the capital with the centres of trade and pilgrimage in Egypt and the Levant was mostly carried on foreign ships. Another blow from the West was the invasion of cheap American silver and European silver coins from 1584 on. This resulted in the collapse of the Ottoman currency system, and state political crises followed the monetary and financial disorder (Inalcik, 1992; Barkan, 1975). Historians in general agree that catastrophic events taking place in the period between 1590 and 1632 led to the irreversible decline of the empire. The empire was then continuously wrecked by crises which extended to all spheres of government – from public order and financial security to succession to the throne. The everlasting crisis threatened the very existence of the state. That the Ottomans themselves were aware of the severity of this crisis is made clear by the observations of the reform writers who openly debated the causes of the empire's ills (Inalcik, 1980, 1972). The Ottomans' decision to enter into a period of protracted warfare with the Habsburgs on the one hand (1593-1606) while at the same time pursuing war in the east against Iran the latter conflict lasting with some interruptions for more than five decades from 1578 to 1639 – must be considered one of the principal causes of the empire's decline.

In particular, the chronic state of war between the Ottomans and the Ṣavafids for control over Azerbaijan and Iraq had a devastatingly destructive effect on the Ottoman state.

The period of most intense *jelālī* depredations in Anatolia was followed in the period 1610 to 1632 by a series of rebellions against the centre by the provincial governors. During this period, the rebel governors sought to destroy the Janissaries as the Sultan's main source of political and military support, thus further weakening the empire's centralist rule and ability to defend itself. At the root of these power struggles lay the intractable problem of the mercenaries and the unresolved question of how their demands for greater recognition as a force in state politics were to be accommodated. During the early decades of the seventeenth century, the mercenary *sekbān* foot soldiers dominated the make–up of the expanded military retinues attached to the service of the provincial governors, and apart from their perfectly reasonable demands for punctual payment and adequate supply, these troops had the desire for booty or for other rewards for their sacrifices in line of duty. As late as the nineteenth century, however, problems associated with the periodic need for temporarily mobilized mercenary troops (especially for the wars against Russia) continued to plague Ottoman military planners.

During the period when the provincial scene was dominated by rebellious governors, the reins of government were effectively in the hands of the Janissaries in the capital. A Janissary–led coup in 1622 ended with the execution of Sultan Osman II, an event without precedent in previous Ottoman history. Around this time a triumvirate consisting of the top officers of the Janissary corps was formed, and its voice carried such weight in Ottoman politics that it was able to dictate its terms both to the palace and to the government (see Plate 58). The Ottoman reform writers of the period attributed this development to the weakening of Sultanic authority through power–sharing arrangements. In their view, an undivided and absolute sultanic authority was the essential precondition for keeping mutually opposing forces in society in proper balance. By taking the reins of government firmly in his own hands when he became an adult in 1632, Murad IV (1622-40) succeeded in bringing the dictatorship of the Janissaries to an end. Sultan Murad had also put an end to the provincial disturbances and in this way sultanic authority was firmly re–established. The neutralization of Europe as an effective threat to the Ottomans during the period of the Thirty Years War (1618–48) gave Murad the opportunity to renew the Ottoman conflict with the Ṣafavids undistracted by other strategic concerns. In 1638 he retook Baghdad. In the decade which followed, during the reign of an ineffectual ruler, Sultan Ibrahim I (1640–8) and during the minority years of his successor, Mehmed IV (1648–87), the issue of sultanic authority surfaced again. Once more state authority was divided between the proponents of rival factions while at the same time the ongoing Ottoman campaigns against Venice aimed at dislodging them from Crete resulted in defeat for the Ottomans. For the time being, the Ottomans had completely lost their control at sea, and the Venetian blockade of Dardanelles placed the capital itself in jeopardy. At this juncture, the palace was left with no option but to hand over the reins of government with dictatorial powers to an experienced vizier in the person of Köprülü Mehmed Pasha who assumed office in 1656. The aged vizier proceeded to subdue the Janissaries by forceful means and assigned potentially dangerous or openly rebellious provincial governors to the war fronts in Dalmatia and Crete. In other words, Köprülü Mehmed, with the full backing of public opinion, made a successful bid to restore centralized state authority. By eliminating the Venetian blockade he removed the threat to the capital, but the effort to capture Candia which lasted over twenty–four years from 1645 to 1669 was successfully concluded only in the time of his son and successor Fāzil Ahmed Pasha. During the period of recovery inaugurated by the Köprülü family it was a relative of the Köprülüs, Qara Mustafa Pasha, who deceived himself into thinking that the Ottomans could reassert their supremacy over eastern and central Europe. He entered the Ukraine at the head of a large army and won the initial campaign against Russian forces in 1678. Later, in 1683, Qara Mustafa opened a campaign against the Habsburgs and surrounded Vienna with a huge army. All Europe anxiously followed the events as their collective fate seemed to hang in the balance. At this time the Habsburgs were already at war in the west with France and felt compelled to cease hostilities in light of the general peril facing Christendom. Under papal guidance, a Holy League comprising the Habsburgs, Venice and Poland was formed, and after long negotiations with both parties the Russians finally threw in their lot with the Holy League. The Holy Roman Emperor with the full military support of the German princes succeeded in evicting the Ottomans from Hungary, and the League's armies advanced for a time as far as the plain of Kossovo at the heart of the Balkans. During the long war which continued over a sixteen year period between 1683 and 1699, the Habsburgs occupied Hungary, Venice occupied the Morea (1686) and the Russians occupied the fortress of Azov (1696); this coordinated general anti–Ottoman attack of a united Europe orchestrated by the Holy League determined the empire's fate for centuries to come. Europe, which had lived since 1453 under the constant threat of attack being launched by the superpower which bordered it to the south–east, was finally relieved from the spectre of war by the terms of the treaty signed at Karlowitz in 1699. As for the Ottomans, the defeat and the retreat imposed by the combined forces of the Holy League forced them to acknowledge Western superiority once and for all, and finally convinced them that their only means of survival lay in the imitation of Western methods and institutions. In the period following Karlowitz the empire's traditional rivals, the Habsburgs and Russia resumed their many–pronged attacks against Ottoman territories along the northern shore of the Black Sea and in the Balkans preparatory to a final invasion of the empire's heartlands. Alarmed by this prospect and what it implied for their own commercial interests in the Ottoman east, Western states sought to bolster the empire and preserve its integrity. The 'Eastern Question' emerged as a premier concern in the European balance of power which was now divided between two major power blocs composed of those nations pursuing pro–and anti–Ottoman foreign policies. In this period, the foreign policy of the Ottoman Empire relied on support from the Western powers–in particular France and England – to protect it against the threat posed by the expansionist aims of the Habsburgs and Russia.

This dependence on Western support in the diplomatic arena strengthened the process of westernization which had begun to manifest itself in the Ottoman state. Beginning from the time of Peter I, Tsar of Russia (1682–1725), the Ottomans began to attribute the Russian tsar's successes in the battle against them to the tsars' westernizing policies. During the eighteenth and nineteenth centuries, the Ottomans undertook westernizing reforms of their own in earnest.

The Question of the Ottoman Decline

During the last three decades, an extensive literature has poured forth asking the question why nations under the Ottomans remained backward. The answer was sought in the social structure of the Ottoman Empire. It was argued that the empire typified a feudal state or that it typified a state at some stage in the 'Asiatic Mode of Production'. The former argued that it was feudal because the society was divided into two principal classes, the ruling military élite on the one hand and the masses of dependent reaya with few political or civil rights on the other hand. The surplus product of the latter, it was argued, was appropriated merely by force for the élite with no economic articulation. Those who identified the Ottoman Empire as one of the Asiatic empires with a strong centralist bureaucracy and a command economy, believed that there was no possibility for change which could lead to economic growth and social evolution in this socio-political structure. It is believed that the fundamental cause of the stagnant character of the Ottoman economy and society was the state ownership of arable lands, which resulted in the complete control of peasant production and labour. In this situation, there was no possibility for the agricultural economy to change and to adapt to market 'economy. In this major economic sector, a stagnant subsistence economy prevailed for centuries.

Similarly, a rigid regulatory regime imposed upon the crafts prevented urban industries from developing. Studies on Ottoman social structure based on archival evidence confirm the theory that Ottoman state control of agricultural land and peasant labour was indeed one of the main causes of the Ottoman failure in social and economic change. But, it must be added, this is a reductionist approach which ignores all other fundamental political and economic conditions which made possible the development of a capitalist economy among the western societies in a particular period of their history. In fact, the Ottoman Empire had a specific agrarian-social structure it strove to maintain throughout its history in the Balkans and Anatolia. It was a foundation stone for the Ottoman social-political system to maintain an agrarian system based on small peasant family-farms which were called *çift-khāne*. *Çift-khāne* was an economic-fiscal unit consisting of a peasant household with a farm of a size workable by a pair of oxen, sufficient to sustain the household and meet reproduction and tax obligations. The Ottoman bureaucracy took every necessary measure to maintain these agrarian-fiscal units and it was basically successful in eliminating the trends aiming at converting peasant farms into big estates. The basic policy to ensure it consisted of putting all arable land under state ownership called *mīrī*.

Recent studies argue that the population explosion which the empire experienced in the mid-sixteenth century resulted in a profound crisis in the Ottoman society as a whole. Since no technical innovations were introduced or no changes in the state-controlled Ottoman landholding system occurred, the extensive traditional agricultural system based preponderantly on wheat and barley production could not keep pace with the population increase. It is true, under population pressure peasants moved and settled in the *mezraa*s which were the arable lands of abandoned villages nearby and marginal lands, or new lands opened in the forest and swamp areas. Ottoman survey books provide evidence of such activities in the sixteenth century.

It was to resist Austrian-German soldiers equipped with hand-guns that the Ottoman government felt the necessity to replace the provincial cavalry, the sipahis, which used only outdated conventional weapons, with the Janissaries and mercenaries. The Janissary corps was expanded but this was expensive and as a result the state had to organize companies of 50 to 100 musketeers from among the wandering peasants under the command of officers sent from the Janissary corps to Anatolia. It was an easy investment for a peasant youth to buy a musket and be enrolled as a mercenary (manufacture of muskets ceased to be a state monopoly and cheap types were available at this time).

Dismissed in peace time, such mercenary companies turned into brigands living off the villages to survive. Just as France had experienced a horrible period of anarchy at the hands of *compagnies d'armes* during and after the Hundred Years War, Ottoman Anatolia too was devastated by bands of unemployed mercenaries known as the *jelālīs* during the years 1593-1610. The critical point in this development was that landless peasants were now given the opportunity to organize themselves to fight for survival. The Balkans would experience the same type of depredation and devastation during and after the wars against the Habsburgs and Russians in the eighteenth century when the Ottoman government introduced the same enrolment method in the poor mountainous areas of Albania and Rhodopes.

Communication in Ottoman Society

For a social and cultural history of the Ottoman Empire it is of key importance to begin with a comprehensive view of the forms and techniques of communication.

Education: *Madrasa*, Mosque, Palace and Dervish Convents

Madrasas or theological seminaries existed in the Ottoman realm since Sultan Orhan's time (1324-62) and there was a state organization of the hierarchy of *madrasas* from the fourteenth century. A comprehensive reorganization was introduced by Mehmed II (1451-81) under the supervision of the famous astronomer, 'Alī Qushdju. A second reorganization was made under Süleymān I (Inalcik, 1973).

Politics, culture, and religion being inseparable in Ottoman society, we have to look at the religious institutions for social-political expression and activities. In the second half of the sixteenth century, *madrasas* in Anatolia became centres of discontent and rebellion for the unprivileged. Peasant youth or urban destitutes flowed to the *madrasas* as students, since being a student, *sukhte,* guaranteed exemption from taxation.

Sometimes they created their own *'madrasa'* on a remote mountain and they also organized gangs which roamed the country robbing the people under the cover of collecting canonically approved alms. These gangs proliferated to the extent that the government declared them to be gangs of bandits, and abolished all such small provincial *madrasas. Sukhtes* caused such extensive social upheaval that historians call these disorders the *sukhte rebellion.* This situation resulted in the concentration of higher education in the three capitals of the empire, Istanbul, Bursa and Edirne.

In the Ottoman Empire, the mosque too was place where public opinion was shaped.

In the mosques, professors gave lectures, not only for students but also for the public outside their *madrasas.* We know of cases where a simple soldier, a Janissary, attended such lectures and became a member of the 'ulamā group. After the Friday prayers a preacher, *khatīb,* came to the pulpit and gave religious advice. Some preachers covered current affairs and events in their preaching. Every sermon ended by mentioning the name of the Sultan and giving a short prayer for him. This was interpreted in Islamic practice as recognizing the legitimacy of the sultan's authority. No Muslim ruler was legitimate unless his name was mentioned on the coinage and in the *khutba,* Friday sermon.

Speaking of oral communication, we cannot ignore various kinds of formal or occasional meetings. It was a venerated custom with all Muslim rulers to have periodic sessions with the 'ulamā at the palace, and all of the outstanding scholars of the time were invited to these meetings. At such meetings religious questions, theological as well as juridical, with some practical relevance to current issues were discussed. Such meetings often resulted in bitter rivalries among the 'ulamā. They were particularly frequent under Mehmed II. In one of the meetings, he encouraged the leading 'ulamā to write on the famous theological question of whether God is intelligible through reason or faith.

The Palace school and its role in Ottoman high culture deserves special attention (Miller, 1941; Inalcik, 1973). Palace education aimed at training the sultan's servants, who were mostly of servile origin called *ghulām* or *ķul,* to become the political élite. The 'Perfect ghulām' was the one who became a blind instrument of the sultan's absolutist regime and shared a cosmopolitan culture with other élite groups in the Islamic world, in particular with their counterparts in Iran and Mughal India. Their political philosophy, artistic taste and manners were standard, basically originating from pre-Islamic Indo-Iranian cultural heritage. Common to all the political élite groups were refinement, exclusivity and the disdain of folk culture of the land. Ottomans, in the formative period of their empire, endeavored to learn this sophisticated, cosmopolitan culture from the Timurid and Iranian examples. For instance, the *Qābūsnāme,* a Persian manual for the gentleman or prince, was translated several times during this period.

Conformist dervishes received donations in the form of religious endowment, or *waqf,* and built convents, *zāviyes* and *khānqāhs.* These were gathering places where members of the order came together for rituals. Usually religious music and dancing, *semā,* were performed to attain a mystical experience, and a religious meal followed the ritual (Birge, 1937). The government expected these establishments to fulfil the function of a sanctuary for the poor, the uprooted and travellers. Apparently such convents or lodges also provided a forum for discussion of current affairs. Religious orders such as the *Melāmetiyye,* radical in their anti-government beliefs, survived only as underground organizations. The government persecuted *melāmetī* leaders.

Militant wandering dervishes, similar to minstrels, preached in the bazaars and in public places, and they had a powerful influence on the populace of the towns as well as in rural areas. Dervishes called *Baba*s or *abdal*s, spiritual leaders of the semi-nomadic Turkmens or Yörüks, led the most dangerous insurrections in central Anatolia or in Dobrudja, the centre of the Yörüks in *Rumili* in the fifteenth and sixteenth centuries.

Popular meeting places and public entertainers

The *boza*-house and coffee-house were places of socializing in the bazaar area. (*Boza* made of fermented millet is a drink typical of Central Asiatic pastoralists). Before the coffee-house became a place of social gathering, its function was fulfilled by the *boza*-house. Since certain kinds of *boza* were intoxicating and since the *boza*-house became an arena for political gossip, government control was exercised through a monopoly system. Each town had a limited number of *boza*-houses rented by the government. The qadi was in charge of inspecting them. As would happen later with the coffee-house in the middle of the sixteenth century, the *boza*-houses were labelled 'the nest of trouble makers and nasty gossip' and were often shut down by the sultan's decree.

In rural areas the Turkish minstrel who wandered from one place to another was the most popular element in communication. Mostly active in the countryside, playing his *qopuz* or *saz,* an instrument originally used in Central Asia by shamans, these minstrels were responsible for the transmission of the most varied and colourful folk literature productions, religious, popular-mystical, naturalistic-realistic and epic. The minstrel was the mouthpiece of religio-political propaganda, particularly that addressed the oppressed Shī'ī sects of Anatolia, the Qïzilbash, whose beliefs, aspirations, and complaints the minstrel voiced. Minstrels such as Pir Sultān Abdal became the instigators of popular protest movements. Rural classes, peasants and pastoralists voiced their aspirations through these popular minstrels.

In towns and cities the bazaar, *charshï* or *sūq* area was the place of contact and communication for the whole urban population. Christians, Jews and Muslims belonged to the same guilds in the bazaar and intermingled there while in the residential part of town each group lived in its own quarter. As a rule, government offices, the cathedral mosque and the law court were also situated in the bazaar area, and government announcements were made by a herald in the bazaar square (Inalcik, 1971; Wirth, 1975; Faroqhi, 1984, 1987).

Written Communication

Islamic culture is one based on the written word. The Qu'rān, was collected in book form under the third caliph, Osman. Book writing and dissemination of knowledge in Islamic society were determined by two principal concerns: propagation, teaching and consolidation of Islam, and the preparation of a bureaucracy in order to increase, in the most efficient way, the power and wealth of the sultan-caliph. Accordingly, books were classified in two principal categories, those on religious and related areas (*'ūlūm*) and those on practical uses *(funūn).* The last category included literary sciences *(ādāb)* as well as such sciences as mathematics *(hisāb* and *siyāqa),* geography, history, astronomy and zoology. The practical sciences were supposed to serve in the last analysis 'religion and the state' *(dīn u dawla).* For example, it was the desire to increase the tax base that stimulated writing or translating books on agronomy. Astronomy provided knowledge on weather conditions as well as the determination of good omens for the sultan's decisions. At the beginning of each year, the palace astronomer presented to the sultan an almanac with a list of good and bad dates. Of course, occasionally independent minds emerged, engaged in science for the sake of science. Ottoman mathematician Molla Lutfi

(d. 1494) was one of them, but the corps of 'ulamā had him hanged at the square of the At-Meydanï in front of a huge crowd of spectators. Intellectual life and book production had to be and was in harmony with the needs and requirements of a traditional, patrimonial society. Tradition and social equilibrium, not change or 'progress' was the ideal of that society. Nizām al-Mulk's classic book on the art of government, *Siyāsetnāme,* described the ideal social order as a compartmentalized society of status groups with no mobility allowed. It was only in the nineteenth and twentieth centuries that 'westernizers' in the Middle East came up with the new ideas that change and 'progress' were good, minimizing the concept of a society in 'perfect equilibrium' on the basis of the values of eternal truth and tradition.

Music and dancing in the dervish convents were condoned by some of the 'ulamā only when they helped stir and elevate the spirit to religious-mystical perceptions. On the other hand, it should be noted that honesty and earnest concern for careful examination and accuracy in religious sciences trained 'ulamā with a scholarly discipline. Ottoman sultans employed 'ulamā in bureaucratic services especially in the first two centuries when a fully competent group of bureaucrats had not yet emerged. Sultans also needed the 'ulamā's authoritative opinions in organizing their conquests according to the precepts of Islam. While the 'ulamā had a *madrasa* education, the bureaucrats had their basic training in the bureaus as apprentices to master bureaucrats in the same way artisans became masters of their profession. Specializing in some practical sciences, however, some of the 'ulamā entered the secretarial profession.

The Ottoman zeal in collecting and preserving the scholarly heritage of the Islamic world in many libraries in Istanbul made it possible for the Ottoman scholars to compose encyclopedias. Today the Istanbul libraries are considered to house the best and largest collection on Islamic sciences in the world. The encyclopedia of sciences *(Mewzū 'āt al- 'Ulūm)* by Tashköprülüzāde, and that of Hajjī Khalīfa (Kātib Chelebi) entitled *Kashf al Zunūn* are the best known among many such works.

Ritual as Communication

While rites, ceremonies and festivals had particularly important social functions and meaning in Islamic society, Ottoman parades and processions also showed features common to other Mediterranean societies. Islamic rituals had a powerful effect for stirring intense emotions and leading masses to common action. Every military campaign and victory celebration started and ended at the Aya-Sofya (Hagia Sophia), cathedral mosque of the capital city where the sultan, dignitaries, army commanders and a great crowd of believers came together and prayed for success. During the campaign, at the encampment sites, vast open air squares called *namāzgāh* were used so that thousands could pray together before God and produce a powerful feeling of solidarity.

The direct contact of the ruler with the ruled was considered a fundamental principle of government in Islamic culture (Inalcik, 1973). The mirror-for-princes literature recommended that the sultan make use of outings such as a religious ceremony or a hunting party to get in direct contact with ordinary people and receive their written complaints *(riq'a)*. This was an ancient Middle Eastern custom interpreted as the sign of the ruler's concern to protect the people from the abuse of power by his agents to whom he entrusted delegated powers. The presence of the ruler at the imperial council and the right of every subject to bring his complaint to the council were considered the foundation of good government and justice.

Festivals of Iranian or Islamic origin, celebrated on certain days of the year such as the birthday of the prophet, the night of his voyage to heaven and especially Ramadān, the month of fasting, became the occasions of ceremonies. At the *'īd al-adhā* festival (in colloquial Turkish *Qurban* festival) thousands of sheep were slaughtered and distributed to the poor by the sultan and well-to-do citizens. At the *'īd al-fitr* relatives and friends visited each other, old discords were forgotten and a new life full of hope began for everybody. It was a strict rule that the younger and the lesser in rank paid visits first.

Nowrūz, the beginning of the New Year, on the spring equinox, a prehistoric rite in origin, became an indispensable part of the imperial ritual celebrated by the Ottomans in all earnestness.

Festivals on the occasion of the circumcision ceremony of the sultan's son or wedding of his daughter were organized as events of great importance. In fact, the Ottoman festival was characterized more by its ritualistic, political, and social meaning than by its being an occasion of pure entertainment. It was an occasion to show a spirit of peace and reconciliation (And, 1963/1964). Vassal princes and dignitaries offered their presents and were honoured by costly caftans and other gifts at the festivities in which social-political bonds were strengthened. The strict rules of protocol observed at these meetings established rank and hierarchy among the ruling group. Bringing together the ordinary people with the ruling élite and letting them share the joyous atmosphere of the festival fulfilled the important social function of reestablishing bonds of attachment and trust in the otherwise rigidly compartmentalized hierarchical Ottoman society.

Since circumcision was believed to be, like baptism in Christianity, the beginning of a new stage of life, it was as an occasion for particularly long and grandiose festivals. The festival of the circumcision of the prince Mehmed in

1582, a particularly grandiose one lasting more than fifty days, was described in a magnificent festival-book, the *sūrnāme,* illustrated with superb miniatures. People of all avenues of life in the city participated in these festivals.

In this atmosphere mass conversions to Islam occurred and thousands of non-Muslims came to join the circumcised Ottoman prince. The purpose was to show the wealth and might of the ruler to the whole world. This becomes evident in the fact that foreign rulers were always invited through special envoys. A special kiosk was erected to accommodate the representatives of European princes at the 1582 festival of Prince Mehmed's circumcision. In these festivals everyone was considered to be the guest of the sultan and was served food during the festival. Such details as the permit to plunder the dishes after the public banquets are reminiscent of the Central Asiatic *toy* and *shölen* which had an important ritualistic meaning in the Turco-Mongolian khanates.'Feeding his people' was considered to be one of the most important duties of a khan. Providing public feasts symbolized it and neglect of it sometimes resulted in rebellion.

Such grandiose festivals required a careful organization and lavish spending. Public entertainment, dinners and fireworks were carefully scheduled and everything took place in perfect order.

An imperial festival for the accession to the throne or for the birth of a prince or for a major military success was organized not only in the capital of the empire but in all cities. The *At Meydanï,* the ancient Roman Hippodrome in Istanbul, was the square in which festivals usually took place in the capital.

An important type of unofficial customary festival in Ottoman society was organized by handicraft guilds. On the first day of the traditional New Year festival, members of each guild, Muslim and non-Muslim, celebrated it together going out for an excursion. This expressed and renewed the guild brotherhood and solidarity.

Ottomans and Westernization

Although the Ottomans borrowed many European cultural elements, this did not result in their assimilation to European culture, mainly because the Ottomans retained their value system which is an intrinsic principle of their culture embodied in the religion of Islam.

Let us study a specific case. Ottomans borrowed firearms as early as the 1380s through the Balkan states, while it appeared in Hungary about 1354 (Petrovich, 1975). By 1378 canons were made in Dubrovnik. In order to resist the Ottoman onslaught the Balkan states made use of firearms from 1380 onward. Ottomans appeared in the western Balkans in 1385 where firearms were already used quite extensively. Cannons appeared to have been used at the battle of Kossovo in 1389. Dubrovnik became the major manufacturing centre for firearms and was a supply centre for other Balkan states. Already in 1393 big guns capable of firing shots of 300 pounds were cast in Dubrovnik. A contemporary eyewitness, a German captive at Nicopolis (1396), Schiltberger states that Bāyezīd I used cannons in his campaign against Karaman in 1397. Arquebuses and hand guns appeared in the Balkans in the 1430s. In the fifteenth century, the makers of guns were mostly foreigners including Italians, Hungarians, Germans and Frenchmen. In making cannons first blacksmiths were employed and over time expert gun-makers took over. Although initially the Ottomans hired foreign experts or employed captives, they themselves learned the art and became quite sophisticated in making cannons and arquebuses. The Hungarian cannon-maker, Urban, hired by Mehmed II, is a well known example. He made history by producing giant cannons for the Sultan to demolish the walls of Constantinople. Ottoman artillery was among the best in Europe and was responsible for the capture of such fortresses, thought impregnable, as Rhodes and Nicosia.

Throughout Ottoman History, sultans invited foreign experts to join their services. A special chamber of European engineers and specialists called *Efrenciyān* was created at the Sultan's palace as early as the sixteenth century. In the Topkapï Palace archives, Leonardo da Vinci's application to come to Istanbul and perform construction works for the Sultan was discovered (Babinger, 1958).

The circumstances under which the Ottomans borrowed the Hussite *Wagenburg* tactic is of particular interest. The Ottomans quickly adopted the tactic which had given John Hunyadi unquestionable superiority over the Ottomans in the field. Consisting of an arrangement of war wagons mounted with guns in a circle like a mobile fortress, this innovation was one of the important factors in the Ottoman victories in the east over the Iranians and the Mameluks. These Muslim rivals of the Ottomans were delayed in equipping their own regiments with firearms. In Iran and India, cannon-makers came mostly from Ottoman territory. Two Ottoman cannon-makers helped Bābur, the founder of the Mughal Empire in India, gain military superiority over his rivals. Ottoman expertise in making and tactically using firearms gave them a reputation throughout the Arab lands and India such that Ottoman mercenaries called *Rūmī* (Anatolian Turk) were in great demand in all these countries. In their struggle against the Portugese and Iranians, Ottoman sultans sent soldiery equipped with firearms or experts to the Central Asiatic Khanates, Muslim states in India and to the Atjeh Sultanate in Sumatra in the mid-sixteenth century. Following the same methods as in the making of firearms, Ottomans also had their own shipyards as early as the fourteenth century and by the end of the fifteenth century organized powerful navies to challenge Venetian sea power. In their dockyards of Gallipoli Greeks and later on engineers from Genoa and Dubrovnik worked for them. Ottomans, however, lost the race with Europe in war technology in the seventeenth century. Subsequently, they suffered severe defeats because they were able only to borrow techniques without the cultural and social conditions and institutions specific to the West which secured creativity in such tools.

The French *Encyclopédie* became available to Ottoman students in the Ottoman engineering school, and it is believed that ideas of the French Revolution were not unfamiliar in Turkey at the end of the eighteenth century (Lewis, 1953). The idea of revolution in the sense of fundamental change in the society as understood in modern Europe was conceived in the Ottoman Empire as a fundamental reform, implemented from above through state power. Until 1950 such reforms were introduced exclusively through the efforts of the bureaucracy as necessary expedients for the survival of the state since a civil society in western sense never fully developed in the empire. Thus, the periodization of Ottoman history must be based on its fundamental reforms. Although the empire's fate became closely dependent on the political and economic changes in Europe, particularly in the eighteenth century, its historical evolution cannot be considered to have had complete parallelism with Europe. However, it is a fact that decisions on fundamental bureaucratic reforms came under pressure from Europe in Ottoman history, a fact which is also true for other countries outside Europe.

BIBLIOGRAPHY

Allen, W.E.D. 1963. *Problems of Turkish Power in the Sixteenth Century.* London.

And, M. 1963-4. *A History of Theatre and Popular Entertainment in Turkey,* Forum. Ankara.

Babinger, F. 1958. Vier Bauvorschläge Leonardo da Vinci's am Sultan Sultan Bayezid II (1502-3). *Nachrichten der Akademie der Wissenschaften in Göttingen. Phil. His. Kl., no. II.*

Bacqué-Grammont, J-L.; Kroell, A. 1988. *Mamlouks, Ottomans et Portugais en Mer Rouge.* Cairo.

Barkan, Ö.L. 1975. The Price Revolution of the Sixteenth Century. English transl. J. Mc Carthy, *International Journal of Middle East Studies,* vol. VI, no. I.

Birge, J.B. 1937. *The Bektashi Order of Dervishes.* London.

Braudel, F. 1949. *La Méditerranée et le monde méditerranéen à l'époque de Philippe II.* Paris. [English trans. Reynold, S. 1972. *The Mediterranean and the Mediterranean World in the Age of Philip II.* New York.]

Faroqhi, S. 1984. *Towns and Townsmen of Ottoman Anatolia, Crafts and Food Production in the Urban Setting.* Cambridge.

_____. 1987. *Men of Modest Substance: House-Owners and House Property in Seventeenth-Century Ankara and Kayseri.* Cambridge.

Fischer-Galati, S.A. 1959. *Ottoman Imperialism and German Protestantism.* Cambridge, Mass.

İnalcık, H. 1969-89. The Ottoman Turks and the Crusades. In: Hazard, H.V.; Zakour, N.P. (eds) *The Impact of the Crusades on Europe.* Setton, K.M. (general ed.). *A History of the Crusades. Vol. VI.* Madison, University of Wisconsin Press.

_____. 1971. "Ghulām". In: *Encyclopaedia of Islam,* second edition (EI^2), III.

_____. 1971. "Imtiyāzāt". (EI^2), III.

_____. 1971. "İstanbul". (EI^2), IV.

_____. 1972. "The Ottoman Decline and its Effects upon Reaya". In: Birnbaum. H.; Vryonis, S. (eds). *Aspects of the Balkans,* pp. 338-54. The Hague.

_____. 1973. *The Ottoman Empire: The Classical Age, 1300-1600.* London, Weidenfeld and Nicolson.

_____. 1980. "Military and Fiscal Transformation in the Otoman Empire 1600-1700". *Archivum Ottomanicum VI,* pp. 283-337.

_____. 1987. "When and How the English Cotton Goods Invaded the Middle East". In: İnalcık, H.; H. İnan, (eds). *The Ottoman Empire and the World Trade,* pp. 374-83. Cambridge.

_____. 1991. "Ottoman Galata, 1453-1553". In: Eldem, E. (ed.). *Première rencontre internationale sur l'Empire Ottoman et la Turquie moderne, 1985,* pp. 60-6. İstanbul.

_____. 1992. "Economic Situation in Turkey". In: Inalcık, H. *The Middle East and the Balkans under the Otoman Empire.* Bloomington.

İnalcık, H. ed., with D. Quataert, 1994. *An Economic and Social History of the Ottoman Empire.* Cambridge.

Halil İnalcık

Kortepeter, C.M. 1972. *Ottoman Imperialism during the Reformation, 1578-1608.* New York.
Lewis, B. 1953. "The Impact of the French Revolution on Turkey". *Journal of World History,* vol. I, pp. 105-25.
Miller, B. 1941. *The Palace School of Muhammed the Conqueror.* Cambridge.
Petrovich, D.J. 1975. "Fire-arms in the Balkans". In: Parry, V.J.; Yapp, M.E (eds). *War, Technology and Society in the Middle East.* London, Oxford University Press.
Willan, T.S. 1955. "Some aspects of English Trade with the Levant in the Sixteenth Century". *English Historical Review,* LXX.
Wirth, E. 1975. "Die Orientalische Stadt". *Saeculum.* 26, pp. 75-94.

3

Political Modernization in Turkey

We can best describe the original features of Ottoman-Turkish traditional society by going back to the times of Süleyman I (1520-1566). In the period immediately before the political modernization of the nineteenth century, we find only more or less degenerate forms of the original Ottoman institutions, and new social and political developments threatening the basis of those institutions. The generation of reformers confronting the period of decline after the sixteenth century avowedly sought to restore the Golden Age of Süleyman I. Under the impact of the defeats in Hungary between 1683 and 1699 the Ottoman Turks first became aware of the superiority of the West; the reforms thereafter increasingly acknowledged Western influences, first in the military field and then, in the nineteenth century, in administration. The decisive modernization movement, accompanied by a basic change in the concept of state and society, began with the national revolution after the First World War.

The hesitations and delays in the Turkish modernization process were due to the fact that, until the twentieth century, Turkey was an empire comprising nations of different cultures and that the dynasty became at a certain time the only focus of common loyalty. On the other hand, the political and social superstructure of the empire was still based on the *sharī'a* (Turkish: *şeriat*), the unalterable religious law of Islam, and this politico-religious structure culminated in the office of the sultan-caliph.

The position of this Ottoman ruler and the developments which reduced his power and ultimately led to modernization will constitute the main theme of this essay.

I. The Ottoman Ruler and Ottoman Society

Tursun Beg, Ottoman statesman and historian of the late fifteenth century, stressed that harmony among men living in society was achieved only by statecraft, which kept each individual in his proper place as determined by his ability. As the instrument of social order, statecraft possessed two aspects or sanctions: the authority and power of the ruler and the divine reason or *sharī'a*. Insofar as the rules instituted by the ruler did not have a perpetual character, he should always be present in a human society. He should have absolute power to determine the place of each man in the social scheme. Always seeking to strengthen his position by expanding his revenues and his armies, he should serve society as a whole by consolidating public security and order. Tursun Beg's rational arguments were manifestly designed to prove that every society must have one ruler with absolute power and with the authority of issuing regulations and laws outside the religious law. The values which this ruler was to conserve were social order and security under justice. These ideas constituted the basic political philosophy of the Ottomans.

The absolute power of the Ottoman ruler found further support in the old Oriental maxim that a ruler can have no power without soldiers, no soldiers without money, no money without the well-being of his subjects, and no popular well-being without justice. Repeated in Turkish political literature from *Kutadgu Bilig* in the eleventh century to the Gülhane Rescript of 1839, this formula was regarded as the summation of practical statesmanship. Kâtib Çelebi in the seventeenth century particularly stressed the central position of the sultan in the state. Though absolute power was ascribed to the caliph in the Islamic community, the theorists stressed that absolute power was simply a means of implementing the religious law.

The Ottoman rulers first made this theoretical absolutism a reality by establishing a type of administration that concentrated power in their persons. This they achieved notably by eliminating all kinds of aristocracies in the conquered lands, by entrusting executive functions only to slaves trained in the court *(kuls),* and by enlisting the *ulema* in their service. The sultan's slaves were entrusted with executive power and the *ulema* with the administration of law, including the supervision of all legal and financial matters. Both of these branches of administration were attached to the central government but each was independent of the other. A governor had no authority to give orders to a local judge *(kadı)* appointed by the sultan. If a conflict arose between the branches, it was appealed directly to the central government. The same judges administered both the *sharī'a* and the subsidiary laws and regulations directly issued by the sultan. On the other hand, the *şeyhülislām,* the highest authority in formulating opinions on points concerning the *sharī'a,* had no right to interfere directly in the government or in legal administration. Once, when Şeyhülislâm Ali Cemali came over to the seat of the government to protest against a decision of sultan Selim I (1512-1520) which he thought contrary to the *sharī'a,* the sultan denounced him as interfering in state affairs. But in the eighteenth century it became established practice to seek the *şeyhülislām*'s opinion on every governmental matter of importance. The limitations so imposed on the government by the *sharī'a* and by religious authority in the period of decline made the application of reforms especially difficult. The all-embracing *sharī'a* became the stronghold of traditionalism in Ottoman government and society—introducing, as we may note in passing, a major difference between the Turkish and the Japanese modernization processes.

Ottoman social policy conformed closely to the traditional view that for the sake of social peace and order the state should keep each man in his appropriate social position. In the first place, Ottoman society was divided into two major classes. The first one, called *askerī,* literally the "military," included those to whom the sultan had delegated religious or executive power through an imperial diploma, namely, officers of the court and the army, civil servants, and *ulema.* The second included the *reaya,* comprising all Muslim and non-Muslim subjects who paid taxes but who had no part in the government. It was a fundamental rule of the empire to exclude its subjects from the privileges of the "military." Only those among them who were actual fighters on the frontiers and those who had entered the *ulema* class after a regular course of study in a religious seminary could obtain the sultan's diploma and thus become members of the "military" class. It was, in fact, the sultan's will alone that decided a man's status in society. In the period of decline, Koçi Beg and others asserted that a major cause of the disorganization of the empire was the abandonment of this fundamental rule in favor of letting subjects become Janissaries of fief *(tīmār)* holders.

The subjects in turn were divided into Muslims and non-Muslims, townspeople and peasants, sedentaries and nomads, each with a different status, as reflected in their tax obligations. Taxation was indeed the most important factor in determining the subject's status. Those who were granted certain tax immunities in return for public service actually constituted an intermediate group between the simple subjects and the "military," who were wholly tax-exempt. Living for the most part on state-owned lands as tenants, the peasantry were subject to special taxes and were divided into groups according to the taxes they paid, the status of each being individually recorded at regular intervals. Peasants were not allowed to leave their lands, nor could they settle in towns.

These laws reflect a rigid social organization imposed by the will of the Ottoman ruler. But in the late sixteenth century a profound transformation took place which may be attributed ultimately to economic and military changes in Western Europe. During this period, for example, in order to resist German infantrymen, the Ottomans discarded their *tīmār* cavalry in the provinces and increased the force of Janissaries, who were by this time equipped with firearms. This neglect of the fief holders within the army was followed by the disorganization of the land and taxation system upon which their status had been based. Simultaneously, the shift of international trade routes to the Atlantic Ocean and the invasion of the markets of the Levant by American silver resulted in the disorganization of the rigid Ottoman fiscal and economic structure.

Already during this period of "decline", the sultan and his bureaucracy, who sensed immediate danger to the state from outside, adopted the idea of reform, although they thought of it as reform along traditional lines. The Japanese, at a much later date, experienced the same challenge from outside and their emperor, too, personified the idea of reform. But the Japanese reform movement found national support at least among some leading classes in the society, while in the Ottoman Empire the major ruling classes took a reactionary stance. In the Ottoman Empire reform remained a concern of the sultan and his immediate collaborators alone. *Ulema* and a rising semi-feudal landed aristocracy in the provinces, called the *a'yān,* resisted any innovation that might disturb their vested interests.

II. The Decline of the Sultan's Power;

The Janissaries, the *Ulema,* and the Rise of the *A'yān*

In the capital of the empire the politically influential groups were the military corps at the sultan's Porte, particularly the Janissaries, constituting the "military" proper, and the *ulema,* the learned in Islamic sciences, who were vested with authority to express and apply the commands of the *sharī'a.* In the provincess, too, the *ulema* and the Janissaries at one time possessed commanding power, but in the eighteenth century the *a'yān,* a group of provincial magnates, came to be the most powerful class throughout the empire.

The Janissary corps constituted the original foundation of the centralist government and the principal support of the sultan's absolute power. It formed a standing army at the Porte, which was directly attached to the person of the sultan and which he could use at any time to strike at an internal or external foe. In addition, Janissary garrisons were stationed in the main strongholds in the provinces. In the large cities they occupied the forts, which no one else, not even a governor, was allowed to enter. In the period when central authority grew weaker, these Janissaries took over the actual control of the government in such distant parts of the empire as North Africa, Baghdad, and Belgrade. In the capital they determined who would wield control. As early as 1446, Murad II had accepted the throne only after obtaining their consent in a public meeting. In the first half of the seventeenth century they strengthened their grip on the government. In 1628 for the first time a former commander of the

Janissary corps was appointed Grand Vezir with the support of the *şeyhülislām,* the head of the *ulema.* In the 1630s Koçi Beg complained that the balance established earlier between the power of the Janissaries and that of the provincial forces was gone and that the Janissaries invaded all sectors of the empire. The vezirs, courtiers, and heirs to the throne all sought their aid to attain power. The Janissaries furthermore obtained for themselves additional privileges, among them that of engaging in trade. Hence many of them joined the class of small shopkeepers and were thus affected by the government's financial policy as was the rest of the Istanbul population.

Let us observe also how the *a'yān,* a powerful class of magnates, rose in the provinces. Traditionally the Ottomans granted the craftsmen and merchants in the towns a distinct and honorable status and recognized the most influential and wealthy among them as their natural leaders. Organized in so-called *ahi* unions, the craftsmen had played a major social and political role in Anatolia from the thirteenth century onward; their leaders, the *ahis,* acquired control of the administration in many Anatolian towns. Under the centralist government of the Ottomans, they were gradually reduced to simple guild masters, but each guild continued to elect its own master, called *kāhyā,* to supervise the application of the guild's rules and to act as its representative before the authorities.

Above the guildmasters were the *a'yān* (notables) and the *eşrāf,* the most influential residents of the city whom the government always addressed on matters directly concerning the town population. We find these *a'yān* and *eşrāf* present even in fourteenth-century Ottoman cities. Whenever an imperial order was to be communicated to the townsmen, the local judge convoked the *a'yān, eşrāf,* guildmasters, and *imāms* (district clerics) of the town, because "these were," our source adds, "the agents and representatives of the people, who did what they said to do." Among the population, *kāhyās* were elected as representatives of each district of the town and, from very early times, a town *kāhyā,* represented the whole municipality. The local *eşrāf* included the head of the descendants of the Prophet in the town, the head of the local *ulema,* and the mufti, the local agent of the *şeyhülislām.* Though their influence derived originally from religious services, the *eşrāf* were usually among the well-to-do citizens.

The *a'yān* were the most influential and wealthy citizens in a town except for the *eşrāf.* Most of them came from humble origins, many being minor local officials or Janissary officers who had risen by exploiting their official position.

As pointed out earlier, the tax and land-tenure system of the empire underwent a transformation during the upheavals between 1595 and 1610. The new conditions enabled the *a'yān* to become feudal lords in the provinces, replacing the fief holders in the state-owned lands as lessees or tax collectors. In the meetings of *a'yān* and *eşrāf* under the judge, the most important issue was usually the distribution among the people of the total tax assessment of the district. After the decline of the earlier timariote army, the central government, in inureasing need of money to support the enlarged Janissary army, resorted more and more to extraordinary assessments, which were allotted to the counties. These special taxes and the assessments for local expenses were farmed out to individual persons by the council of *a'yān* and *eşrāf*, who often used these responsibilities to increase their own wealth and influence. They usually added to the assessment books items for themselves, or collected additional dues for their services. They often neglected to send the assessment books to the central government for inspection, and thus levied taxes without government control. In 1705 in Manisa, a city in western Anatolia, the populace became outraged by such abuses, and invaded the judge's court where the *a'yān* and *eşrāf* were sitting.

But usually the *a'yān* managed to show themselves to the people as their protectors. They occasionally sent the sultan petitions for tax exemptions, which bore their own signatures though they were confirmed by the judge. They contended with oppressive government officials sent by the sultan. They were so influential in their areas, all in all, that the sultan's governor and judge often became simple tools in their hands. Without their cooperation, the authorities could not collect taxes, levy troops, or maintain public security.

The *a'yān* gained their wealth and power through leasing state-owned lands as well as by tax farming. The larger part of such lands ceased to be assigned to fief *(tīmār)* holders and were leased by the state to local notables, *a'yān* and *ağa*s (*a'yān* usually had the title of *ağa*s, but *ağa*s mentioned together with *a'yān* meant lesser *a'yān* in the provinces), and more than fifty percent of agricultural lands in the empire were state-owned leaseholds. Large areas of endowed land and land assigned to officials and favorites were similarly exploited. The *a'yān*'s influence on, and close cooperation with local authorities, favored them in these leasing operations. Later, in the eighteenth century, the leases were made for lifetime and priority rights to the leases were granted to the sons of lessees.

Tax farming, too, was extended after the dissolution of the old *tīmār* system near the end of the sixteenth century, and local notables benefited from their involvement in this profitable business.

In the period of decline, the sultan's governors themselves employed the *a'yān* as their local agents in financial and administrative matters under such various titles as *mütesellim*, *voyvoda*, and *subaşı*. Increasingly in need of new troops for its prolonged wars, furthermore, the state encouraged the *a'yān* to equip forces at their own expense under their direct command. Thus in the eighteenth century the groundwork had been laid for the rise of a powerful semifeudal aristocracy in the provinces of Anatolia and in the Balkans. Many of the *a'yān* families were able to maintain their position for several generations and founded local dynasties. Actual clashes sometimes occured among rival *a'yān* seeking to extend the area of their leasehold. Some of the most powerful among them even forced the government to confer upon them the official titles of vezir or pasha, thereby consolidating their control of the provinces in which they held their estates and becoming able in time to challenge the sultan's authority. The latter tried in his weakness to play one *a'yān* against another, but often only with the result of making his ally excessively powerful. Tepedelenli Ali Pasha, actual ruler of southern Albania and northern Greece, was the most famous example of a pasha of *a'yān* origin.

III. The Revolutions of 1807 and 1808:

The Struggle for Power among Janissaries, *Ulema,* and *Âyan*

A brief account of the revolutions of 1807 and 1808 will illustrate the part which the Janissaries, *ulema*, and *a'yān* played in political developments in the Ottoman Empire at the turn of the nineteenth century.

Selim III (1789-1807) has been regarded as the father of Ottoman-Turkish Westernization and as an exponent of general reform in the state. He was indeed interested in Western civilization in its various aspects. Ebu Bekir Ratib, his envoy to Vienna in 1791, brought him a detailed report not only of the military and administrative establishments but also of technology and social advances as embodied in such institutions as the postal system and hospitals. Selim gave positive instructions to his newly appointed ambassadors to Western capitals to study the administrative as well as the military institutions of those states and encouraged the staffs at the embassies to learn Western languages and observe all the things that they considered useful. At home before he began his reform he invited the foreign officers in his service, among whom was a French officer in the Ottoman army, to submit appropriate reform proposals. But Selim's main motive for reform was his determination to restore the military power of the empire and throw back the Russians, who had recently conquered the Muslim-inhabited lands north of the Black Sea and now threatened Istanbul itself. His state philosophy was not very different from that of his predecessors. He reasoned, that there could be no power without an army, no army without sufficient sources of revenue, and no revenue without justice and prosperity among his subjects. In his decrees introducing military reforms he pointed out that his ancestors had given him guidance and that the *sharī'a* permitted Muslims to use "the enemies' tricks to overcome them." What was new and antitraditional in his measures was the introduction not only of European weapons but also of the sciences, training procedures and uniforms of Europe. Western scientific thought challenged traditional Muslim thought, and the European uniforms challenged traditional symbols.

He also issued reform decrees on governorship, *a'yān* leases of the domains, currency, and the status of the *ulema*, but all these followed absolutely traditional lines.

Despite his personal conservatism, Selim III created in Ottoman society a trend toward Westarnization and a sense of the necessity for rapid and progressive change. The *ulema*, representing religiously sanctioned traditions, opposed him for the most part. The reforms found support only among some of the higher *ulema* who either sought the favor of the sultan or considered the reforms necessary to the ultimate interests of Islam and caliphate. These supporters, too, appealed to the *sharī'a* to justify their position.

The true reasons for the opposition to Selim were to be found in the social situation. His efforts to create a regular army under his direct command threatened the dominant position in the state of the Janissaries, on the one hand, and of the *a'yān*, on the other. In addition, his financial measures created widespread discontent in the country and turned public opinion and the *ulema* against him.

To finance the new army, Selim created a treasury of the "New Order" and allotted to it the revenues of an important part of the domain leaseholds. To find additional resources he also raised the rates of the various dues. Since the dues paid for the imperial diplomas conferring an office, immunity, or fief were among these, he thereby alienated a number of influential people. The first reaction came from the *a'yān*. When the sultan in 1806 planned to extend the military reform to the Balkans by a transfer of "new troops" from Anatolia, the *a'yān* in the Balkans gathered together in Edirne and opposed his further advance. Selim retreated, and this marked the beginning of his fall. The conservatives at once seized power under the leadership of Hilmi Pasha, the new Grand Vezir who had once been the commander of the Janissaries, and *Şeyhülislâm* Ata'ullah, a fanatic supported by the reactionaries. The opposition of the Janissaries to the New Order was understandable enough: it was no less than an instrument of their own destruction. They also rallied the populace of Istanbul, who were afflicted by the new taxes and by the inflation following Selim's debasing of the currency. The sultan's price-fixing and terrible threats against profiteers had proved useless. The abolition of Janissary pensions in the possession of non-military persons had also affected a number of people in the capital. Finally, Selim had let a group of favorites draw up his reform plans and control their application. Exploiting his ambition to restore the power of the sultanate, many of these favorites in fact set out to gain wealth and power for themselves. The responsible government officials hated them and in time turned against the sultan himself. In their eyes the reformist sultan had merely brought back the arbitrary rule of a handful of favorites.

In brief, the population of Istanbul was, as our analyst says, split into two camps, partisans of the New Order, and its enemies. Finally in 1807 the Janissary *yamak*s rose against the reformist sultan. All the Janissaries, *ulema*, and the populace of Istanbul joined them, seeking the abolition of the New Order and of the treasury created for it, and the execution of the favorites. The head of the *ulema*, Ata'ullah, gave a formal opinion *(fetva)* for the deposition of Selim III, in which he said that Selim was unfit for the caliphate because he had let irresponsible men usurp power and use it against the Muslim population. The rebels made an agreement with the new sultan, Mustafa IV, providing that they would not be prosecuted for their past actions; in return they themselves promised not to interfere in state affairs any more. Our anlyst notes that such a pledge on the part of the sultan was unheard of in Ottoman history. The Janissaries and their conservative allies were now in control of the whole governement and busy with the purge of Selim's partisans. Mustafa's authority was not heeded outside the walls of his court.

The *a'yān* were quick to seize power from the hands of the Janissaries. The *a'yān* of Rumelia under the leadership of Alemdar Mustafa Pasha, formerly an *a'yān* of Rusçuk (Russe), marched against the capital together with the imperial army then on the Danube. Alemdar seized Istanbul, suppressed the Janissary leaders, and demanded Selim's restoration to the throne. When it turned out that Selim had been put to death in the meantime, Alemdar made Mahmud II sultan and became himself Grand Vezir and dictator. In his diploma of appointment to the Grand Vezirate it was stressed that he should be most careful to act in accordance with the *sharī'a* in all state affairs, to cooperate with the Janissary corps and *ulema*, and enforce the ancient laws of the Ottoman sultans. Under Alemdar, nevertheless, there was a violent reaction against the enemies of the New Order, about one thousand of whom were executed in two months.

Previously the *a'yān* had not made a united front against the Janissary corps. In 1806 those in Rumelia had cooperated with the Janissaries while some powerful *a'yān* in Anatolia supported Selim's New Order. But now the *a'yān* of Rumelia and Anatolia united against the reactionaries, less out of sympathy for the reforms than from a desire to control the central government and guarantee their position in the provinces. Soon the joint forces of the *a'yān* flocked into the capital with their armies, terrifying the Janissaries and the court.

Following the example of the Janissaries, they, too, made the sultan sign an agreement called *Sened-i İttifak* (Covenant of Union). In the introduction of this document, it was emphasized that the division and conflicts within the government and among the *a'yān* in the provinces were the main causes of the desperate situation of the empire and that this covenant proposed to revive the empire. The main provisions were as follows: vezirs, *ulema*, high officials, "dynasties" of major *a'yān* in the provinces, and military corps in the capital promised always to respect the sovereign authority of the sultan and the orders of the Grand Vezir, who represented in his person the sultan's absolute power, and to take united action against any rebellion. The important article 5 declared that just as the signatories promised collectively to safeguard the person and authority of the sultan and the order and security of the state, so the security of the provincial "dynasties" was to be protected by joint action of the signatories in the event that any law-abiding "dynasty" was assailed by the "state" or by vezirs in the provinces. The "dynasties" further undertook not to punish any lesser *a'yān* under their own authority without first consulting the central government. Each "dynasty" was to respect the boundaries of the other's area of control, and all were to take joint action against any transgressor. In article 2, the "dynasties" and lesser provincial notables sanctioned a state army and promised to conscript soldiers for it in the face of any opposition, including opposition from the military corps in the capital. In the same article, they promised to cooperate in the collection of state taxes for the sultan in the provinces. They further pledged themselves to protect the population under their authority and observe carefully the tax regulations agreed upon among the state, ministers and provincial *a'yān* (article 7).

The document was drawn up in the form of a regular contract according to the *sharī'a,* the parties being the state and its officials, *ulema*, generals of the military corps in the capital, and representatives of the provincial "dynasties." It will be noted that the "state" but not the sultan himself was mentioned as a party in the document. He took no oath as the others did, but for confirmation put his imperial seal upon the covenant, even though he had been warned by his closest advisers that it would severely limit his absolute power. The several "dynasties" stood surety for each other. In the postcript it was made clear that the covenant was to be the perpetual and unalterable basis for the regeneration of the empire. As such it was to be signed by every Grand Vezir and *şeyhülislâm* upon his acession to office, and these were to see that it was observed in every detail. A copy of it was also to be deposited with the sultan, who would see in person that it remained in force forever.

This important document has been interpreted in very different ways, often without sufficient recognition of its historical meaning and background. Like Magna Carta, it was a limitation upon the king's power imposed by local magnates; it was not, like Magna Carta of popular conception, a basis for liberal-democratic development. It clearly indicates the diminution of the sultan's power and the rise of the provincial magnates. In it the "dynasties" acknowledged many traditional rights of the sultanate: the supreme authority of the sultan, the independence of his government, and the rights of the state to conscript soldiers and collect taxes directly in the provinces (articles 1-4). At the same time it clearly stated that as long as the "dynasties" did not infringe upon the central authority, the government had to respect their status and their established rights. The "dynasties" and grandees of the empire, furthermore, were arrogating the right to take common action against anyone, including members of the sultan's government, who violated the provisions of the document. Article 4 provided that if the Grand Vezir violated the laws and fell into corrupt practices, it was the duty of all to sue him and check the abuses. But the document did not constitute any special organization which might carry out such a suit. What the "dynasties" wanted, in fact, was precisely to assure themselves of a degree of autonomy incompatible with a centralist and progressive government.

IV. The Restoration of the Sultan's Power in the Empire:
His Bureaucracy Takes the Lead in Modernizing the State

The rule of the *a'yān* did not last long. The court and members of Ottoman bureaucracy as well as the population of Istanbul were in a state of terror and rather welcomed the counter-attack of the Janissaries which put an end to *a'yān* rule. To reestablish his authority in the provinces, Mahmud II (1808-1839) could only rely on the Janissaries, who now become more disobedient than ever. In 1812, nevertheless, immediately after the conclusion of the peace treaty with Russia, Mahmud began to suppress the principal *a'yān* in the provinces. He crushed some of those who resisted him by sending into their territories troops commanded by the neighboring governor. Others he was able directly to deprive of their titles and leases so that they themselves were forced to submit and their sons to accept humbler positions. But in 1821 Tepedelenli Ali Pasha, the most powerful among the pashas of *a'yān* origin, raised truly massive resistance. The Greek insurrection followed his revolt.

Mahmud's war against the refractory *a'yān* resulted in the dispossession of many of them and restored much of the sultan's authority in the provinces. Yet hundreds of these notables remained at the head of local administrations and in possession of large leaseholds. Still constituting the most influential class in the provinces, they often appeared to the passive local populations in the guise of protectors against oppressive governors and an arbitrary central authority. Later, when the masses were given the opportunity to participate in political life, men of this class were to play a major part in political leadership.

In 1826, during the most critical period of the Greek insurrection, Mahmud II at last made the fateful decision to get rid of the Janissaries. Having done away with these as well as the rebellious *a'yān* in the porvinces, he would then possess unlimited power to reorganize the empire as the conditions of the time required.

Before the destruction of the Janissaries, Hâlet Efendi, a favorite whom they had supported, had been virtual master of the state. Thereafter, Hüsrev, a reformer left over from Selim's time, was given the task of creating a new army and became the major force in the empire for fifteen years. He was a product of the old Ottoman *kul* (imperial slave) system. This institution, established to provide wholly reliable instruments for the exercise of the sultan's absolute power, had been clearly defined by Kemal Pasha-zâde at the beginning of the sixteenth century. Hüsrev, its last great representative, had himself trained many slaves who became generals and governors of the empire. It would remain, of course, for westernized diplomat-bureaucrats to introduce truly modern reforms in the Ottoman state.

Muhammed Ali, who had become pasha of Egypt in the manner of pashas of *a'yān* origin, proved more dangerous than Tepedelenli. From 1833 on, he threatened to extend his power to all Asiatic provinces of the empire. His influence was felt even in Anatolia, where the *a'yān* and conservative masses hostile to Mahmad's reforms were sympathetic to him. He defeated Mahmud's new armies in 1833 and 1839. It was during this critical period that a new generation of reformers, of whom Mustafa Reşid Pasha was typical, emerged to save the empire from total destruction. Differing wholly from the military reformers like Hüsrev, these men were chiefly diplomats who had become acquainted with international conditions and with the structure of Western states during service in European capitals. They came out of the age-old bureaucracy which formed the third class of Ottoman state functionaries, the other classes being the *ulema* and the military. Their training was a practical one in the state bureaus, differing from that of the military, who were mostly trained under the *kul* system, and more markedly still from that of the *ulema*, who came from the rigidly formal religious seminaries. Thanks to their services in diplomacy and finance, the bureaucrats gained an increasing influence in the administration from the eighteenth century on. Devoted exclusively to the secular interests of the state and free from formalism and the bonds of tradition, they were ready to become faithful instruments of radical administrative reform. In 1821 when the Ottoman government had to replace the Greek interpreters with Turks, a Translation Office was created at the Sublime Porte, and Western languages were taught there, the first teacher being a professor from the military engineering school. This Translation Office, like the embassies which Selim III had established in Western capitals, became an educational center for a new generation of Westernized administrators and intellectuals. Âli Pasha, future Grand Vezir and reformer, and Fuad Pasha, collaborator of Reşid, received their first education in these centers.

Confronted with the disaster at Navarino in 1827 and Muhammed Ali's starling successes, Mahmud II heeded the advice of his reformist diplomats who saw the necessity of gaining the sympathy and confidence of Western powers and modernizing the Ottoman administration. Accordingly he introduced, between 1831 and 1838, some administrative and social reforms which can be regarded as the first decisive steps toward Westernization. Principal among these were the creation of state departments and of a council of ministers with a prime minister, the establishment of two high councils for military and civil reform, the use in the administration of civil servants with fixed salaries, the founding of a modern postal service and of secular professional schools, and modernization in clothing and state protocol. But Mahmud's most significant achievement remained the restoration of the sultan's power in the provinces and in all branches of administration.

After his success on a diplomatic mission to London in 1838, when war was pending with Muhammed Ali of Egypt, Reşid Pasha gained an increasing influence over Mahmud II and was able to persuade him that the disposition of Egypt would finally be decided in Western capitals. The very survival of the Ottoman state, in his view, was dependent on a modernization of its administration which would enable it to enter the concert of European states. The Ottoman defeat at Nezib in 1839 was followed by the death of Mahmud II, and thereafter everyone, including his great opponent, Hüsrev, looked to Reşid for salvation and became receptive to his reform projects. The most radical Turkish decisions to reform, we observe, were almost always made in time of crisis.

On November 3, 1839, an imperial rescript, read by Reşid Pasha at Gülhane, intiated the era of reform called *Tanzimat* in Turkish history. That document said in summary: The empire had been declining for one hundred and fifty years because the religious law and imperial laws had been disregarded. In order to restore its prosperity and strength, new legislation was required which should be based on the pirinciple of securing the life, honor, and property of all subjects. Taxation and conscription laws would be revised in accordance with the demands of justice. The tax farming system would be abolished and each citizen taxed in proportion to his means. Every accused person should be publicly judged. These guarantees should be extended to all subjects of whatever religion or sect.

A high council of reforms *(Meclis-i Vālā-yı Ahkām-ı Adliye)* would devise, after free debate, bills fulfilling the purposes agreed upon, and those in turn would be submitted to the sultan to be confirmed and published. Since all the bills would be drawn up for the sake of resuscitating Islam, the state, and the empire, the sultan promised to take an oath not to disregard them. The *ulema* and grandees of the empire were to take oaths to the same effect, and those who broke their word were to be punished without respect of rank and position according to the provisions of a penal code. These dispositions, finally, were to be made public throughout the empire and communicated officially to all the ambassadors of friendly powers resident at Istanbul.

In this rescript the main features of the European constitutions of the 1830s are quite skillfully combined with traditional Ottoman institutions and with practical necessities. A number of references to the *sharī'a* obscured from conservatives the revolutionary content of the document, and indeed the traditional state philosophy was genuinely apparent in it: The rescript said that the state needed armed forces which in turn required money, that state finances could remain in good order only if the subjects were protected against injustices, and so on. The basic principle of legislation, also, was discovered not in natural rights but in the practical necessity of resuscitating the empire. In brief, state power remained the ultimate goal as before; the people were still regarded as mere subjects of the state.

It should be remembered that in classical Islamic thought no principles of law could exist apart from the *sharī'a*. But with the Ottomans there had always in fact been an independent category of laws called imperial laws or *kānūn*s which were derived directly from the sovereign will of the ruler. For their justification it was asserted that, though applying to situations not covered by the *sharī'a,* they were necessary for the well-being of the Islamic community. The Ottoman sultans had promulgated hundreds of such *kānūn*s concerning public law, state finances, taxation, economic life, and criminal law. The Gülhane rescript was promulgated on the same principle, the legislation which it envisaged being thought necessary to regenerate the state. The document itself was rendered in the form of a decree.

When all this is said, it remains nevertheless clear that the rescript introduced revolutionary ideas and institutions into Ottoman society. Among them was the sultan's promise, confirmed by an oath, to respect the laws to be made pursuant to its principles and the establishment of a council for legislative activities with the guarantee of freedom of debate.

When he composed the decree, Reşid had intended to impose limits on the despotic power of the sultan. In his letter to Palmerston, dated August 12, 1839, he confessed this intention: "Les puissances de l'Europe," he wrote, "savent à quel degré était progressivement parvenue la tyrannie des Empereurs ottomans depuis la destruction des Janissaires.... Lorque malgré la considération, si forte du voisinage, l'Autriche et la Russie, quelqu'en soit le motif, permettent à la Walachie et à la Servie, d'adopter une constitution, auune puissance ne sauraitelle jamais vouloir empêcher que les populations musulmans obtiennent rien que de simples sûretés pour leur [sic] vies et pour leur fortune."[1]

A further revolutionary element in the document was the extension of the guarantees in it to all subjects. Later, in 1846, the sultan could confirm these principles in a speech saying: "The differences of religion and sect among the subjects is something concerning only their persons and not affecting their rights of citizenship. As we are living all in the same country under the same government, it is wrong to make discriminations among us." The revolt of the Greeks and the European crusade for Greek independence had taught a severe lesson to the Ottomans. Now, possessing equality before the law, the non-Muslim subjects would, it was expected, no longer feel that they were a segregated and oppressed element in the state and would no longer strive for independence from it. The Western powers, too, would appreciate this change in favor of the Christians in the empire. It must be noted that with their demands for equality, freedom, home rule, reforms in taxation, and land ownership the non-Muslim subjects were contributing to the Westernization of the Ottoman-Turkish state. Perceiving their peculiar position and the intervention of the West on their behalf, the sultan was moved increasingly to secularize public institutions. As sultan-caliph, he began to distinguish as best he could between his offices as ruler of all Ottoman citizens equally and his office as caliph of only the Muslims in accordance with the *sharī'a*. The significant concession made to the non-Muslims caused apprehensions among the Muslims in general, who regarded it as the destruction of the caliphate and denounced the Westernization movement as a whole. The fanatical ones stigmatized it as apostasy. The division thereby brought into focus between Westernizers with chiefly secular views and conservatives attached to the rule

---

[1] F.E. Bailey, *British Policy and the Turkish Reform Movement,* Cambridge, Mass., 1942, 275.

of the *sharī'a* remained for many years the principal schism in Turkish political life.

In brief, equality before the law and the securing of life, honor, and property for all subjects were the revolutionary ideas in the rescript. Reşid himsel asserted that the *Tanzimat*, the reforms introduced with the rescript, would change the imperial regime completely. The change in the concept of the state was further visible in the various decrees in which the sultan announced that the laws were made solely for the subjects' benefit.

We can ascertain the sincerity of Reşid's professions when we study the measures by which he undertook to put into effect the principles proclaimed in the rescript. Reşid showed his zeal to make the rule of law a reality by the haste with which he published a penal code.

In the provinces, administrative councils were established, the members of which were the governor, his two secretaries, the local judge, the mufti, the local military commander, four notables, and, if there was a Christian community in the province, the *metropolit* and two Christian notables. The notebles were to be elected by the people. The provincial councils and smaller councils in the dependent towns were to discuss freely all administrative matters and were to sit as criminal courts. The High Council of Reforms in the capital constituted a court of appeal for them. With the establishment of the provincial councils, Ottoman subjects, non-Muslims in particular, may be said to have received for the first time a voice in the local administration, though in actual fact these councils were composed of the local high officials, *ulema*, and notables, and differed little from the old councils of notables under the judge. Sometimes, paradoxically enough, the local *a'yān* and *eşrāf* used their new positions in local administration to obstruct the Tanzimat and incite the conservative masses against it.

Introduced with the intention of protecting both the peasants and the public treasury, financial reforms followed soon after the proclamation of the rescript. To secure greater justice in taxation Reşid abolished the tax immunities and exemptions affecting such influential groups as *a'yān*, *ağas*, *ulema*, and the military, as well as the exemptions connected with religious endowments. The affected groups started an intense propaganda campaign against the reforms. The survey and census embarked upon for purposes of the reform gave them an opportunity to incite the conservative masses, and they spread rumors variously that the government had determined to double the taxes or to abolish them altogether. The abolition of tax farming affected the large group of tax farmers and credit agents and the substantial number of officials profiting from it in dubious ways. It must be recalled that most of the tax farmers were local notables who had gained wealth and influence through this activity. Again in order to extend the state's protection over the peasantry Reşid abolished forced labor and usury. One of the first decisions of the High Council of Reforms read: "In the Balkans most of the notables used to think that the peasants were their serfs, and employed them for their own services without any compensation. Also they did not permit them to leave their estates to work elsewhere and they interfered even in their marriages. Now the sultan has never accepted such abuses, and those who oppose this order [abolishing them] will be punished according to the provisions of the penal code recently published." Another decree pointed out that the usurers were getting twenty per cent per month for the money they lent to the peasants. Never able to pay their debts, they were eventually deprived of all their possessions. The usurers also used to appropriate the peasants' crops at below market prices. Now the government reduced the rates of interest and permitted the peasantry to pay their accumulated debts in installments.

The government had ordered the officials in the provinces to explain to the people in mass meetings the principles embodied in the Rescript of Gülhane. In some areas in the Balkans the peasants became so impatient to see the results of the reforms that they attempted desperate actions. Seeing that the Tanzimat had not brought any immediate relief in their tax burden, for example, and that they were still subject to forced labor, the Bulgarian peasants around Nish rose up under their own lesser notables. Further uprisings in 1849 and 1850 in the Vidin area were even more serious. Most of the agricultural lands in this area were originally state-owned. But local Muslim *ağa*s had the exclusive rights to lease them and in fact possessed them as their own estates. Rejecting the popular demands and organizing a local militia *(başıbozuks)*, the *ağa*s fell upon the rebels, and it required regular government forces to end the struggle. The High Council of Reforms in Istanbul decided first to abolish the existing administrative council and granted the Christian peasants the right to lease the state-owned lands themselves. These radical decisions proved impracticable, however, and the situation did not change much subsequently. Similar reactions occurred in Anatolia. The *a'yān* of Bala near Ankara, for example, was prosecuted before the High Council of Reforms for evading tax payments, subjecting the peasants to forced labor, inciting people to rise against the government. The difference here was that the Muslim population, under the influence of the local *ulema* and *a'yān*, were extremely conservative, whereas the Christian subjects in the Balkan, under the influence of nationalist leaders, were in a mood to rebel.

These examples indicate how difficult it was for Reşid to effect his reforms and how various were the social forces arrayed against him. The privileged classes of the old regime, especially *ağa*s in collaboration with the *ulema*, were asserting that the grant of civil equality to the non-Muslims and the "indifel" was pure disregard of the *sharī'a* and would ruin the state and religion. To control them, Reşid had hastily published his penal code so that he might legally prosecute offenders against the government's reform measures. Many reactionaries in the capital as well as in the provinces, including even old Hüsrev, were punished. In Ankara a mufti, member of the administrative council, was condemned for inciting people to rebel against the reforms.

In line with his efforts to introduce a Western system of administration, Reşid decided to entrust public service in the provinces exclusively to salaried civil servants appointed by the central government and to abolish all forms of dues and bribes which the *a'yān* and officials of all degrees had been accustomed to accept. In seeking to create a corps of civil servants to implement the reforms. Reşid was directly threatening the position of the provincial *a'yān* who, as agents of the governors-general, then occupied most of the local administrative posts in Anatolia. Reşid was intent on changing those features of the organization of the empire which were inherited from feudalism. His administrative reform meant, in the last analysis, profound social reform. One of his radical measures after the abolition of tax farming was to appoint revenue collectors *(muhassıls)* in the provinces who were attached directly to the central government. But he failed to find enough civil servants trained for the job and was forced after all to employ local notables, who often followed the old practices.

It was later decided to found special secular schools to supply the civil servants so urgently needed. In these schools and in the military academies a body of Westernized officials were trained who were destined to play a decisive part in the modernization of Turkey. The resistance to Reşid's reforms caused his fall in 1841 (he was then foreign minister). The newly introduced institutions had not worked well; the new system of tax collection especially was a failure. Reşid had relied solely on the sultan's favor, which he had gained through his services in solving the Egyptian question. His successor in power was Rıza Pasha, the Minister of War, who like many old-type reformers believed chiefly in military reorganization as a means of resuscitating the empire. Tax farming came back with him, and radical reforms in the administration generally were judged to have been ill-timed. When in 1845 Reşid came back to power he gave priority to training the bureaucrats needed to implement his reforms; to his end he created a High Council of Public Education and projected the foundation of a university.

In the same year the government took the bold step of asking each province to elect two delegates and send them to Istanbul to consult on the reforms to be undertaken. These delegates were "elected from among the prominent and respected people." The assembly seemed in concert as simply an extension of the provincial administrative councils. Yet it remains the first representative assembly ever convoked in the Ottoman capital. Though the *a'yān* who appeared at the sultan's Porte had enough and soon returned home, the conservatives were appalled. Serasker Said Pasha went so far as to denounce Reşid for intending to proclaim a republic. Perhaps more significant in its consequence was the promulgation of a commercial code borrowed from France which established tribunals of commerce, the first secular tribunals of the Ottoman state.

For two principal reasons the bold steps taken by Reşid remained without effect. In the first place, the current severe economic depression was identified in the popular mind with the West and its ways—not improperly, since the cheap and plentiful products of Western industry, invading the Turkish market under the capitulatory regime, were ruining the native industries. Contemporary consular reports give us vivid descriptions of these happenings. In the second place, disgruntled persons were accusing the reformist Sultan Abdülmecid (1839-1861) of letting Reşid abuse the power of the sultanate. The highly centralist and authoritarian system of government espoused by Reşid and his followers became the particular target of the rising Ottoman-Turkish intelligentsia, who saw in it a despotism harmful to the empire. Organized as the secret society of the Young Ottomans in 1867, these intellecuals embraced the romantic nationalism then prevalent in Europe and advocated a constitutional regime which would introduce elements of Western civilization while preserving traditional Islamic-Turkish culture. For the first time we find a group of progressives acting independently of the government and opposing the official reform program. The Young Ottomans were the real forerunners of the nationalist and democratic movement in Turkey.

The major characteristics of modernization in this early period can be succinctly summarized.

A program of modernization was first adopted by the state as a measure of self-defense against an aggressive and imperialistic Europe. The superiority of European military techniques and organization was recognized as early as the end of the seventeenth century. This perception was a necessary psychological preparation for the later cultural borrowings from the West.

Second, systematic modernization started with military reforms in the eighteenth century, especially under Selim III. From 1830 on, the process was extended to administration and public institutions, a trend which culminated in the proclamation of the Ottoman constitution of 1876.

Third, the state was the initiator of the modernization movement and changes were imposed from above, the sultan using his absolute power to create the bureaucratic machinery necessary to effect changes.

Fourth, the masses, the great majority of whom were living in a closed rural economy, were generally dependent on the *a'yān, ağas,* and clerics, who were vitally interested in keeping them attached to the traditional institutions. Even in the period between 1800 and 1850 these groups actively resisted the reforms imposed by the state; the Turkish-Muslim population of the empire remained indifferent or even refractory in the face of change in general.

Fifth, a desire to satisfy non-Muslim subjects and the Western powers definitely encouraged the Ottoman state to adopt secular laws and institutions. The Western powers were interested in furnishing the empire with liberal institutions, which they thought would guarantee at once the integrity of the empire and their own economic interests in it.

Sixth, around 1860 a small group of Turkish patriots with a Western outlook emerged and carried out, in the newly introduced press and in a number of literary periodicals, a vigorous campaign against the sultan's absolutism. His reform measures were, they believed, both arbitrary and contrary to the real interests of the Turkish-Muslim population.

In the Turkish modernization movement, finally, the principal difficulties stemmed from the religious basis of the traditional society and state. In general, the Tanzimat reformers and intellectuals, though wanting to Westernize the administration and to borrow modern techniques, believed it desirable to preserve such basic traditional institutions as the *sharī'a,* religious courts, and religious schools. It was thought that these might be taken out of public affairs and relegated to their own sphere. Later, radicals who wanted wholesale Westernization and national sovereignty like that of European states were to blame the failure of the Tanzimat upon this dualism. But no concept of the nation-state was in fact realized until Atatürk called the Turkish Republic into being after the dissolution of the empire in 1919.

4

Change in Ottoman - Turkish Society

Eighty two years ago, on October 29,1923, the Grand National Assembly proclaimed Turkey a republic. This resolution put an end to the six-century-old Ottoman sultanate and established a nationalist-democratic state, on those lands of the Empire traditionally inhabited by Turks. This was possible by the success of a two-fold revolutionary movement which began in Anatolia, in 1919, under the leadership of Mustafa Kemal Atatürk. A difficult three –year struggle ensued against both the sultan's government in İstanbul and the victorious Allied Powers, which ignored the Mudros Armistice in pursuit of their imperialistic end in Asia Minor. In this two-fold struggle, the leaders of the revolution employed against their enemies the most effective weapon of the time; the priciple of national sovereignty, the right of the Turkish nation to determine its own destiny. Recognizing this masterful strategy, a young English writer, Arnold Toynbee, wrote that, indeed, Mustafa Kemal was defending the most exalted principles of the West-against the West itself.

Under the circumstances the concept of an independent Turkey could be realized only in terms of a Western type nationalist-democratic state. The close relations between the Turks and the West, especially in the nineteenth century, conditioned the developments in this direction. It is important to see the actual scope and nature of these relations.

The outstanding characteristics of the Ottoman-Turkish modernization movement in the eighteenth and nineteenth centuries were that it was regarded as a measure for preserving the state in the face of crises, and that it took the West as a model. This movement was not a process of change brought about by dislocations within the society, but was a series of reforms or changes introduced from above, by the state, accordance with its own concepts and requirements. The reforms were the work of the military-civilian bureaucrats. It was they who conceived and formulated the reforms, and also put them into practice. Often the masses, who did not fully comprehend the real nature of the measures, viewed them as part of the political oppression of the ruling group. This was especially true when the reform projects led to the imposition of additional financial burdens on the people. Consequently the masses clung to the traditional values and adopted a passive attitude to reform.

The Ottoman-Turkish modernization was gradual and piecemeal. It first manifested itself in the adoption of arms and military techniques. Later, with the upsurge of admiration for the Western material culture, the imitation of the West in its outward forms followed. Finally, in the second half of the nineteenth century, the upper classes tried to adopt the Western lifestyle and world-view.

In some respects there was direct historical continuity between the Atatürk revolution and Ottoman modernization, and the two shared certain common characteristics. At a time of extraordinary crisis, when the very existence of the Turkish nation was endangered, the concept of a nationalist-democratic state emerged as the only radical solition for Turkey's survival. The large class of military-civilian bureaucrats, which represented the continuity of the state, not only assumed the leadership of the revolutionary movement but also determined its objectives, planned its course,and undertook its execution. Their reform projets can be viewed as a radical expression of the modernization trends, which manifested themselves in the Ottoman society before World War I.

In the history of the modernization movement in Turkey the Tanzimat represents a period the adoption of the Western legal and administrative institutions. In 1839, when the Ottaman state was faced with the danger of total collapse, it accepted the reform projets of those bureaucrats who had served as diplomats at European capitals. In this plan, a masterful reconciliation of liberal principles with traditional forms of government was presented as the only means for the survival of the state. These Western liberal principles were: equality of all before the law, recognition of certain fundamental rights guaranteeing the security of life and property of subjects, public trial of persons, creation of a council with powers of legislation and supervision, and the introduction of popular representation into provincial councils. All these measures were permitted by the Sheriat, Islamic religious Law, on grounds that they were nothing but techniques required for the safety of the Islamic community. In fact, in the Ottoman legal system, such regulations emanating from the sultan's will always co-existed with the precepts of the Şeriat. During the Tanzimat era, development of a secular legal system had gotten underway, with the adoption of European legal codes-first a practical measure to regulate the commercial transactions with the growing European colonies at the commercial centers of the Empire.

On the other hand, the Turkish-Muslim masses viewed with suspicion and distrust the liberal measures adopted under pressure from non-Muslim communities in the Empire or forced upon the state by the Western powers, which had considerably expanded their commercial interests within the Empire.

As the measures imposed by the bureaucrats took extreme forms as was the case in the attempt to introduce, at least partially, the Code Napoleon in 1867 the resistance of the conservatives stiffened further.

In the 1860s the Islamists distinguished between Western technology and Western culture. The latter, in their view, was a product of a set of values peculiar to the West. They claimed that technology alone was required to meet the crisis of the Ottoman society; therefore, adoption of technology would suffice. These ideas were widely debated in the privately-owned newspapers a new means of communication introduced into Turkish society in the 1860s. Meanwhile a *Western* literary form, the novel, began to spread the Western world-view, with its life styles and value systems. Perrot, who traveled in Anatolia during this period, noted that the educated youths in Anatolian cities yearned to travel to Europe. For them, Paris was the new Mecca. Also increased trade relations with Europe resulted in the rise of sizable European colonies and of Levantine quarters in Pera, Salonica, İzmir and Beirut, transforming these cities into attractive centers of a new lifestyle. These developments marked the beginning of the era of true modernization in Turkish-Islamic society. Along with bureaucratic reformers, a Turkish intelligentsia came into being.

The new intelligentsia were not only champions of a modernized Islam, but also of the Western parliamentary system which promised popular participation in government. It is significant that Abdülhamid II attempted to suppress this grass-roots movement by incorporating its leaders into the bureaucracy with high salaries, as well as by using his police force against them. In 1876 the deposition of Abdülaziz and removal from office of his corrupt government by the action of the modernized War College *(Harbiye Mektebi)* was an event foreshadowing future developments.

In the period of crisis between 1875 and 1876, the first Ottoman Constitution imposed by the bureaucratic elite on the state was no more than a logical extension of the Westernization trend in government introduced during the Tanzimat. Its real social basis may be sought in the class of provincial *ayan* and *eşrāf* and in the rapidly growing class of non-Muslim commercial bourgeoisie-both of which bore the burden of the arbitrary measures imposed by the central government. Despite a restricted system of elections, these discontented elements came to dominate the parliament and they directed their criticisms boldly and freely against the Palace and bureaucrats. However, the parliament lasted only five months, and the subsequent period under Abdülhamid II witnessed the elimination of Westernizing Tanzimat reformers and rise to prominence of Islamists, who advocated the necessity of borrowing only technology from the West. In the eyes of the Muslim masses extreme

Westernization ventures of the Westernizing elite were responsible for the disastrous outcome of the 1876-77 Russo-Ottoman War. The idea of a parliament was no longer favored and the Constitution became inoperative.

Among the real causes of the reaction of the Turkish-Muslim majority were increasing economic and financial exploitation by Western powers under the system of capitulations and consequent dislocations in the traditional socio-economic structure collapse of the handicrafts industry and of the guild organization, as well as the monopoly of commerce by non-Muslims who were the agents of Western capitalism. This reaction was at the same time directed against the advocates of radical Westernization. The traditional Ottoman society defended its own social structure and value system with increasing zeal, while its resistance became increasingly rigid and limited in its outlook. By and large, the period between 1830 and 1908 was one of socio-economic collapse, as well as resistance to modernization by the masses. On the other hand, the members of an elite group, who left the government bureaucracy and emigrated to Europe, came to represent an increasingly radical movement for modernization. They were pioneers in the concern about socio-economic issues and the problems of culture and social structure. These modernists, through their contacts with the schools of French sociology, sought a scientific basis for their projects of reform and modernization. Their impact on the history of Turkish thought has been more far-reaching than originally thought. Following the Young Ottomans of the 1860s, who were inspired by Montesquieu and Rousseau, the Young Turks under Abdülhamid's regime sought in August Comte's positivism and in La Playe's theories scientific solutions to the problem of social change in Ottoman society. Later, with Ziya Gökalp, positivism was to predominate Turkish intellectual movements.

In 1909, at the first Congress of the Committee of Union and Progress, Ziya Gökalp, disciple of Durkheim and Gaston Richard, was entrusted with the task of formulating and spreading, among the youth, the value system of "the new life". Gökalp emerged as the first objective and comprehensive thinker of Turkish modernization. He was unique in that, unlike his predecessors, he did not view modernization simply as a political phenomenon, but rather as a scientific-sociological one, with a valid program of action. Taking as his points of departure the concepts of collective consciousness and the distinction between culture and civilization, he established national consciousness and the nation as the highest stage of social development. He perceived modernization only in terms of the adoption of "civilization", while "culture" consisting of value systems, could not be adopted. Civilization, on the other hand, was a product of human reason and was, therefore, universal and could be acquired through education. Ziya Gökalp defined modernization as the capacity to manufacture and use the tools employed by the most advanced nations, yet he argued that national culture should be preserved and its sources developed. He believed that the sudden and coercive changes that occur in adopting another civilization might undermine the national system of values and might result in a cultural vacuum and deterioration. Therefore, the modernization movement should parallel a gradual development in national culture. Later, these ideas of Ziya Gökalp came into conflit with those of Atatürk, who rejected the distinction between culture and civilization and favored the rapid method of revolutionary change imposed from above. In 1924 this controversy became the subject of a lengthy and heated discussion at the Grand National Assembly; Atatürk's approach to madernization triumphed.

After 1909, under the Committee of Union and Progress, which put an end to Abdülhamid's reactionary regime, the ideas of reform and modernization were expressed in diverse but powerful movements. Thanks to the rapid expansion of the press, these ideas were debated by people of all classes. This period provided the intellectual environment for Atatürk and the future founders of the Republic.

In the same period, following the tragic disappointment of the Balkan Wars in 1912, a keen sense of self-criticism and a search for radical solutions dominated Turkish public opinion. Ahmed Hilmi, a member of the new intelligentsia, saw in Europeanization the only means of survival. In his book *Europeanization (Avrupalılaşmak)* he wrote:

> All our misfortunes are an outcome of traditionalism and Easternism. It was not our army or our fleet that was defeated in the Balkan Wars, but our rotten social life and Easternism. I firmly believe that we shall neither maintain our existence nor independence by our Asian and Eastern Way of life or culture. We should no longer be enslaved by age-old customs and should accept novelty and progress as the basis for all things...... Turkey is in need of leaders with moral courage.

> Europeanization will in no way reduce the value and the importance of our religion. In fact, perhaps through Europeanization we may be able to resurrect the ancient civilization of Islam. True Islam, cleansed of all superstitution, positivistically conceived, was desired, and to achieve this end the reformists advocated a return to the "pure and untainted Islam" which was believed to have existed at the time of the Prophet and the Four Caliphs.

Ziya Gökalp believed that the Şeriat was an outcome of historical processes and it could undergo further changes to meet the new requirements. The radical reformers, among them Dr. Abdullah Cevdet and his followers, however, advocated an unconditional adoption of Western civilization and laicism, formulating for the first time the radical reforms of Atatürk. Among the proposed reforms was the romanization of the script, since the Arabic script was regarded as one of the causes of backwardness.

Another important development of the period was the emergence of the notion of a national economy. Beginning in 1913, the government actively attempted to abolish the Capitulations. The problem facing Turkey was one of exploitation by the capitalist-imperialist powers and by their protogées, the non-Muslim commercial bourgeoisie, which was made possible under the system of Capitulations.

The era of the Committee of Union and Progress was one of considerable reduction in the size of the Empire. The period of dismemberment and of wars began with the Austrian occupation of Bosnia and Herzegovinia in 1908. followed by the Italian attack on Cyrenaica (Trablusgarp) and continued with brief intervals for eleven years, until 1922. These wars left the Turkish nation in a state of total exhaustion and confusion, while the Balkan wars and the subsequent Turkish withdrawal from Rumelia led to tragic migration movement into Anatolia. As a result, the Turkish nationalist movement became a predominant force in the land.

In May, 1919, when Greeks, with the blessings of the Allies, began to occupy Western Anatolia, many speakers, addressing the emergency council assembled in Istanbul, defended the idea of a Turkish nation. Mustafa Kemal had already been in Anatolia for a week. Turks faced with the necessity to fight for themselves and not for the Empire were for the first time united with a national zeal. They found a charismatic leader in Mustafa Kemal, the hero of the Dardanelles, who would unite the nation and lead it in its struggle.

The birth of the Turkish state was, above all, an outcome of the struggle for survival. In 1919 the leader grasped the significance of this historic moment and expressed the essence of the nationalist revolution to the entire nation in the proclamation, "It is the will of the nation that is supreme, and determines the destiny of the state and of the nation".

We have tried to analyze the development of the change in attitudes towards modernization in Turkish society. Since the beginning, this attitude was persistent in preserving traditional values. Ziya Gökalp tried to justify this attitude by distinguishing between culture and civilization, thus trying to impart a scientific character to it. Atatürk completed the trend of constitutionalism with the proclamation of the Republic. He carried secularization to its extreme end. He took out of the Constitution the stipulation that "the Turkish state is an Islamic state" by 1928, adopted the Swiss civil code, secularized the educational system by abolishing religious education, and entrusted education to the secular state.

Atatürk rejected the distinction between civilization and culture. He viewed Western civilization as a whole and saw no reason to discriminate among its various components, and thus he launched the nation into a path of total and radical Westernization. He defined culture as "the result of all things a society achieves in its governmental, intellectual, and economic life". According to him, civilization was nothing more than this. His campaign against the symbols of traditional society should be seen as actions undertaken to achieve a total change in attitude. Viewed in this context, the "Hat Reform" should not strike us as trivial. In Eastern society headgear was a most important symbol, signifying a person's social status and allegiance. Under the Ottomans, the nature of the headgear to be worn by each socio-religious group was determined by decree of the sultan. Similarly, Atatürk enforced by decree the wearing of the European style of headgear as a symbol of Westernization. Though enforcement came four years after the abolition of the Caliphate, it seems to have had a more profound impact on the traditional masses. There were men who preferred to stay at home for days rather than to go out and wear the hat. In addition to enforcing reforms in dress, the alphabet, and the calendar, and in adoption of surnames, Atatürk also imposed changes in social customs and even in music and the arts.

In this movement of total acculturation the definitive role of the educational institutions was fully recognized. Atatürk believed that total modernization could be realized only for future generations. In order to educate the youth, to whom he entrusted the Republic, he established a state monopoly over all teaching and schoolbooks, and excluded all traditional elements from the educational process. In practice, however, largely due to financial and social difficulties, this educational campaign could not reach all the people. The result was two types of citizens with different world-views and cultural attitudes, who lacked an understanding of each other. This dichotomy in cultural attitudes has assumed such proportions at times as to play a more important role in Turkish political life than the existing economic and political differences.

In the process of total modernization the most serious and the most difficult task was the creation of a modern national economy. Since the War of Independence, the politicians of both the right and the left have always claimed that Turkey's most crucial problem was that of economic development. In 1923 Mustafa Kemal convened in İzmir a congress of economic affairs, attended by more than 1.000 delegates from all parts of Turkey. In his opening speech he stressed the fact that without a national economy there could not be national sovereignty, and he criticized the exploitation by foreign capital. He also stated that under Ottoman rule, Turkey had been reduced to a colony, and that it was absolutely essential to abolish the Capitulations. It is to be remembered that the Congress coincided with the spirited debates on the Capitulations at the Lausanne peace conference.

During the administration of the Republican People's Party (RPP: *Cumhuriyet Halk Partisi)* foreign capital was viewed with suspicion. It was in this period that railroads and other enterprises, operated by foreign companies, were nationalized and laws were enacted to encourage the rise of a Turkish entrepreneurial class and the birth of a national economy. However, these attempts failed to attain any significant degree of success. The world-wide Depression of 1929 triggered an economic crisis resulting in a sharp fall in prices of agricultural products and in a reduction in exports and imports. The Depression thus not only affected state revenues, but also the fortunes of the peasantry. The policy of etatism, with strong protectionist measures, was thence enforced with grater vigor, and Turkey entered an era of planned industrialization.

Yet etatism in Turkey never departed from its initial objective, the ultimate creation of an economy based on private enterprise and capitalism. Etatism in the industrial sector meant large-scale undertakings by the state in the establishment of factories, building of railroads, etc. The justification given for these extensive state enterprises was that Turkey lacked the entrepreneurs and the private capital to undertake such enterprises, required for economic development. These investments by the state laid the groundwork for the economic expansion of the period after 1950. On the other hand, due to large deficits and a low level of profits, state enterprises were economically unsuccessful.

During the early years of the Revolution, modernization was regarded as a matter of survival. This sentiment was clearly expressed by Atatürk himself in 1923: "Whatever happens, the country will become civilized, modern, and prosperous. This, for us, is a question of survival." On another occasion he expressed the need for a rapid tempo of change as indispensable for modernization: "These steps should be very rapid and very long .... Our century is characterized by speed".

For this reason he chose speedy, definitive, and active methods in enforcing the measures for modernization and acculturation. He called all these measures inkılâp, revolutionary change. Today, when confronted by movements adverse to modernization, Atatürk's reforms (inkılâp or devrim) are defended with revolutionary fervor. When progressive policies are formulated toward modernization, his name and "eternal leadership" are once more invoked for legitimization.

The great leader, before enforcing his reforms, prepared the public by making tours of the country. Then he proceeded to codify them in the form of laws which he passed through the Grand National Assembly. Lastly, he backed his measures with the entire force of the state and the army. This method was essentially that of the Ottoman reformists. Atatürk's uniqueness lays in the definitiveness and suddenness of his revolutionary changes. These were not mere reform measures; he attempted to base these radical changes on the will of the nation.

In practice, however, Atatürk's decisions for modernization were imposed from above, and this practice had significant consequences. In the Ottoman state, it was the sacret duty of the sultan and his military-civilian bureaucracy to ensure that the Muslim subjects abided by the rules of the Şeriat and to organize every facet of their lives in accordance with the religious law. The subjects, on the other hand, owed absolute obedience to their trustee, the state. Under the Republic, the system of trusteeship continued, with the ruling class still claiming to have the knowledge of the true path and the right to lead the masses in that path-which was now called modernization.

In imposing the measures of acculturation, Atatürk derived power from his great charisma and from the trust and love of the people which he had acquired as savior of the nation *(Halâskâr Gâzî)*. Nevertheless, this reverence for the person of Atatürk did not stop the traditional society from reacting strongly to his modernization measures, thus forcing him to rely more and more on the bureaucratic elite. The large group of uneducated people who resisted modernization were left outside the sphere of political life. After 1930, the one-party system increasingly developed into an authoritarian regime. Finally, the fundamental principles of the Republic People's Party were incorporated into the Constitution.

The central argument of the bureaucratic elite was that the uneducated masses, not conditioned in the direction of modernization, would use the right to vote to impair democracy and modernization. This group of men demanded restrictions in the right to vote, in the name of modernization and of an enlightened and progressive democracy. Similarly, at the present time the socialist elite, which has found itself poorly represented in the parliament, has employed the same line of reasoning. However, the 1973 elections proved that economic and social factors, as well as tradition, are important in voting patterns. At any rate, it should be remembered that, since Atatürk's time, the Turkish social structure and political life has undergone considerable development. The leaders of the one-party system had declared that their ultimate goal was the attainment of the present state of affairs. It is not easy to determine the real extent of their contributions in preparing the groundwork for present developments.

The history of the Turkish Republic must be devided into two major periods. Between 1923 and 1950, the Turkish society may be divided, as it was under the Ottomans, into two main classes: the ruling group or bureaucratic elite which controlled the state, and the masses under the trusteeship of the elite. The ruling class represented a highly centralized government; it imposed measures for modernization, controlled the economy and the educational system, and regarded any organization outside itself as harmful to the existence of the state. This government sometimes employed methods closely resembling the Ottomans. Onerous taxes and forced labor imposed on the peasantry were reminiscent of the most criticized and resisted Ottoman taxes, the *avarız* and *imdadiye*.

Recent research has revealed that, under the Ottoman regime, the provincial *a'yān* and *eşrāf*, traditionally representing local people before the government authorities, constituted a class which resisted the oppression of the representatives of the central government and played a significant part in political life. During the War of Independence and in the early years of the Republic, this class had cooperated with the leaders of the Anatolian revolution and with the founders of the Republic against the sultanate.

5

The Caliphate and Atatürk's *İnkilâb*

My focus in this paper will be on how Atatürk's *inkilâbs* or "revolutions" actually constituted one total revolution during which the events occurred in sequence as links of one whole historical process. I believe most of the historians of Atatürk's revolution are often too dependent on his historic speech, *Büyük Nutuk,* which he delivered after the major *inkilâb* was already completed in 1927. The *Nutuk* is one and undoubtedly the most important source for the period. But basically it was delivered before a party convention for explanation and justification of the *inkilâb* and the tactics used for its victory.

It will be seen that historically the separation of the Caliphate from the Sultanate and the abolition of the latter set off a sequence of events and movements which led to the major *inkilâbs* including the abolition of the Caliphate and other secularizing reforms in the period 1922-1927.

The most urgent problem subsequent to victory over the Greek army was to make the allied powers recognize the objectives of the Indepencence War in a formal treaty. This in turn raised the fundamental question of the country's regime: who was going to represent the Turkish state in the coming peace conference. The claim of the Sultan's government to this effect triggered the great *inkilâb*. Mustafa Kemal reacted by declaring that absolute sovereignty of the Turkish state is embodied in the Grand National Assembly (GNA). Only three days after the Sultan's claim, Kemal proposed to the GNA the separation of the Caliphate from the Sultanate and the abolition of the latter (November I, 1922). A fortnight later the Sultan Vahideddin fled aboard an English warship, still claiming to be the Caliph of the Muslims of the world. A new Caliph, Abdülmecid Efendi, was elected by the GNA. Then the question came up whether the new Caliph was to be considered the head of state and would enjoy political power in the Turkish state. The question was asked by many deputies including the *hoca*s, Muslim clerics, and the most influential nationalist leaders and companions of Kemal, Rauf, and Refet. At the GNA, Kemal stressed that the Turkish nation now replaced the state of Osman in sovereignty and took its destiny in its own hands. "National sultanate and sovereignty," he said,[1] "is embodied only in the GNA composed of the representatives of the nation. As to the question of the future of the Caliphate, history provides examples of the Caliphate continuing side by side with the Sultanate. Now that the Sultanate is gone the Caliphate will stay as the spiritual and religious center of the whole Muslim world. The Sultanate now is replaced by the powerful body of the delegates of the nation and from now on it will be able to take care of the nation's affairs towards a modern prosperous society." In these words Kemal declared the fundamental revolutionary change in the regime of the country and summarized its future policy. There was no place for the Caliphate in the new Turkish state. The expression, "national sultanate" was chosen by him to argue that sultanate meant secular sovereignty and now it was assumed by the nation. The Caliph's position in the Islamic community was interpreted in a quite unusual way. It was presented as a purely spiritual dignity as in Christendom. And actually those who tried to support Kemal in the press compared the Caliph to the Pope.

Before the GNA proceeded to elect a new Caliph, Kemal saw to it that the candidate to the post, Abdülmecid, son of Sultan Abdülaziz, vowed by signature that he agreed to this interpretation. The document signed contained the following points: Abdülmecid shall bear the title of Caliph of all Muslims. The manifesto that he was going to publish to the Muslim world was instructed to him emphasizing the fact that the election was duly made by the representatives of the nation, that is, by the GNA[2]. Thanking the Muslims all over the world for their support to the Turkish nation in its struggle for independence and to the Ottoman dynasty which he said had always been the defender of Islam he added that "the high office of the Caliphate and in particular the exalted duty of the *imâmet, which is a trust by God,* asked for their continued support. He signed the manifesto as *Halîfe-i Muslimîn,* the Caliph of the Muslims and *Khâdim al-Haramayn al-Sharîfayn,* the Servant of the Two Holy Cities of Islam[3]. In a message to the press he asserted that the Caliphate is a trust (without mentioning whose trust) and would be happy to perform thereby a service to the nation" like other citizens[4]. Although the idea

---

[1] *Atatürk'ün Söylev ve Demeçleri,* vol. I-III, İstanbul: Türk Inkilâp Tarihi Enstitüsü Yayımları I, 1945, s. 270; *Hilâfet ve Millî Hâkimiyet, hilâfet ve millî hakimiyet mesâili hakkında muhtelif zevâtın makâlât ve mütâliâtından mürekkep bir risâledir.* Ankara: Matbuât ve İstihbârât Müdiriyet-i Umumiyesi Neşriyâtı'ndan no. 32, 1339/1923, 216

[2] Gazi Mustafa Kemal Atatürk, Nutuk, II, İstanbul: Turk Devrim Tarihi Enstitüsü, 1961, 696; Utkan Kocatürk, *Atatürk ve Türk Devrimi Kronolojisi,* Türk Inkilâp Tarihi Enstitüsü Yayımları, Ankara 1973, 238.

[3] *Hilâfet ve Millî Hâkimiyet,* 211-12.

[4] *Ibid.,* 214-15.

of imâmet and that of God's trusteeship could not easily be reconciled with the nationalist interpretation of the Caliphate, in his letter to the GNA the newly elected Caliph agreed that the election was made "in accordance with the Constitution which guarantees absolute sovereignty of the Turkish nation."[5] Contradiction was apparent and both sides, the *inkilâbcı*s and *hoca*s began a heated controversy on the question as to whether the Caliph could remain as a simple spiritual dignitary in Islam, whether he could receive his authority from a community or from a group, and whether the acts of the GNA could be valid without his ratification. All these points were raised in a treatise published by Hoca Şükrü Efendi, deputy of Karahisar. He claimed that according to Islamic principles the Caliph should be the head of the Islamic state or the head of the GNA, and that his ratification was necessary to make the acts of the GNA valid laws for the community or nation[6]. However, some other *hoca*s supported the nationalist interpretation an *inkilâbcı*s joined them in using as an argument Islamic law and history[7]. Ağaoğlu Ahmed, referring to the Islamic sources, *hadîth* and *siyar* and recognized authorities on Islamic sciences, said that the prophet himself made a clear distinction between worldly affairs and religion, and that, in early Islam, under the first four rightly guided Caliphs, between 632 and 661 A. D., the Caliphate was elective and the affairs of the Islamic community were taken care of by consultative bodies as in a republican government and that a republican government conforms best to the spirit of Islam. In brief, Ağaoğlu found all the principles of the Kemalist revolution in early Islam-republicanism, national sovereignty, liberty, equality and brotherhood, and even populism. He identified national sovereignty with *icmâ-i ümmet,* consensus of the community. He asserted that the Caliphate belongs originally to the *umma,* Islamic community as a whole, and the Caliph has to be elected by its delegates. The concept of divine monarchy, he argued, comes from Persian tradition, and is totally foreign to the original Islamic spirit and practice[8]. Rasih Efendi, a *hoca,* Muslim scholar and GNA deputy, emphasizing the important place of social action in Islam, asserted that exercise of political power is to be entrusted as a trust *(emânet)* to the most capable person or body for the good and salvation of the Islamic community. The most important issue was to defend and maintain the independence of the Muslims. Islam, he said, is incompatible with bondage. Islam is based on the absolute equality of Muslims. Brotherhood and equality are the foundations of the Islamic community. Islam commands management of their affairs in *shûrâ,* that is in consultation. Citing

---

[5] *Ibid.,* 215.
[6] F. C. "Hoca Şükrü Efendiye Cevap", *Hilâfet ve Millî Hâkimiyet,* 177-85.
[7] Hoca Ubeydullâh, "İslâm'da Hilâfet", *ibid.,* 186-90.
[8] Ağaoğlu Ahmed, "Tarihî Celse", *ibid.,* 11-32.

verses from the Qur'an in his article he asserts that government by a body elected by Muslims is the only valid form of government based on Islamic foundations. [9] Many *hoca*s using exclusively Islamic arguments supported Hoca Rasih's view. [10] Later Mustafa Kemal was going to use all the Islamic arguments to defend absolute sovereignty of the nation as represented at the GNA against those who advocated sovereign rights of the Caliph in the Islamic state[11]. Rasih Efendi's emphasis on independence of the Muslims was particularly important in support of Mustafa Kemal's authority, and Islamic leaders in India would wholeheartedly espouse these Islamic arguments of the nationalists. It should be noted that later Kemal sent a delegation under Rasih Efendi to India.

It is almost needless to add that Islamic arguments for modernization were not new in Turkey or in the Islamic world in general. The so-called modernists had been advocating, on the same basis, reforms in Islamic state and society such as constitutionalism for more than half a century[12]. The movement had gained momentum among the Turkish ulema and intellectuals during the second constitutional period[13].

Ziya Gökalp, the spiritual father of Turkish nationalism, joined in the controversy over the Caliphate. Sociologically, he said[14], national consciousness is a higher stage in social evolution and basic social reality is nationality while the *umma,* the religious community embracing many nations, confers an additional identity to the individual. Turkey reached to the stage of national consciousness during the war of independence. The Caliph as the head of the religious community, he continued, has to be exclusively a religious authority and spiritual guide. His claim to have a political authority in a nation-state can only lead to conflicts detrimental to both nation and religion. As Islam and *umma,* he argued, are also social and religious realities, a Caliph as their head and symbol is necessary for the unity of Islam. In his earlier writings[15] Gökalp had warmly advocated "the re-opening of the gate of *idjtihâd"* for modernizing the Islamic community as far as worldly affairs were concerned. At any rate, Gökalp had exerted strong influence on the *inkilâbcı*

---

[9] Hoca Rasih Efendi, "İslâm'da Hâkimiyet ve Te'sîs-i Hükûmet", *ibid.,* 33-49.

[10] Hoca Ubeydullâh, "Hilâfet-i Sahîha", *ibid.,* 50-54.

[11] Bak. meselâ, *Atatürk'ün Söylev ve Demeçleri,* 62-3, 37, 144-46.

[12] H. A. R. Gibb, *Modern Trends in Islam,* Chicago 1947; "Islâh" *Encyclopaedia of Islam,* second edition, vol. IV, 141-71; Fazlur Rahman, *Islam,* New York: Anchor Books, 1968, 237-315.

[13] Hilmi Ziya Ülken, *Türk Düşünce Tarihi.*

[14] "Hilâfet'in Hakiki Mâhiyeti", *Hilâfet ve Millî Hâkimiyet,* I-I0.

[15] See. Z. Gökalp, *Turkish Nationalism and Western Civilisation,* ed. and trans. Niyazi Berkes, London 1959.

concept of a secular state and law. *Hocas* as well as *inkilâbcıs* writers were concerned with keeping the Caliphate in the custody of the Turkish nation during this period because the English were trying to assume the role of the protector of the Caliphate and were in favor of the idea of recognizing Sherif Husayn of Mecca, a descendant of the Prophet, as the supreme Caliph of the Islamic world. Against this plan the Turkish press argued that the Caliphate can exist and survive only with the support of an independent and strong Islamic state. Islamic leaders in India, notably Maulana Mehmed Ali, Amir Ali and the Agha Khan publicly supported the Turkish nationalist view that only the GNA of Turkey had he right to elect the Caliph, and denounced the English plan as an interference in the internal affairs of Muslims[16].

The question of the Caliphate was further complicated by becoming an issue of power politics among the nationalist leaders. According to the report given in Atatürk's speech in 1927, Rauf, then prime minister told him that "it is difficult for us to make ourselves masters of the general situation; this can be secured by a higher office and the sublime dignity which everbody generally considers to be unapproachable. This office, this dignity and the attempt to substitute it by a body of a different character would lead to disappointment and disaster. This is not to be thought of."[17] The attitude which Rauf, Refet, Kâzım Karabekir and others were going to take later on clearly showed that what they really wanted was to prevent Kemal's taking over the control of all state power. Collective leadership of the Indepence War was going to split up over the issue of the political form which the country was going to take. Now Kemal created an inner circle around him with his closest comrades İsmet, Fevzi and Kâzım (Özalp) to further the *inkilâb*. Incidentally, the word *inkilâb* chosen by Kemal for the revolution he was leading originally meant transformation or radical change without violence. In carrying out the revolutionary changes Kemal's tactic was to introduce them through acts of the GNA which, he always asserted, was the only and absolute holder of national sovereignty. Actually this was his only source of legitimate power and support in using state power first against foreign adversaries during the Independence War and then against his opponents during the revolution in the period 1922-1924. In 1923, when he encountered potential opposition in the GNA, including from some of the army generals, on the issue of the powers of the Caliph, he decided to create a political party and to gather the nation around himself as *halâskâr ghâzî,* the saviour of the fatherland[18]. Rauf and other generals had

---

[16] *Hilâfet ve Millî Hâkimiyet,* 129-64.

[17] Mustafa Kemal Atatürk, *A Speech,* Leipzig 1929, 573.

[18] The most important source: Atatürk, *A Speech.* 570-90; A. H Fuad Cebesoy, *Millî Mücadele Hatıraları,* İstanbul 1953; idem, *Siyasî Hatıralar,* 2 vols, İstanbul 1957, 1960; Mahmut Goloğlu, *Devrim ve Tepkileri,* 1924-1930, Ankara 1972, 57-84.

reminded him that at the beginning of the Independence War they had declared before the nation that they were fighting to deliver the Caliphate from captivity. Now Kemal was going directly to the nation to seek its support for the *inkilâb*. Kemal's political campaign in western and central Anatolia in January-March 1923 was designed to back up the Turkish delegation at the Lausanne peace conference as well as "to exchange views," Kemal said, "with people on the questions concerning the present and the future."[19] This campaign was to have a tremendous significance for the events to come in Turkey in the following years[20].

In Izmit he rejected the idea that the Caliph should be considered as the head of state or a dignitary bearing political responsibility. He argued that since the greater part of the Muslim world was at the moment under foreign domination, the GNA took the Caliphate under its protection until the time when other Muslim countries became independent and gave a definitive form to the Caliphate. In the meantime, he said, the new Caliph Abdülmecid will be wise enough to realize his real position and cautious enough not to cause a crisis by inappropriate action or behavior. All along the campaign he addressed himself to two different groups separately, the *halk,* common people, artisans, peasants, landowners and farmers on the one hand, and, *on* the other, *gençler* or *münevverân,* that is students and the intellectual elite. But this cleavage between two sections of the Turkish nation he observed had to be remedied; the intellectuals should go to people and try to eliminate the alienation by evaluating popular national culture[21] an idea that will give rise in later years to the *Halk-evleri,* that is people's houses and other populist movements in Turkey. He saw that this cleavage between *halk* and *münevver* could be fateful for the entire *inkilâb* and for the changes he was planning to introduce in the future. Later, in 1924, by suppressing religious schools along with the Caliphate and establishing one secular educational system he believed that he would create one Turkish nation. In the meetings in every city he visited the *hocas,* clerics came forward as the spokesmen of the *halk,* people, a function established in the traditional Ottoman society. Questions posed by both groups centered around the position of the Caliph and Islam within the new state. Since Kemal's opponents claimed that the Caliphate could not be separated from the state and the new Caliph had to assume real responsibility in the state, the future of the Caliphate had become the most fundamental and emotional issue across the country.

---

[19] *Söylev ve Demeçler,* II, Ankara 1959, 49-50.

[20] Ibid., 50-164.

[21] Ibid., 140.

In his answers to *hocas,* Kemal used the religious arguments forwarded by the Islamic modernists saying that Islam originally depended on consultative government, and the community's sovereignty was an essential principle in early Islam[22]. He said also that sovereignty was later usurped by despots with a theory totally foreign to the original Islamic precepts and thus the exercise of absolute sovereignty by the GNA only means the reestablishment of this right[23]. But on the other hand Kemal must have been aware that the use of Islam for the *inkilâb* was contradictory. The *hocas* were using it confidently against the *inkilâb* before a religious mass ready to listen. On this platform no real agreement was possible, for the reactionary *hocas* were talking about the Islamic *umma,* or community ruled by the Religious Law and its administrator the Caliph, while the *inkilâbcıs* were considering the people as a nation whose government was based on the national will. In the press at the same period Ağaoğlu Ahmed was severely criticized and ridiculed by the conservative *hocas* for defending the *inkilâb* based on the same Islamic sources[24]. In his speeches Kemal carefully distinguished the modernist *hocas* by calling them "the enlightened ulema" while he accused the conservatives of following the example of those ulema who served despotic Caliphs for their own personal interests. Kemal talked about conservative *hocas* as a class with vested interests in defense of the traditional order[25]. Many of them actually made up part of the powerful body of notables in the provinces. He denounced them as enemies of the nation fomenting against the inkilâb which had restored the nation's sovereign rights. Thus, the question of the Caliphate became a cover for the power struggle between the *hocas* who were the spokesmen of the old regime and the *inkilâbcıs* who were determined to change the Turkish state and society towards a modern nation-state.

Kemal emerged as a radical revolutionary when he was speaking to the youth and *münevvers,* an elite with secular and professional education, during the campaign. In Konya, a city known traditionally as being unsympathetic to the Ottoman dynasty, in an emotional speech Kemal declared that "if they (the supporters of the Caliphate) make a wrong move he shall consider it not only an opposition against his personal beliefs and goals but a conspiracy and a deadly danger against the life and existence of his nation. When this happens the only thing that he and his comrades who shared his ideals have to do is to act and fight until their total destruction. "[26] This speech was published in the

---

[22] Ibid., 63.

[23] Ibid., 145; cf. Ağaoğlu Ahmed, ibid., 11-32.

[24] See, *Hilâfet ve Milli Hâkimiyet,* 191-207.

[25] *Söylev ve Demeçler,* 144.

[26] Ibid., 146.

official newspaper, *Hâkimiyet-i Milliye* (26 March 1923). This was a declaration of war against those who hoped to create a movement against the *inkilâb*. Confrontation was inevitable. But it was also essential to save the country from an internal struggle at a time when debates crucial for the future of the nation were being carried on at the Lausanne peace conference. This was the purpose of the political campaign and Kemal used every argument to win over public opinion for his cause. In addition to the notion of the supremacy of national sovereignty he opened an intense campaign to discredit the Ottoman dynasty and history. He reminded people how he Sultan-Caliph had then organized "the armies of the Caliphate" against the national movement and used Greek aircraft to drop *fetwâs* on the nationalist forces condemning nationalist leaders as rebels. Historically the Ottoman Sultan-Caliphs, he said, had always acted as despots and, abusing the good faith of the Turkish people they had wasted Turkish blood across remote frontiers for their vanity.[27]

With a personality combining the idealist and statesman, Kemal was at the same time a strategist, and a pragmatic politician. He asserted in his speeches to the youth that the *inkilâbcı*s definitely were going to win the struggle. The assurance came from the fact that he had full control of the armed forces. What distinguished Turkey at the time from other Islamic countries was that a westernized military elite trained in the professional secular schools took the leadership of the radical modernization process, and the Indepencence War had produced a leader with incomparable charisma and ability. Leadership of the military elite for modernization had become a tradition in Turkey since Süleyman Pasha's coup of 1876 and particularly the second constitutional revolution in 1908. At the beginning of his campaign on January 18, 1923 at Izmit he warned his opponents. "Those who achieved the *inkilâb*" he declared, "have all the necessary power to crush the reaction... It should be clearly understood that the moment a dangerous situation is caused by a dignitary or a person, then, theory stops and action starts."[28] During the same campaign he promised to the reserve and regular army officers as well as to the professional elite that the government shall take measures to improve their welfare[29].

When he was back in Ankara from the tour he had the GNA pass a law to the effect that anyone acting contrary to the GNA's decision on the abolition of the Sultanate and the legality of the acts of the GNA shall be sued under the law of treason to the country[30].

---

[27] Ibid., 100-106, 121.
[28] Ibid., 64.
[29] Ibid.
[30] See, Kocatürk, ibid., 252.

Kemal's political campaign in early 1923 is of crucial significance not only for his major *inkilâb* with the radical changes in the political order of the country, but also for publicly expressing the changes Kemal and his *inkilâbcı* companions were planning for the future. First and above all he made it perfectly clear that the GNA representing national sovereignty was the only source of political power in Turkey and no political responsibility was going to be accorded to a member of the Ottoman dynasty under whatever name or office. He declared the Ottoman state dead and replaced by a new Turkish state. This declaration would logically lead to the promulgation of the republic and the abolition of the Caliphate. On January 16, 1923 in an interview with newsmen he declared that "in order to lead the nation and the country to the level of modern civilization and human progress the government and people have to make rapid and long advances." He spoke of equal rights for women, use of simple Turkish by the preachers at the mosques, and having a modern appearance in attire. At Bursa in a talk with people he said, "any nation claiming to be a civilized, progressive and developed nation is definitely to make statues" and there is nothing, he asserted, religiously wrong in this[31]. The reason for the Prophet to prohibit making statues, he further argued, was necessary in those days to fight idolatry. Today, he said, I cannot imagine any Muslim Turk looking at a statue as an idol. Our nation shall make beautiful statues and this will not make them less Muslim[32]. Kemal found justification and impetus for his plans of the most radical legal reforms when the allied powers at Lausanne stubbornly resisted the abolition of the capitulations on the grounds that Turkey was a backward country and still under Islamic Law. Kemal immediately set up a committee for legal reforms and the Turkish delegation declared that Turkey was under way to adopt European laws in civil matters soon[33]. The convocation of a conference in Izmir on national economy also coincided with the claims of economic independence of Turkey and abolition of capitulatory ties[34]. It is very interesting to observe the paralellism between Turkish claims to be a fully independent modern nationstate and as such to ask for equal treatment at Lausanne, and Kemal's promises of taking radical measures to modernize Turkey during his Anatolian tour in 1923.

While he rejected the attitude of the western powers toward his nation, he at the same time had come to the realization and deeply felt belief that an independent existence for the nation absolutely depended on complete

---

[31] *Söylev ve Demeçler,* 127, 133, 151.

[32] Ibid., 66.

[33] Cemil Bilsel, *Lozan,* II, İstanbul 1933, 79-118.

[34] *Türkiye Iktisat Kongresi, 1923-Izmir, Haberler-Belgeler-Yorumlar,* ed. A. Gündüz Ökçün, Ankara 1968: Atatürk's opening speech, 246, 253.

modernization, and that there is no more fundamental principle than the law of survival in this world. "The law of Inkilab" he declared at Izmit, "is above all existing laws."[35] It was impossible for him to subject the nation to a law, even when this law was in the scriptures, if eventually it led to a servile existence in this world. His whole philosophy of life was based on the Darwinian theory of survival. The pragmatic outlook on life with a belief in the decisive role of actual power for survival is the key to understanding Atatürk's personality, and his tactics in politics and *inkilâb*. In his speeches he always stressed that life is struggle, and that success in this struggle depends on being prepared for struggle. In 1923 at Akhisar for instance he said, "Every nation in this world wants to survive and survival depends on struggle... this country shall definitely become a modern, progressive and developed one. This is a struggle of survival for us."[36] If we are to define Kemalism in terms of a social doctrine we may find it in social Darwinism.

Representing all the traditional forces in the country, the Caliphate had the potential to become the center of reaction to the *inkilâb* and to the modernizing reforms of the future. Kemal expressed the concern during his campaign that the supporters of the Caliphate had plans to bring back the Sultanate.

Always in his logic of struggle for survival, the reaction to the *inkilâb,* he said, is a conspiracy against the life and existence of the nation and the *inkilâbcıs* should use every means to overcome it. The incidents leading to the abolition of the Caliphate in 1924 are well known.

A rather practical matter, the question *of who* actually was the head of the state, came to the fore when the allied powers at Lausanne made it an issue. Conservatives turned their eyes naturally to the Caliph. Subsequently, Abdülmecid's behavior and the attention he was getting in the country and abroad led the *inkilâbcıs* to make a revolutionary move although it was as always achieved through the GNA. Seven months after Kemal's tour in Anatolia, and three months after the signing of the peace treaty, the Republic was promulgated by the GNA and Kemal was elected its first president. İsmet became prime minister. This new *inkilâb* further estranged the Rauf group from Kemal, and when the rumours of the Caliph's resignation spread, the opposition beseeched him not to do it because this as Lütfi Fikri, chairman of the Istanbul bar, put it, "would thrust the world into a calamity."

A letter supporting the Caliph written by the Indian Muslim leaders to İsmet Pasha was published in an Istanbul newspaper before it reached the addressee. This as well as Rauf s visit to the Caliph in Istanbul, made Kemal and İsmet decide to make the final move and abolish the Caliphate through the

---

[35] *Söylev ve Demeçler,* 63.
[36] Ibid., 93.

GNA. In the following four years the GNA enacted revolutionary laws designed to complete the secularization of the state and society which actually constituted the logical consequences of the revolutionary *élan* and of the great *inkilâb* which took place in the period 1922-1923. All the pre-requisites for a nation-state were formally enacted and promulgated [37].

What was accomplished by the abolition of the Caliphate and the immediate measures of secularization was a radical revolution. As Count Ostrorog, a judicial consultant to the Ottoman government and a close observer of the changes in Turkey in 1924 pointed out[38], this was "one of the most considerable events that has happened in the history of the East since the fourteenth century."

The abolition of the Caliphate on March 3, 1924 and the suppression of an insurrection in Eastern Anatolia in the following year marked the final victory of the *inkilâbcıs* over the religious establishment. But secularization introduced by the unification of public instruction under a secular administration and promulgation of the Swiss civil code as Turkey's law in 1926, meant a much more radical revolution for Islam. Free from the intricacies of the Islamic theology and jurisprudence the *inkilâbcıs* went further and asserted that religion is only a matter of the conscience of the individual. In his speech before the abolition of the Caliphate Kemal declared that "For salvation in the next world and happiness in this world of the nation it became imperative to move decisively and without delay to free our consciences and religious beliefs which are sacred and sublime from politics and from all its accretions which have proved to be only an instrument for all kinds of shady and unstable games of interests and ambitions."[39] "The word of Revolution was not pronounced" Count Ostrorog observes,[40] "but activities soon manifested themselves that were indeed not Evolution but such a Revolution as the world of Islam had never seen... what has been done is somewhat more than reform, something that tends to revise fundamental tenets supported by an established doctrine and an ancient observance, not reform but reformation.... It may even become the starting- point for an important renewal of Islamic thought developing on terms of an independent liberal exegisis."

Half a century has passed since Kemal's revolution but Count Ostrorog's hope has not been realized. On the contrary the reaction came in its most

---

[37] Kocatürk, ibid., 260-66, and the sources referred to there; and Gologlu, *Ibid.*.

[38] Count Léon Ostrorog, *The Angora Reform,* London: University of London Press 1927, 14.

[39] Atatürk, *A Speech,* 576-78; Kocatürk, *op. cit.* 266: *Zabıtlar Ceridesi,* Devre II, cilt VIII, 3-6.

[40] Ostrorog, *op. cit.* 70.

fundamental form aiming at subjecting the state and society more than ever to the *Shari'a* as established by the great *imâms* of the eighth and ninth centuries. Those governments which followed Kemal's revolution and modernization program even partially have been either totally destroyed or forced to change their policies.

Mustafa Kemal Atatürk was a statesman but above all a revolutionary who believed that rapid modernization was a matter of life and death for his nation, and that could be achieved by revolution legitimized by the modern principle of national will against a concept of divine authority. His modernization pattern can be classified in the terminology of political scientists as a forced one from above by a modernizing leader. "Man" as C. E. Block observes in *The Dynamics of Modernization (*157), "is not a captive of history despite the undeniable persistence of historically evolved traditions... The character of the policies of modernization adopted and the way that they are implemented depend to a considerable degree on leadership." But, he added, "instant modernization is not within the realm of possibility." Modernization is the end result of an historical process of a more or less long period. It was not an accident that Turkey could achieve the most radical revolution in modern Islam, and is today the least affected Muslim nation by the upsurge of Islamic fundamentalism. By revolution and with the strong backing of a group of *inkilâbcı*s as well as with the approval of a large section of the population, Atatürk was able to eliminate the control of a powerful clerical hierarchy and to introduce the legal and political conditions for rapid social development and modernization.

B

TURKEY and EUROPE

6

Turkey and Europe: A Historical Perspective

The earliest known Neolithic site of Hacılar and Çatalhöyük, dating back to 7000 BC "stands out as an incomparable prehistoric centre of culture. It was here that man created one of his first great works of art" (Prof. Dr. Ekrem Akurgal, *Ancient Civilisations,* p. 3). Agriculture was then practised, as revealed by the excavations. Anatolian civilisation seems to have been retarded and remained at the stage of a village civilisation until 2500 BC when the Bronze Age started with the Hatti. The Hatti gave their name to Asia Minor which was then called the Land of the Hatti. Before the Hittites, an Indo-European people, began to arrive from 2200 BC, the Hatti had reached a high level of urban civilisation, writing in cuneiform from the beginning of the eighteenth century BC. The Hatti's cultural influence, particularly in religion and state organisation on the Old Hittite Kingdom (1750-1450 BC), was paramount. The Hatti language was different from all other Near Eastern languages. In its basic structure it has common characteristics with the Altaic or Turkic language family.

Other known inhabitants of Asia Minor before the Hittites were Luvians, an Indo-European people living in southwest Anatolia. The Hurrians, whose language showed an Altaic structure, occupied the southeast around 2000 BC. They came under the strong influence of Babylonian culture. The Hurrians were followed by the Mitanni, an Indo-European people in eastern Anatolia. The newcomers, the 'people of Hatti', from which the Old Testament name Hittite was derived, spoke an Indo-European language called Nesian (Hittites called themselves *Nesi* or *Naşi).*

With the invasion of these Indo-European tribes between 2200 BC and 2100 BC, a new period began in Asia Minor. The Hittites founded the first strong state uniting the whole of Asia Minor under their rule (1450-1200 BC), and annexed Aleppo and Babylon. The name Asia comes from the Hittite word *Assuwa.* In Syria they clashed with the Egyptian empire of Ramses II in 1299 BC, leading to the the earliest known peace treaty signed at Qadesh, 1299 BC. At the excavations in the Hittite city of Kültepe there came to light the first state archives of mankind.

Scholarship underlines the artistic and cultural influence of the early Asia Minor civilisations on Aegean and Greek culture (Akurgal, *Orient und*

Okziden, Baden-Baden, 1966). Archaeological excavations, to which in the 1930s Atatürk gave impetus, delivered solid evidence that before the Aegean culture flourished in Ionia, Anatolia had become the cradle of great civilisations. Atatürk regarded the Hittite state as the prototype of the modern Turkish state in Asia Minor with its territorial boundaries and its capital in the central plateau.

While the central plateau and mountainous east came under the strong influence of the highly developed Mesopotamian civilisations in the early periods, later on Western Anatolian cultures, as uncovered in Troy and the western coastal areas, represented a different cultural tradition coming from the Aegean. In fact, throughout its history Anatolia became the bridge for the transmission and fusion of oriental and Western cultures from the Bronze Age to the present time. The Ionian civilisation in western Anatolia was a product of the coexistence of Greek people with the natives of Asia Minor (Akurgal, *Ancient Civilisations,* p. 17).

Scholarship has established that no fewer than seventy languages have been used in Anatolia up to the present time and that more than twenty different ethnic groups live today in Turkey. In the nineteenth and twentieth centuries hundreds of thousands of refugees from the Caucasus, the Crimea, Bosnia, Bulgaria, Greece and Albania, who felt themselves to belong to the Turkish culture came and were settled by the government in various parts of Anatolia. It is suggested that every third person in Turkey today belongs to one of these refugee groups. The explanation is that under the Turkish states which succeeded each other in Anatolia and the Balkans in the course of the last millennium, all of these indigenous and immigrant peoples acquired a common Turkish identity. Very long coexistence and common historical experience under a unified state structure gave rise to one Turkish culture and a common culture is the solid foundation of the Turkish nation today. Ideological attempts to break up this unity are against the historically formed, organic existence of the Turkish nation of today.

The Ionian civilisation, which gave to the Graeco-Roman civilisation the principle of national thinking and science, flourished in western Anatolia with Greek colonies on coastal regions and a highly developed trade during Hellenistic and Roman periods, blending Greek civilisation with the Orient's wisdom and mysticism, Anatolia then appeared as the world's richest and most advanced region. The ruins of magnificent cities from this period witness to this golden age of the peninsula.

In the following period, Asia Minor became the scene of an inconclusive struggle between the Caliphate and the Byzantine Empire, and declined until the time when, under the Seljuk sultanate of Konya, it recovered its past prosperity. With the Seljuks, the Turkish-Islamic period of Asia Minor began.

The great Seljuk empire in the east, encompassing central Asia and Iran, vigorously continued the struggle against the Byzantines who lost the final confrontation at the battle of Manzikert in 1071. Then, the whole peninsula to the Aegean was flooded with Turkish tribes.

The first period of the Turkish invasion and settlement under the local Turcoman dynasties ended with the unification of Asia Minor, except for the western regions. Under the Seljuks of Konya, the peninsula rose once again to be one of the most prosperous and advanced areas of the world and at the crossroads of the then flourishing east-west trade (trade privileges, for example, were granted to Venice in 1220). Anatolian cities of the Seljuks can be compared to those of the Graeco-Roman period, with the difference of their oriental characteristics. The Seljuks built on trade highways magnificent caravansaries comparable to Western cathedrals. In the classical period of this refined civilisation, Konya became the most celebrated centre of oriental mysticism with Mawlana Jalaleddin Rumi and other great mystic philosophers of the thirteenth century. Under the Seljuks, Islamic religion and civilisation became prevalent in Asia Minor.

The task of Islamisation was completed under the second period of the Turcoman principalities, which arose on the frontier areas and conquered Byzantine western Anatolia. The Ottoman state in its first stage was one of these Turcoman principalities. The frontier military tradition and the Seljuk cultural heritage made it possible for the Ottomans to create one of the most powerful and enduring empires of the world, replacing the Byzantine Empire in İstanbul and the Balkans.

Although ethnic and cultural identity in Anatolia has been Turkish for the last millennium, it represents in fact a synthesis of ' various cultural and ethnic heritages which have been juxtaposed and fused in the long history of the peninsula. Archaeological and anthropological research shows that in daily life, beliefs, language, toponymy, arts and anthropological features of the Turkish nation today there are numerous elements from the bygone people and their civilisations. Five main periods in this long evolution can be identified: I. the Hatti and Hittite period, 2500-900 BC; II. the Urartian civilisation in eastern Anatolia and Phrygian, Lydian and Carian civilisations in western Anatolia, 900-300 BC; III. the Minoan and Ionian-Greek civilisations in Western Anatolia and the Aegean, a Persian interlude (546-334 BC), and Hellenistic civilisation, 900-30 BC; IV. the Roman and Byzantine period, 30 BC-AD 1071; V. Turkish Asia Minor-a. the Seljuks and Turcoman principalities, 1071-1307, b. the Ottomans, 1307-1923, and c. the Turkish Republic, 1923 onwards.

1. The Ottoman Empire's Place in World History

In this synopsis an attempt will be made to review Turkish-European relations in past political, economic and cultural perspectives. The dividing line in these relations is, without doubt, the rise of the modern nation-state of Turkey.

In the period 1250-1500, the Levant, that is the eastern Mediterranean region with its hinterland of economically integrated countries, was the world's most lively region for the exchange of goods and ideas between east and west before the great European discoveries. The Ottomans unified under their rule the entire region conquering first Anatolia and the Balkans from the Euphrates to the Danube and from the Crimea to the Aegean islands in the period 1300-1453. In 1453 they conquered Constantinople/Istanbul despite the threat of a Western crusade, thus creating a compact empire around the imperial capital and the Straits. In the early sixteenth century they annexed to their Empire the Arab lands of Syria, Egypt, Arabia and the Yemen (1516-1517), thus taking under their control the trade and pilgrimage routes through the Indian Ocean and the Red Sea, which involved them in a long struggle against the Portuguese. In the east, at various dates they extended their rule as far as Tabriz (1517, 1534, 1585), Georgia (1549) and the Caspian Sea (1585) in an effort to establish full control of the silk route from Tabriz to Bursa and from Tabriz to Aleppo. By annexing Iraq (1534) and gaining access to the Gulf (1534) they participated, along with the Portuguese and the Iranian Safavids, in the flourishing trade of the Indian Ocean through Hormuz, Basra and Baghdad.

In 1453, the full control of the Straits (the Dardanelles, Marmara Sea and the Bosphorus) gave the Ottomans a strategic position in establishing full control over the trade of the Black Sea and East European countries (for instance the conquest of the Genoese colonies of the Crimea in 1475, and the first commercial agreement with Muscovy in 1497).

The first Ottoman grant of trade privileges, or capitulations, to the Genoese in 1352, and subsequently to Venice and Florence, guaranteed the continuation of the grand commerce of these maritime republics with the Levant, thus securing the economic prosperity of Renaissance Italy. The Ottoman sultans extended the same trade privileges to France in 1569, to England in 1580 and to the Netherlands in 1612. At one time, half of the foreign trade of France was with the Levant, while England's Levant Company, pioneer of such trade companies, established the basis of that country's commercial expansion in the world and of its capitalistic development. In those early centuries when the Ottoman emperors represented a superpower in the East, they granted such privileges only to those nations judged as friendly. Capitulations became a kind of bilateral, binding treaty only when Russia elicited such capitulations in 1783.

Extended at each renewal and practically mandatory, the capitulatory privileges with a low rate of three per cent customs dues became a means for the European economic exploitation of the Middle East and were responsible for the collapse of its native handicraft industries in the period 1600-1900. In the 1840s, England's exports to the Middle East jumped to one-third of its whole foreign trade. In brief, it can be said that in the period 1500-1990, the Ottoman Empire, whose territory comprised Asia Minor, the Balkans and the Arab lands of the Middle East, played one of the most crucial roles in the economic development of Europe.[1]

2. The European State-system and the Ottoman Empire, 1500-1815

Medieval Europe was supposed to make up one unified *Respublica Christina* under the Pope and the Holy Roman Emperor. This unity began to dissolve with the rise of national monarchies in the fifteenth century. Then, the crucial issue in the realignment of the rising powers in Europe was, on the one hand, how to keep the balance of power among the rival national monarchies and, on the other hand, how to keep the balance of power between the national monarchies and the Holy Roman Empire under the Habsburgs. In the sixteenth century the Ottoman Empire, rising as a superpower in the east, in rivalry with the Habsburgs, played a crucial role in the struggle.

In his struggle against Emperor Charles V, the French King Francis I (1515-1547) admitted that the only power capable of checking Charles V's domination of Europe was Süleyman the Magnificent (1520-1566). Francis's successor Henri II (1547-1559) had to borrow, through the Jewish banker family of Mendes, large sums of money from the Ottomans to finance his wars against the emperor. Again, the French prince Henri was able to gain the Polish throne (1573) only with the strong support of the Ottomans who opposed a Habsburg-backed king in Poland. The Ottomans also encouraged and promised aid to the Protestants in Germany as well as to the Dutch in rebellion against the Habsburgs in the Low Countries. Historians today unanimously underline the fact that Protestants obtained significant concessions from the emperor because of the impending Ottoman pressure from the east. Later on, when Elizabeth I (1558-1603) of England was under threat from the Spanish Armada, she tried to stir up Ottoman naval action in the Mediterranean against Spain. Examples can be multiplied to demonstrate how significant a role the Ottoman state played in maintaining the balance of power in Europe in the sixteenth

---

[1] For the Ottoman Empire's economic relations with Europe now see H. İnalcık, ed. with Quataert, D. *An Economic and Social History of the Ottoman Empire,* Cambridge University Press, 1994.

century. In general, the Ottoman state pursued a policy aiming to ensure that none of the European powers became powerful enough to unify Europe under its domination.

In the end, two superpowers, the Ottoman and Habsburg empires, reached a kind of balance in east-central Europe and the Mediterranean, and made a truce in 1547 which stabilised the Ottoman territories in Europe and opened a new period of balance of power in Europe. Following the Catholic reaction and the Thirty Years War (1618-1648) in Europe, the France of Louis XIV (1643-1715) challenged the emperor, which emboldened the Ottomans to resume their expansionist policy against the Habsburgs, The Ottoman siege of Vienna in 1683 resulted in a coalition around the Habsburgs against the Ottoman Empire (the Holy League of 1684). England and the Netherlands, worried by the French advances in the Rhine valley, were endeavouring to achieve peace between the Ottomans and the emperor. English and Dutch pressure on the Habsburgs during the peace negotiations at Karlowitz in 1699 were duly appreciated by the Porte which subsequently granted to them new commercial privileges. This was the beginning of England's special influence in the Ottoman Empire which would last until 1878. This is also the date at which the Ottomans finally recognised European superiority in military technology and decided to imitated. European experts were invited to modernise the Ottoman army.

During the long war of 1683-1699 another very important development took place-the Russian Empire, joined the Holy League and entered the Black Sea region by capturing Azov (Azak) in 1696. Now Istanbul itself was under threat. Equally important was that Russia then was admitted into the European state-system as a result of its joining the Holy League, whereas the Ottoman Empire remained outside the system until 1841.[2]

3. Russian imperialism, the Ottoman Empire, the West, and the so-called Eastern Question

In the eighteenth century, Russia, now officially recognised as part of Europe, pursued a plan of replacing the Ottoman Empire in İstanbul, the tsar claiming to be the protector of the Christian populations of the Balkans. Weakened and threatened by Russia and the Habsburgs, the Ottomans, along with the Western powers, now became more than ever an advocate of the balance of power in

---

[2] For Ottomans and the European state system, see H. İnalcık, *The Middle East and the Balkans under the Ottoman Empire,* Bloomington, 1993; H. İnalcık, *The Ottoman Empire: The Classical Age, 1300-1600,* London, 1973; D.M. Vaughan, *Europe and the Turk, A Pattern of Alliances,* Liverpool, 1954.

Europe. This Ottoman policy became particularly apparent in the protest against Poland's partition between Russia, the Habsburgs and Prussia (1772-1795). Once more, the Western powers, France and England, joined the Porte in this policy. In the wake of the Russians' spectacular military successes against the Ottoman armies during the war of 1768-1774, the Russian annexation in 1783 of the northern Black Sea countries, inhabited mostly by Muslim peoples of Turkic origin, alarmed the whole of Europe. Russia now had an exclusive trade monopoly in the Black Sea and had become an imminent threat to İstanbul and the Straits. The Porte now sought aid and guarantees from Western powers for its territorial integrity. This new situation was labelled in European diplomacy as the Eastern Question, showing Western concern to preserve the Ottoman Empire, considered necessary for the European balance of power. (Incidentally it is totally misleading and is a mistake in Western literature to call the Ottoman Empire simply the Turkish Empire; identifying the Ottoman state-a patrimonial, dynastic empire-with the present-day nation-state of Turkey, which came into existence in 1923. This mistake is often responsible for the unjust anachronistic treatment by European states of the issues concerning modern Turkey.) This Western policy, however, did not go so far as to make the Ottoman state a member of the European state-system under the guarantees of international law. It was mainly religious ideology that was responsible for the Europeans denying the fact that the Ottoman state had long become part and parcel of the continental state-system. However, it is to be noted that Protestant countries, particularly England, overriding the Pope's prohibition of the sale of strategic materials to the 'infidel', used to export to the Ottoman Empire high quality powder and steel as early as the sixteenth century. It is also to be remembered that the Ottoman government systematically supported Lutherans and Calvinists throughout Europe. In the Ottoman Empire, too, while pragmatic-minded bureaucrats put the state's interests above everything else, the *ulema,* representing Islamic ideology, endeavoured to impose, most of the time without success, their influence on state policies.

4. European Security Systems and the Ottoman State, 1815-1878

One century before the establishment of the League of Nations and the United Nations, Fürst von Metternich, the Austrian statesman, considered Europe not as a continent in which separate nations and states were in constant struggle against each other, but as one single integrated European republic. This unity, he said, could be achieved only by the "co-operation of the states", not through the control of one dominant state. As a protection for and guarantee of the peace and existing monarchical order in Europe, a league of the four leading powers should have the right of supervision over revolutionary movements anywhere in Europe. At the Congress of Vienna the Quadruple Alliance of 1815, in accordance with the Metternich System, made the decision to assemble annually to review the situation in Europe, thus creating a permanent mechanism to maintain the status quo established in Vienna. Regardless of the specific nature and function of the Metternich System, all its arrangements can be considered as the precursor of the international organisations of the twentieth century. [3]

The Porte was not represented at the Congress of Vienna in 1815. The Ottoman statesman and historian, Cevdet Pasha, notes[4] with regret that the Ottoman Porte then failed to seize the opportunity to participate in the Congress of Vienna. Since, he argues, in a later stage of the congress all those European states which were connected with the issues discussed in one way or another sent their delegates, obviously the Ottoman state also had the right to participate in the negotiations, at least on the problems directly concerning the Ottoman Empire. Unfortunately, he points out, the Porte was deeply engaged in so many urgent problems within the Empire-the struggle against the rebellious provincial notables in particular-that such important external events escaped the government's attention. Charles Talleyrand, the French diplomat, Cevdet adds, raised the issue of an agreement among the European Great Powers about a joint guarantee for the territorial integrity of the Ottoman Empire in the instructions sent to the French delegation. Ottoman participation in the Congress, Cevdet suggests, might have been useful in checking Russia's ambitious plans. Along with the French and the Austrian governments the English government, too, supported the idea that "the Ottoman Empire should be included in the general treaty guaranteeing the status quo in Europe which [Canning, British statesman] hoped would be a result of the congress."[5] Upon Russia's rejection, the idea of a general guarantee for the Ottoman Empire was dropped.

It was to isolate the Ottoman Empire from Europe that, in the Holy Alliance of September 1815, Tsar Alexander I insisted on the Christian nature of the Alliance. Let us add here that down to our days, such a policy is the cornerstone of Greek diplomacy against Turkey. Predicting the future, Metternich's overriding concern was that the dismemberment of the Ottoman

---

[3] H. R. von Srbik, (1925), "Metternichs Plan der Neuordnuung Europe 1815/15", *Mitteilungen des österreichischen Instituts für Geschichtsforschung,* 60, 109-126; H.W. Schmals, *Versuche einer gesarnteuropalischen Organisation, 1815-1820,* Aarau, 1940; H. Tuncer, *Metternich'in Osmanlı Politikası (1815-1848),* Ankara, 1996.

[4] *Tarih-i Cevdet,* 2nd edition, İstanbul, vol. XI, 1309 H., 156-161, 181.

[5] Anderson, *The Eastern Question,* 47-8.

Empire in the Balkans and the ensuing collapse of the European balance of power, would result in a general war.

Developments during the Egyptian crisis of 1832-1833 fully justified Metternich's apprehensions. The Russian Empire had reached a dominant position in European politics following the fall of Napoleon, hoping to replace the Ottomans in İstanbul. In 1832, in the desperate situation caused by Mehmed Ali of Egypt whose armies had invaded Anatolia, Mahmud II (1809-1839) had to recognise Russia's special status in respect of the Straits with the treaty of Hünkar-İskelesi in 1833, virtually making the Ottoman sultan a vassal of the tsar and changing the European balance of power in favour of Russia.[6] The tsar had profited from the hesitant policy of Western powers during the first phase of the Egyptian crisis. During the second phase of the Egyptian crisis (1837-1839), France's pro-Egyptian attitude obstructed Western co-operation over the problem of the integrity of the Ottoman Empire. In the critical situation in the wake of the Ottoman defeat at Nizib (June 24, 1839), on the initiative of England and Austria, the Great Powers including Russia, France and Prussia, delivered a unanimous note to the Porte and assumed the responsibility of bringing a solution to the crisis. Thus, the concert of Europe was restored in the face of the dangerous situation in the east which seriously threatened the balance of power in Europe, and aimed at neutralising Russia's exclusive position. England, which had obtained vast commercial privileges in the Ottoman dominions through the treaty of 1838, decided to support effectively the integrity of the Empire and the *Tanzimat* reforms. This was the beginning of the period covering the years 1839-1878 when England's influence in the Ottoman Empire became preponderant in all fields. All the Great Powers, except France, agreed among themselves in London (July 15, 1840) to force Mehmed Ali to abandon his plan of an Arab empire matching the Ottoman sultan's. At this point, although rivalry among the members of the European concert continued, the concern to keep the balance of power in Europe brought them together, the fate of the Ottoman Empire having become the most important issue in nineteenth century European politics.

Actually, policies or excuses for interference in the internal affairs of secondary states followed by the Great Powers in the period 1815-1878 were not very different in essence from those of our time, except that they are now globalised to control world issues which can lead to a general war.

---

[6] In the secret article of the Hünkar İskelesi treaty it is specified that in return for Russia's military aid to the sultan, "the Sublime Ottoman Porte shall confine its action in favour of the Imperial Court of Russia to closing the strait of the Dardanelles, that is to say, to not allowing any foreign vessels of war to enter therein under any pretext whatsoever."

In 1841, a very important document signed by the five powers with France joining the Alliance re-established the old status concerning the Straits, superseding Russia's privileged position. "The ships of war of the foreign powers" were prohibited to enter the Straits of the Dardanelles and the Bosphorus and the five Great Powers would "engage to respect this determination of the sultan, and to conform themselves to the principle above declared." The particular importance of this agreement was that the Great Powers were united in accepting the principle as binding on themselves, which became part of the public law of Europe. It is interpreted as the first step toward the Ottoman Empire's inclusion in the European concert. This became apparent when the tsar attempted to make the sultan recognise his protectorate over the Christian subjects of the sultan in 1853. The British and French governments decided to support the Porte against Russia (the Crimean War, 1854-1856). By the treaty of Paris (March 30, 1856) the Great Powers admitted Turkey into the European concert. Article VII says: "Their majesties engage, each on his part, to respect the independence and the territorial integrity of the Ottoman Empire".

In return, the Porte promised (The Hatt-i Hümâyûn of 1856) fundamental reforms to improve the conditions of its subjects. By a special agreement, Britain, France and Austria jointly guaranteed Ottoman sovereignty and territorial integrity and infraction of them was to be a *casus belli*. Historically, this meant the culmination of the long process of integration of Turkey with Western Europe.

5. Ottoman Reforms and the Emergence of Modern Turkey

The westernising reforms of the *Tanzimat* period (1839-1877) were responsible for the adoption of a series of Western law codes, judicial organisation with secular law courts, introduction of the French-style provincial administration (1864), and, for the so-called *millet* system, which made it possible for the Christian minorities to have their own religious autonomous administration with representative councils. These liberal westernising reforms culminated in the declaration of a constitution and the convocation of a parliament in 1876-1877. However, the disastrous war of 1877-1878 with Russia, during which the Western powers remained neutral, resulted in the loss of large territories in the Balkans. Dismemberment of the Empire created such a deep disillusionment amongst the Turks that, under Sultan Abdulhamid II (1876-1909), a strong Islamist reaction against Western influence became state policy. Also, radical changes were happening in European politics and the balance of power in the wake of the Berlin Congress (1878), with the emergence of a unified Germany and the ensuing triple alliance making Russia a partner of the Western powers. Taking advantage of the Ottoman helplessness in the wake of the Russian advances in the Balkans and the Caucasus, England managed to take the lion's share in the partitioning of the Empire by occupying Cyprus (1878) and Egypt (1882) as well as penetrating the Gulf and the Red Sea. Thus, the security of the British Empire was believed to be guaranteed. These changes also entailed a complete re-orientation in Ottoman foreign policy. Abandoned by the West, faced with Russian imperial ambitions and the Greek *Megali Idea* of restoring the Byzantine Empire, the Ottomans turned to Germany (Kaiser Wilhelm II's visit to İstanbul in 1899).

The events in the course of World War I, the defeat of the Allied fleet at the Dardanelles in particular, showed the world the key strategic importance of Turkey and the Straits. Another historic importance of the struggle at the Dardanelles was that Turks found, in the person of a young, brilliant soldier named Mustafa Kemal (later Atatürk) a national hero who was destined to be the deliverer of the homeland of the Turks in Asia Minor and Europe from the Greek invasion in 1919-1922. At the end of World War I the prime minister of Greece, Eleutherios Venizelos, a consummate diplomat, succeeded in obtaining the full support of the Allied powers for the realisation of the Greek dream of reviving the Byzantine Empire. On 15 May 1919, the Greek forces landed at İzmir under the protection of an Allied fleet, an episode which vividly recalled the Navarino operation of one century earlier. The story of the ensuing events is well known. Dictated by the Allied powers, then occupying the capital of the sultanate, the Treaty of Sèvres of 1920 (articles 65-83) granted Greece İzmir and its hinterland, and distributed large territories in Asia Minor as booty to the Allied powers. No one then could anticipate that the use of the Greeks for the Allied scheme of partitioning the Turkish homeland would be a fatal mistake, and would arouse the whole Turkish nation in staunch resistance to the Allied verdict. Following a three-year struggle (1919-1923) a new nation was born. The point to be stressed is that in his fight against the Greeks and the victors of World War I, as well as against the Caliph's manoeuvres in occupied İstanbul, Mustafa Kemal always made sure that important decisions went through a national Assembly on the principle of the absolute sovereignty of the Turkish nation. Thus, the War of Independence signified a national revolution which asserted the Turkish nation's determination to end the Ottoman dynasty's imperial-patrimonial rule once and for all, and to join on equal footing the club of the European nation states. In 1922, Arnold Toynbee, then visiting the Turkish-Greek front, declared that the Turks were fighting there with Western ideals against the West itself. In the peace conference of Lausanne (July 24, 1923), the Turkish delegation's insistence on equality with European states was the recurring theme of every issue discussed. Capitulatory privileges, which had reduced the Ottoman Empire to the conditions of a semi-colony of the Western powers, became the subject of the most heated discussions causing the rupture of the negotiations for three months (the recent attempt to give Turkey secondary status in the European Union is interpreted as another sign of how Europe still regards Turkey as the continuation of the Ottoman Empire). During the period of 1923-1928 the Grand National Assembly (GNA) in Ankara, acting as the sole representative of the Turkish nation enacted, under the leadership of Mustafa Kemal, a series of revolutionary laws all aiming to make Turkey a modern nation state, democratic and secular. Atatürk and his *inkilâpcı* group in the GNA, considered the total westernization of the country as the absolute precondition for Turkey's becoming a member of the Western family of nations. Atatürk introduced his revolutionary *inkilâb*s one after another: Declaration of the Republic (October 29, 1923), abolition of the caliphate (March 24, 1924), adoption of the Swiss civil law (October 4, 1926); the law for a unified secular education (March 2, 1926); changes in the constitution to secularise the state (1928); the adoption of the Latin alphabet (October 1, 1928), and finally reforms making the Turkish citizen appear as a European and to give him a national Turkish identity. The last *inkilâb*s about the alphabet or dress may be looked on as symbolic, but in fact they are crucially important for cultural, social and political identity in a traditional society. Seeing stiff resistance from a deeply traditional society, Kemal's attention turned to the education of the youth of the country. The enactment of the law of the 'Unification of Education' of 1926 must be looked on as one of the most prudent *inkilâb*s. His hope was that youth brought up under an absolutely national, secular education system would be the guarantee of the new Turkey. Through educational and cultural institutions, Atatürk hoped to create out of a traditional community a modern nation on the model of Western nations.

7

The Turkish Impact on the Development of Modern Europe

Since a Euro-centric view of history in the West began to be replaced by a true world history concept, the history of the Ottoman Empire, which lasted in a very important part of the world for over five centuries, is attracting new interest. A number of contributions recently made in Europe and America on the problem of the place of the Ottoman Empire in European history can be considered as a sign of this growing interest. Although some of these new studies were still not free of certain biases, mainly because they did not make use of the Ottoman evidence, they, however, explored new ideas and had new orientations.

Under the light of these publications we are now able, for instance, to speak of how the Ottoman state became an important factor in the balance of power of European politics. Even during the first stage of the Italian wars from 1494 to 1525 the Ottoman state was an important part in Italian diplomacy. Fr. Babinger and J. Kissling in their studies based on the Italian archival material, and S. Fisher, Pfefferman, Schwoebel, D. Vaughan in their more general treatment of the subject showed how the Italian courts maintained diplomatic relations with the Ottoman Sultan. It is true that the Western archives do not yield much on the subject, for political and military matters were concealed in such negotiations and never put in writing. But sometimes even if an Ottoman military intervention was not really desired the rumor of a secret alliance was used as an intimidation. Hard-pressed Italian states used as a last measure the threat of calling on the Ottomans. In 1525 the French followed actually this Italian policy when their king was made prisoner by the Emperor. The Ottomans welcomed this opportunity to invade Hungary in 1526 and open a sea front against the Emperor in the Mediterranean in 1532 just as in the past they had exploited the situation in Italy against Venice. From 1480 onwards the Ottomans always thought of an invasion of Italy. Two factors made them hesitate for a decisive move, the possibility of resistance of a Europe united under the Pope and Emperor, and their own naval weakness to open an overseas front. In 1537, however, Suleyman thought it was the time for such a move. As early as 1531 the Venetian ambassador was writing to the doge, "Sultan Suleyman says, 'To Rome, to Rome,' and he detests the Emperor for his title of Kayser (Caesar), he, the Turk, causing himself to be called Caesar." Ottoman attempts to capture from the Venetians strongholds along the Adriatic coast and the isle of Corfu in 1537 and 1538 were in fact a preparation for the invasion of Italy. France was then an ally of the Ottomans. They were reinforced by the French navy at the siege of Corfu. But the King and Emperor saw the great danger for the whole of Christendom in Europe. In July 1538 Francis made peace with Charles V at Aigues-Mortes and what is more he promised to take part in a crusade against the Ottomans. Two months later Barbarossa, Grand Admiral of the Sultan, succeeded in routing a powerful crusading fleet at Prevesa. Then, this victory became useless without French alliance.

What I am trying to emphasize is that the Ottomans became an active part in the second stage of the Italian wars and there was a moment when the Western contenders for Italy saw that the balance of power was lost in favor of the Sultan. It must be added that the Ottomans fully appreciated the value of the French alliance and also supported the King financially. In 1533 the Sultan sent Francis a sum of one hundred thousand gold pieces to enable him to form a coalition with England and German princes against Charles V. Two years later the French King asked the Sultan to send him a subsidy of one million ducats. Later on in 1555 the French King Henri II, pressed for money, floated a loan in France with the interest increased from 12 to 16 percent, and at this time many Turks, pashas among them, found it profitable to invest in this loan. The King borrowed 150,000 scudos from Joseph Nasi, Jewish tax farmer of the Sultan. On his part the French king appreciated the Ottoman Alliance as the principal power to check the Habsburg supremacy in Europe. In 1532 Francis I admitted to the Venetian ambassador that he saw in the Ottoman Empire the only force guaranteeing the continued existence of the states of Europe against Charles V.

In brief one can say that the Ottoman Empire played an important role in the balance of power in Europe in the sixteenth century and consequently in the rise of the nation-states in the West. This role continued with the Ottoman support and encouragement to the English and Dutch in the period after 1580 when these nations proved to be the champions of European resistance to the Habsburg attempts at supremacy.

In the sixteenth and seventeenth centuries support for Protestants and Calvinists was one of the fundamental principles of Ottoman policy in Europe. Already in 1552 Suleyman tried to incite the Protestant princes in Germany against the Pope and Emperor. He said in his letter to them that he himself was about to embark on a campaign and promised on oath that they would not be harmed when he entered Germany. Melanchton was directly in touch with the Patriarch of Istanbul, who was in effect an official of the Sultan. Later on in a letter to Lutheran princes in the Low Countries and in other lands subject to

Spain, the Sultan offered military help and saw them as standing close to him, since they did not worship idols, believed in one God and fought against the Pope and Emperor. Under Ottoman rule Calvinism was propagated freely in Hungary and Transylvania, which became a Calvinist and Unitarian stronghold in the seventeenth century. It is convincingly argued that Ottoman pressure on the Habsburgs was an important factor in the extension of protestantism in Europe.

Further, it should be pointed out that the Ottomans contributed to the rise of Muscovy by supporting, as a great power in the politics of Eastern Europe, the Muscovy-Crimean alliance against the Jagellons and the Golden Horde, which then tried to establish or restore their hegemony in the region. When the Ottomans realized the danger for their Black Sea and Caucasian interests in the Muscovite supremacy and expansion in the middle of the sixteenth century it was too late.

Now, I would like to deal in a more detailed way with the economic relations of the Ottoman Empire with Europe.

Speaking of the Ottoman economy one can certainly not ignore the attitude of the Ottoman ruling class towards the productive classes and the problem of its economic policy in general.

At the outset it must be emphasized that the Ottoman state was not a nomadic empire the models of which could be found in the Euroasian steppes. It was a typical Middle East empire with all its age-old adminiistrative principles and institutions. It was concerned primarily with the protection of the settled populations under its rule and promotion of their agricultural and commercial interests. It should be added that this policy was not based on purely economic reasoning but mainly on the financial ends of the state. Even if in the thirteenth century nomadic elements in the Ottoman frontier society played a certain role, the Ottoman state had soon become a typical Islamic sultanate with the basic structure of a Middle East state. Its legislation and actions leave no room for doubt on this point. We know, for instance, that the longest internal struggle the Ottoman state had to make in the fifteenth and sixteenth centuries stemmed from the basic fact that it endeavoured in the interests of the settled population to take under control the seminomads of the Uzun-Yayla in Inner Anatolia and of the Taurus range from the Euphrates to Western Anatolia.

The economic system of the Ottoman empire and its basic economic principles derived from a traditional view of state and society which had prevailed since antiquity in the empires of the Middle East. These principles, since they determined the attitude and policy of the administrators, were of considerable practical importance.

In the Muslim state, as in earlier states in the Middle East, all classes of society and all sources of wealth were regarded as being obliged to preserve and promote the power of the ruler. Hence all political and social institutions and all types of economic activity were regulated by the state in order to achieve this goal. The populace was regarded as forming two main groups—those who represented the ruler's authority (the administrators, the troops, the men of religion), and the ordinary subjects, *ra'āyā'*. The former were not concerned with production and paid no taxes, while the latter were the producers and tax-payers. A main concern of the state was to ensure that each individual remained in his own class; this was regarded as the basic requisite for politico-social order and harmony.

To increase revenue from taxation the governments of Near East States appreciated the necessity of developing economic activity and promoting the greatest possible increase in production from all classes of the *ra'āyā'*.It was recommended that cultivated land should be increased by the digging of canals and that trade between different regions should be promoted by the construction of roads, bridges and caravanséeries, and by ensuring the safety of travelers.

Within the class of the producers, the tillers of the soil and craftsmen were subject to a code of regulations distinct from that of merchants; the methods of production and profit margins of the former were under strict state control, since, in this view of society, they were the classes who produced the essential necessities of life and whose labors therefore were most intimately connected with the preservation of social and political order. That a peasant or a craftsman should freely change the methods of production was not countenanced; his activities were permitted only within the limits of the ordinances laid down by the state. In Near East society, it was only the merchants who enjoyed conditions allowing them to become capitalists. "Merchant," *tüjjar,* in this context, means the big businessmen who engaged in interregional trade or in the sale of goods imported from afar. Craftsmen who in the cities sold goods manufactured by themselves and trades-people who sold these goods secondhand fell outside the category of "merchant." The merchant class was not subject to the regulations of the *hisba*, that is, rules of the religious law to ensure fair deal in the market.

In an Ottoman Mirror for Princes, Sinan Pasha's *Ma'ārifnāme* written in the second half on the fifteenth century, the ruler is advised:

> Look with favor on the merchants in the land; always care for them;
> let no one harass them; let no one order them about, for through their
> trading the land becomes prosperous, and by their wares cheapness

abounds in the world; through them the excellent fame of the Sultan is carried to surrounding lands, and by them the wealth within the land is increased.

Going through the state papers issued by the Ottoman Chancery one is struck by the fact that the administration was always most concerned in applying the principles summarized above.

The Ottoman government's concern for promoting commerce and protecting the interests of the merchant class found its expression in various ways.

It was mainly with the purpose of encouraging trade that the Sultans granted capitulations to the foreigners. It should be emphasized that a capitulation had never been considered as a contractual bilateral document and it maintained its character of a grant of concession by the Sultans until the eighteenth century when they had to give the same privileges to the Habsburgs and Russia. Before this actual change the Sultan retained the authority to decide unilaterally when the pledge of friendship on the opposite side was broken and the capitulation rendered void.

Once its nature as a concession granted by the Sultan is established a capitulation was, however, granted with certain political, financial and economic expectations. The determining factors were usually the opportunities of acquiring a political ally within Christendom, of obtaining scarce goods such as woolen cloth, tin, steel and paper, and especially bullion and increasing customs revenues, the principal source of hard cash for the imperial treasury.

The Ottoman empire was not self sufficient economically as it is sometimes claimed. It was vitally important for its economy and finances to import western silver. Its import was encouraged by tax exemption and measures were taken to hinder its flow to the Eastern countries where gold was cheaper. The Europeans knew well that the Ottomans were dependent on their commerce in the Levant and when they had to bargain for a special privilege in the capitulations their chief weapon was to use the threat that they were going to boycott the Ottoman ports.

A new period in the economic history of the Ottoman Empire started with the annexation of the Arab countries between 1516 and 1550 which actually gave it the control of the trade routes between the Mediterranean and Indian Ocean. It is now commonplace knowledge that the Near East continued to receive spices directly from India and Southeast Asia throughout the sixteenth century. According to the Ottoman records, in 1562 customs levied on spices transported from Mecca to Damascus alone amounted to 110 thousand gold ducats. What is interesting to note is that most of the spices imported there went to Bursa and Istanbul to be shipped further north. To give an interesting example, in 1547 we find a Hungarian merchant in Bursa selling kersey and buying a great quantity of spices.

In this period the newly rising nation-states of the West, France, England and the Netherlands, became most anxious to get trade privileges in the Ottoman Empire. The belief was that the Levant was, as in the past, the most promising field for economic growth. It was not solely on religious grounds that the Marrano family of Mendes, then controlling the spice trade in Europe, came to settle in the Ottoman capital in the 1550s.

The Ottomans had always favoured the rival nations, first the Genoese, then the Ragusans and Florentines against the Venetian dominance in the Levant trade in the fifteenth century.

As to the Western nations, the French made their first progress in Syria and Egypt after Selim's renewal of the Mamluk capitulations in 1517. But they really began to replace the Venetians in the Levant trade only after the Ottoman-Venetian war in 1570-73. Incidentally, the so-called French capitulations of 1536 had never been concluded. The first official Ottoman capitulation to the French is dated 1569. The other Western nations were then to sail and trade under the French flag. At the beginning of the 17th century the volume of French trade in the Levant rose to thirty million French livres, making up one half of France's total trade at that time. Later on when the English and Dutch proved to be even stronger rivals of the Habsburg power than the French, the Ottomans did not hesitate to favor these nations too by granting them capitulations, to the English in 1580, and the Dutch in 1612. Except during the civil war between 1642 and 1660 the English had the lead in the Levant trade in the seventeenth century. According to a contemporary source the Levant market for the English cloth which was the main article for export, expanded by one-third and was one-fourth of all English manufactures exported to the Levant. As W. Sombart put it, without recognizing the significance of the Levant trade for Western economic expansion it is difficult to comprehend the rise of Western capitalism.

The capitulatory privileges were gradually extended so much that Paul Masson and R. Mantran, two French specialists on the Levant trade, could unanimously assert that in the seventeenth century there was no other state in the world practicing a more liberal policy than the Ottoman empire towards foreign merchants.

The Ottomans had then no idea of the balance of trade, an idea that we find for the first time in a clearly defined form only in the mercantilist England of the sixteenth century. Originated from an age-old tradition in the Middle East, the Ottoman trade policy was that the state had to be concerned above all with the volume of goods in the internal market so that people and craftsmen in the cities in particular would not suffer a shortage of necessities and raw material. Consequently, imports were always welcomed and encouraged and exports discouraged. Hence sometimes we find higher customs rates for exports and even prohibition of the export of such goods as wheat, cotton, hides and beeswax. As for silver and gold no customs dues were levied to encourage their importation and every step was taken to discourage exportation. The Ottomans were definitely bullionists, a stage preceding true mercantilism in the West. The difference with the mercantilist nations of the West was that the Ottomans clung to the guild system as the mainstay of the state and society while Europeans saw in the export of manufactured goods a pirincipal means of getting bullion from outside. In order to achieve a favourable balance of trade they intervened in domestic industries and trade organizations to develop them on capitalistic lines and to export more and more goods and conquer more and more overseas markets. Incidentally, one might speculate that the increasingly unfavourable balance of trade of the West in the fifteenth century pushed them perhaps in this direction and caused a mercantilistic policy to develop, since they had no important commodities other than cloths and minerals to export to the East. The capitulations were complementary to this pattern and it is noteworthy that the mercantilistic nations of the West had been concerned in the first place to found their Levant companies and obtain capitulations. Unwittingly the Ottomans became a part of a European economic system which gave rise to modern capitalism.

8

Struggle for East-European Empire, 1400-1700:
The Crimean Khanate, Ottomans and the Rise of the
Russian Empire*

The empire of the Golden Horde, built by Batu, son of Djodji and the grandson of Genghis Khan, around 1240, was an empire which united the entire Eastern Europe under its domination. The Golden Horde empire comprised all of the remnants of the earlier nomadic peoples who spoke a Turkic language in the steppe area which were then known under the common name of Tatar within this new political framework. The Golden Horde ruled directly over the Eurasian steppe from Khwarezm to the Danube and over the Russian principalities in the forest zone indirectly as tribute-paying states. Already in the second half of the 13th century the western pan of the steppe from the Don river to the Danube tended to become a separate political entity under the powerful emir Noghay. In the second half of the 14th century rival branches of the Djodjid dynasty, each supported by a group of the dissident clans, started a long struggle for the Ulugh-Yurd, the core of the empire in the lower Itil (Volga) river, and for the title of Ulugh Khan which meant the supreme ruler of the empire.

Toktamish Khan restored, the unity of the empire for a short period. When defeated by Tamerlane, his sons and dependent clans resumed the struggle for the Ulugh-Khan-ship in the western steppe area. During all this period, the Crimean peninsula, separated from the steppe by a narrow isthmus, became a area of refuge for the defeated in the steppe. Around 1440 one of the grandsons of Toktamish Hajji Gerey or Giray, entrenching himself in this rich peninsula, succeeded in establishing an independent khanate. He minted silver coins in his name which was an indication of independence and assumed the title of Ulugh Khan. Descending from Toktamish Khan, he and his successors never gave up their right to the imperial patrimony on the whole Golden Horde empire,

---

* Read at the International Conference on "The Crimea: Past and Present", Kiev, 12-13 May 1994.

including suzerainty over the Russian principalities. In actuality, by this time the Golden Horde was split into three independent khanates, in the Crimea, Kazan, and the Saray region in the lower Volga. The latter, ruling over the Ulugh-Yurd, claimed to be the only legitimate successor to the great khanship. Like the secessionist khanates, the Grand Duke of Muscovy, once the Ulugh-Khan's deputy over other Russian principalities, began to act independently, challenging the Golden Horde overlordship. At the same time, in the western part of the region, Lithuania under Jagellons rose as a powerful state, claiming sovereignty on the patrimony of the Golden Horde in the area and challenging the rising Giray dynasty. Thus, by the middle of the 15th century, instead of one dominant imperial power in Eastern Europe there were newly rising states which eventually came to compete for supremacy over the whole region. Because of their relation to once powerful Toktamish Khan, the Giray dynasty in the Crimea seemed to have the best chance to revive the Golden Horde empire under their rule. The khans from another branch of Djodji, in control of the Saray region, embarked upon a long struggle against the Girays. The former made an alliance with the Jagellons while Girays, in turn, allied themselves with the Grand Duke of Muscovy to resist the powerful rival coalition. At this juncture the Ottoman power came to support the Crimea-Muscovy axis against the powerful Lithuania-Golden Horde coalition.

In 1454 the Ottoman sultan Mehmed the Conqueror, immediately after his conquest of Istanbul, sent his fleet into the Black Sea, and procured the allegiance of the local rulers such as the voyvode of Moldavia as well as of the Genoese colonies as tribute-paying vassals. Hajji Giray then cooperated with the Ottomans to claim his sovereignty over Caffa and other Genoese cities on the southern coasts of the Crimea but when later on, another Ottoman fleet threatened Caffa, he asserted that "Caffa was his patrimony". Mehmed the Conqueror knew well that he could not take the Genoese colonies of Caffa without cooperating with the Crimean Khan. In turn, the Genoese tried to protect their colonies by supporting a friendly khan on the Crimean throne among the sons of Hajji Giray and cooperated with the powerful chief of the Crimean aristocracy, the Beg of the principal Shirin clan. The Conqueror's diplomacy, however, managed to make Eminek, the Shirin Beg collaborate to put on the Crimean throne a pro-Ottoman Khan. In 1475, confident of Crimean cooperation, the Conqueror immediately sent a powerful fleet to subdue all the Genoese colonies in the Crimea. Later on, always in cooperation with Eminek Beg, he brought to the Crimean throne Mengli Giray who was captured in Caffa during the Ottoman occupation. Mengli Giray recognized the Conqueror as his suzerain and described his relation to him as his "tikme" (appointee). Thus, while an Ottoman province was organized on the southern shores of the peninsula with Caffa as the seat of an Ottoman sandjak-bey, the Crimean

Khanate became a vassal state of the Ottoman empire. This new situation would create totally new conditions in the struggle for domination in East-Europe. The Ottoman presence proved decisive for the balance of power in the region.

First, the Crimean-Moscovite axis got the upper hand in its struggle against the Lithuanian-Golden Horde coalition, and prepared the way for the final fall of the Golden Horde and the rise of the Moscovite power.

Secondly, it guaranteed the existence of the Crimean Khanate, first against the attacks of the Golden Horde Ulugh-Khans, in the period 1476-1502 and then of Russia as late as 1774.

Thirdly, the Crimea became an integral part of the Ottoman empire, politically, economically and culturally.

Fourthly, Ottoman-Polish rivalry in Moldavia and Ukraine resulted first in the rise of Cossack power and later in the formation of the Ukrainian Cossack state.

Of course, the most important development in East-Europe following the fall of the Golden Horde was the emergence of the Moscovite state as the dominant power in the region. The main factors leading to this situation can be summarized as follows:

In the first place Ottoman-Crimean cooperation in the years 1492-1532 is a period crucial for the rise of the Moscovite power, which is understandably ignored in Russian historiography.

Further, in the period 1470-1550, Russian "westernization", which made available to this originally Byzantine-Tatar state the tools of western warfare technology with fire arms, ensured its supremacy over the nomadic peoples of the Eurasian steppes.

In addition, the role of a central bureaucratic system and skillful diplomacy cannot be underestimated in the emergence of the Russian empire. During the rise of their empire the Russian rulers avoided direct confrontation with the Ottoman empire which was the other great power in the region which possessed the same western warfare technology. It is to be remembered that the Ottomans supplied the Crimean Khans with a soldiery with fire arms only to the extent to which the Khanate did not acquireg too much power to become a threat to the Ottoman domination in the Crimea. Ironically, then no one could anticipate future developments which were bound to make Russia a major threat to the Ottoman rule over the Crirnea and the Black Sea. In its efforts to take over the Golden Horde heritage, Moscow gave refuge to the dissident

Genghiskhanids and Tatar clans on its territory and later on used them for its claim to the succession of the Ulugh Khans of the Golden Horde.

Finally, it should be added that Moscow flourished as an economic power by becoming the principal market place of the furs of Siberia and the north, as well as of European exports, mainly woolen cloth. After the annexation of Kazan and Astrakhan (Ejderhan), Grand Dukes encouraged the English to establish a route to Asia for the spice and silk trade through Moscow-Caucasus or Astrakhan.

Perhaps an equally important development was that Muscovy offered an attractive market place for Tatar tribes, in particular the Noghays in the Astrakhan-Kazan region for horses in exchange for western luxury textiles. Ulu-Noghay tribes were to play a crucial role as allies of Muscovy against the Crimeans in the Muscovite expansion in the Volga basin in the period 1521-1554.

Incidentally, starting from the reign of Ivan III in 1496 the Grand Dukes succeeded in obtaining from the Ottoman sultans trade privileges in the Ottoman territories including Azak (Azov) and Caffa. From 1496 onwards, with the exchange of embassies between Istanbul and Moscow, the traffic between the two countries substantially increased, the main items of exchange being Russian furs and Bursa silk brocades.

Mengli Giray architect of the Crimean-Muscovite alliance against the Lithuania-Poland commonwealth, strongly supported Ottoman-Moscovite rapprochement in the period 1492-1512. In their rivalry with Poland over Moldavia, Ottoman Sultans Selim I (1512-1520) and Süleyman I (1520-1566) continued good relations with the Russian rulers till the Khanate under Sahib Giray (1532-1551) could eventually convince the Ottoman government of the Moscovite threat of invasion of the heritage of the Golden Horde in the Itil (Volga) basin.

Developments during the crucial period 1532-1552 consitute a turning point in the history of East-Europe, a dominant power, emerging again to achieve the political unity of the whole region. The decisive struggle for the Çölden Horde heritage now was between Muscovy and the Crimean Khanate.

After the final blow to the Golden Horde by Mengli Giray in 1502, the Girays twice established their control in Kazan and Astrakhan, first under the Ulugh Khan Mehmed Giray (1512-1524) and then under Sahib Giray (1532-1551). Mehmed Giray had even succeeded in re-imposing tribute on Muscovy as in the time of Toktamish Khan. In neither case did the Crimeans receive full approval of the Ottomans although the latter expressed both times its concern against Moscow's aggressive policy. When by 1551 Sahib Giray achieved his imperial ambition in the Volga basin, the Ottoman Sultan became suspicious. Süleyman took action against him when Sahib Giray put forth his claims also on the Ottoman province of Caffa. Ottoman viziers then forged a plan to get rid of the ambitious Khan, not forgetting, however, the Czar's claims on the Khanate of Kazan. The Sultan then ostensibly appointed Devlet Giray, the Khan of Kazan, actually as Khan of the Crimea in lieu of Sahib Giray. Devlet Giray would first eliminate Sahib and then move immediately to aid Kazan against the Russians. Ivan IV, who had declared himself Czar or Ulugh Khan (the Golden Horde title used by Ivan IV in his letters to the Tatars), watching the developments in Kazan, Crimea and Istanbul, in 1547 saw that the right moment had come to invade the Ulugh Yurd. the Golden Horde's imperial domain in the Volga basin. Devlet Giray succeeded in eliminating Sahib Giray in the Crimea but was too late to march to Kazan before Ivan IV, moving with his huge army, strengthened with powerful artillery, captured Kazan (1552). Making a strategically masterful decision, the Czar had profited from the disorders in the Crimea. Devlet Giray's subsequent campaigns against Moscow did not change the state of affairs and two years later Ivan IV, always supported by the Noghay clans, put an end to the Khanate of Astrakhan, invading the Ulugh-Yurd. Assuming the titles of Tsar Kazanskii and Tsar Astrakhanskii, or Ulugh Khan of Kazan and Astrakhan, Ivan IV asserted his ambition to inherit the Golden Horde empire. The Crimean Khan and the Ottoman Sultan were caught by a fait-accompli although they would never accept Moscow's invasion of the Ulugh-Yurd. Then, the Crimean Khan started a series of campaigns against the Russians. Already in 1563 Devlet Giray warned Russia, saying to the Czar's ambassador Nagoy: "The Sultan has mobilized all Muslims against the Czar who invaded the land of the Muslims; he will conquer Astrakhan and enthrone me as khan there. It is better if you would give Astrakhan to me now so that there will be no war" (Solovyev, IV. 219). However, the Ottoman-Crimean campaign to recover Astrakhan had to be postponed for six years. The Khanate and the Ottoman government neither recognized nor used the title of "Çar" (Tsar') or Ulugh Khan for the Russian ruler as late as the year 1643. The strategic goal of the campaign of 1569 was to expel the Moscovites from the lower Itil (Volga) basin where Saray and Astrakhan stood. An Ottoman army and fleet went up the Don River, reaching the Perevolok (later Stalingrad, now Volgagrad) area near the ruined city of Yeni-Saray and began to dig out a canal in order to lake the ships to the Itil and go against the Russians in Astrakhan. In Astrakhan the Russians had built a strong fortress on an island threatening the caravan road from Central Asia and the traffic from the Caspian Sea. Czar Ivan had already begun negotiations with the Shah of Iran, sending him a much needed artillery unit to be used against the Ottomans. The Shah was warned that once Astrakhan came under Ottoman control, Iran was to be exposed to attacks from the rear, which in fact was one of the Ottoman goals in this campaign.

These details should illustrate well the strategic and ideological issues involved in this first direct confrontation between the Russian and Ottoman empires. Ivan IV already had the control of the Volga basin with the title of Tsar or Ulugh Khan. In his turn, declaring himself the protector of Muslims in the area and of pilgrims and merchants from Central Asia, the Ottoman Sultan wanted to assert his own supremacy in the region against the Czar's ambition to regenerate the Golden Horde empire under his rule. In fact, the war of 1569 was the first confrontation of the Ottoman and Russian empires for domination in East-Europe, the scene of struggle being at this stage the lower Volga basin. The Russian advance in later periods would move the main front to the western pan of the steppe or Desht, including Azak, Ukraine, the Crimea and finally the Black Sea. Now dwarfed by the tremendous growth of the Moscovite power, the Crimean Khanate itself was under the threat of a Russian invasion if the Ottoman empire was not behind it. The question is asked why the Ottoman empire, then at the peak of its military might, gave up the struggle and allowed Muscovy to replace the Golden Horde empire in Kazan and Astrakhan.

In the Ottoman supreme council there was a strong faction who argued that campaigns in the north were too expensive, an adventure which might in the end make the Crimean Khan too powerful while vital issues for the empire in the Mediterranean and Central Europe, they argued, required immediate action. Vizier Lala Mustafa, a rival of the grand vizier Sokollu Mehmed, who supported an active policy in the north, made the council eventually decide in favor the invasion of Cyprus in 1570. Then, the defeat at Lepanto the next year kept the empire critically busy in the Mediterranean.

Also, the Crimean tribal aristocracy, mirzas, embodying the Turco-Mongol steppe tradition, opposed growing Ottoman influence and control over the Khanate and often joined the dissident pretenders to the throne in the Crimea. Russia tried to profit from such resistance to reinforce its influence over the Khanate (incidents of Mehmed and Shahin Girays). Consequently, seeing the reaction against too much involvement in the North, the Ottoman government chose to leave decisions on northern affairs to the discretion of the Crimeans. It is to be noted that, from a tradition established under Mengli Giray I, Russian envoys and ambassadors could not proceed to Istanbul unless they first visited the Khan in Bahçesaray and explained the purpose of their visit to Istanbul. Well aware of this situation, Russian diplomats encouraged the Ottoman non-involvement policy in the north by a subtle diplomacy, at once solemnly denying Crimean accusations that Russians were converting mosques into churches while harassing Muslim populations in the Kazan and Astrakhan areas. Also, the Czars carefully avoided participating in the anti-Ottoman coalitions formed in the west until 1686 when Peter the Great decided to join the Holy League. When in 1637 the Cossacks captured Azak and offered the fortress to the Czar, he wisely declined the offer and the Cossacks had to evacuate the place in 1642.

The Cossack question dominated East-European politics in the seventeenth century. Then, for the Ottomans, the Cossack threat became one of the most urgent problems and in the second half of the century attempts to control Ukraine and the Cossacks of Dnieper brought the three major powers in East-Europe, the Ottoman-Crimean block, Poland, and Russia into a decisive confrontation. Again, the Khanate, under the protection of the Ottomans, played a major role in developments in the region during this period. The Cossacks of Dnieper, equipped with fire arms, a replica of the Ottoman *uç* (frontier) organization of *akındjıs* (raiders), were now making devastating sea raids to the settled areas all along the Black Sea coasts, including the Bosphorus. In the face of this growing threat, the Ottomans had to organize a general command with a *Beylerbeylik* on the western Black Sea coast from Özü to Thrace, build new fortresses on the mouth of Dnieper, and make several major campaigns against Poland and Cossacks during the century. With the creation of the Ottoman province of Kameniçe (Podolski Kaminiec) and the occupation of western Ukraine, the Ottoman empire was then vitally involved in all developments in the region.

It is rightly underlined that the developments in the period 1647-1654 constituted a new turning point in the history of East Europe. Under Islam Giray III (1644-1654) Khmelnitski, the leader of the Dnieper Cossacks approached the Crimean Khanate and the Ottomans in the hope of establishing a Cossack state in the Ukraine which could have been organized as an Ottoman vassal state like Moldavia or Transylvania. But Islam Giray did not receive full support for his policy at the Ottoman Porte. The Ottomans were unable to take advantage of these favorable conditions in the north mainly because of the crisis in Transylvania and the protracted Cretan war against the Venetians in the Mediterranean (1645-1669).

Another significant development was the Polish-Russian agreement of 1647 which terminated the long rivalry between the two Christian-Slavic states and led to the formation of a common front against the Crimea and the Ottomans. This rapprochement was a direct result of the growing Crimean-Ottoman pressure on Poland, from which Russia eventually profited. In 1654, Khmelnitski chose union with Russia under the agreement of Pereiaslav. This was a decisive historic development, similar to the Russian invasion of the Khanates of Kazan and Astrakhan, now making the Moscovite state a dominant power, not only in the eastern but also in the western pan of East-Europe. In the face of the change in the balance of power the Crimean government, however, denounced the Czar's new title of "Tsar of the West and the East" (Magrib ve Maşrık Padişahı) and added that "if you are conceited by relying on your guns and cannons, we ourselves rely on God... If you do not give back to Poland the fortresses which you captured, we are determined to fall upon you and the Dnieper Cossacks." These words meant actually the confession of the hopeless situation of the Crimea in the face of the fire power of the Russian armies. Anyhow, in the end, God did not help the Crimeans. It may be said that until 1654 Russia had been an eastern power (Maşrık Padişahı) and only after that date it became a dominant power all over East-Europe, prepared to play a significant role in European politics. For Russia two areas were left to be penetrated, the Baltic and the Black Sea regions, and to make Russia full member of the European state system. As far as the Ottomans were concerned, the Russian empire now became a neighbor to the Ottoman empire in the Ukraine and an immediate threat to the Crimea and the Black Sea. The Porte and the Crimean Khanate did not recognize the subjection of the Cossacks to the Czar and always claimed suzerain rights over the Ukraine. Becoming aware of the vital threat to its northern Black Sea possessions and the Crimea represented by the union of the Dnieper Cossacks with Russia, the Ottoman government, which was now steered by the energetic Köprülü viziers, decided to drive the Russians out of Ukraine. In 1678, Grand Vizier Kara Mustafa and Crimean Khan Murad Giray invaded Ukraine and laid siege to the strategic city of Çihrin (Cigrin).

The Russian army came to the aid of the besieged city, and fierce battles were fought in front of the fortress. This was the first full-fledged confrontation between the armies of the two empires. Now, the issue of Russian domination of East Europe was to be decided by the result of this struggle in the heart of Ukraine. Despite the Ottoman-Crimean temporary success (Murad Giray Khan's driving back four Russian attacks to relieve the besieged city and the capture of Çihrin), the Ottoman invasion of the Ukraine did not have lasting results. Then, concerned with the developments in Hungary, the Porte realized that it could not sustain a long war against Russia over Ukraine.

The Ottoman invasion of Ukraine was all the same a warning to Russia to not dare exploit its new position against the Ottoman-Crimean possessions. The new balance of power following the Ottoman campaign of 1678 in East-Europe would drastically change only when the Ottoman military might would totally collapse at the hands of the Austrian-German armies in the years 1683-1686. In 1681, the peace treaty signed after the fall of Çihrin had not basically altered the traditional pattern of relations between the Khanate and Russia. Negotiations started in Bahçesaray and the provisions reached there were first ratified by the Khan who reported it in a memorandum to the sultan. Only after that ratification did the ambassadors leave for Istanbul to finalize and obtain the sultan's ratification. In a letter to the Czar the Ottoman sultan said: "The Khan Murad Giray is my agent and intermediary." As noted above it was an ancient custom that no Russian embassy left for Istanbul before he first visited the Khan's Palace at Bahçesaray and received his permission. This practice originated from Mengli Giray's time when the Khan mediated between his ally Ivan III and his suzereign Bayezid II for the establishment of friendly relations between the two countries. Later Mehmed Giray I (1514-1523), claiming to be the heir to the Golden Horde Ulugh Khans, re-imposed the tribute on the Grand Duke. The Ottoman sultans always respected this Crimean claim and carried on their relations with Russia through Bahçesaray when the treaty of Istanbul of 1700 abolished the rule.

The Holy League, concluded between the Holy Roman Emperor, the King of Poland, and Venice with the Pope's consecration in 1684, made great efforts to include Russia in the alliance from the beginning. Tsarist diplomacy tried to exploit its position to elicit maximum profits from both the Ottomans and the Holy League, particularly at the expense of Poland. Hoping to prevent the opening of a new front in the north, the Ottomans and Crimeans were ready to negotiate Russian proposals. These included trade privileges, and the delivery of the salt beds on the Crimean border which were badly needed by the Cossacks. Interestingly, a special request for prayers for the Czar at the Greek Orthodox Patriarchate in Istanbul was among the Russian demands. The sensitive issue of the Cossacks was never brought up by the Ottomans in the course of these negotiations, which meant Ottoman recognition of the state of affairs in the Ukraine.

In the Crimea, the Czar was particularly active at Bahçesaray to prevent a peace settlement between the Khanate and Poland. The latter had achieved nothing against the Ottoman Crimean forces in the years 1684-1686. On the other side, Russia, exploiting the allies' concern to open a new front against the Ottomans in the north, demanded the final confirmation of the Andrussovo treaty with Poland, which meant to confirm the final surrender of Smolensk and Kiev to Russia. Pressed by its allies, Poland finally yielded to the Russian demands. Thus, by skillful diplomatic maneuvers Russia had succeeded in having the Ottoman Empire and Poland recognize its sovereignty over the Ukraine. We shall see that in 1686, Russia's participation in the Holy League would result in the collapse of the Ottoman power in East-Europe and initiate Russian penetration into the Black Sea zone.

Poland was one of the principal losers in this game. The Polish government now abandoned all hope of recovering the Ukraine only with the anticipation that to compensate its loss it would take back Kaminiec, and annex Moldavia and the Ottoman Black Sea port of Akkerman. In a message to the Voyvode of Moldavia, John Sobieski could say: "While the Czar was going to invade the Crimea, the Polish army would join that of the Holy Roman Emperor in Adrianople and then they would march together to capture Constantinople."

The first result of Russia's joining the League was that the Crimean Khan, awaiting a Russian invasion, could not leave the Crimea to join Ottoman forces in Hungary. In 1687 an army of one-hundred-thousand

In the years 1686-1689 the northern borders of the empire were successfully defended whereas on the Hungarian front the Austrian-German armies invaded the whole of Hungary, took Belgrade, and penetrated as far as Üsküp (Skopje) in the heart of the Balkans. The Crimean forces under Selim Giray (1670-1677, 1684-1691 and 1691-1698) joined the Ottoman forces there, and the Ottoman-Crimean forces won their first significant victory against the Austrian armies at the strategic Balkan pass of Kachanack near Üsküp, and the enemy was driven back to the other side of the Sava' River (1689). Selim Giray was greeted in Istanbul as the savior of the "state and religion."

When the Crimean troops were away in the Balkans and Transylvania, Moscow ordered Cossacks to capture the Tatar defenses on the border. In 1695, the Cossacks under Pani made a daring raid to the region between Akkerman and Özü on the Black Sea coast. However, all the Polish attempts to capture Kaminiec and to invade Moldavia were unsuccessful. Now with French support, the Porte made attempts to achieve a separate peace with Poland. In 1692, the new Khan Safa Giray told the King that Kaminiec could be evacuated and the Crimean sovereignty rights over the Ukraine given up if the King agreed to a separate peace. The Khan and the Ottomans said they would even join the Poles in their fight against Russia to recover the Ukraine, Smolensk, and Chernigov. Later, during the negotiations at Karlovetz in 1699, Sobieski would say in a letter to his people that acquisition of a few places in Moldavia could never be considered a compensation for the losses to Russia.

Thus, sovereignty over Ukraine continued to be one of the principal issues during the war years. It is interesting that Selim Giray in his third khanship, told the Poles that the Khanate would never give up its rights over the Ukraine.

Czar Peter I, now changing Russian strategy, decided to capture the Ottoman Azak first which would ensure his communication with the bases in his home country. To intercept aid to Azak, Cossack ships were already cruising in the Sea of Azak in the spring of 1695.

During all along the long war, Crimeans and Ottomans had the luck to have in Selim Giray a wise and brave leader. In 1695, his intelligence showed the bitter reality that Azak and Crimea were under the imminent danger of a Russian invasion and Ottoman military aid was now absolutely necessary on this front. Instead, totally unaware of the Russian plans and ignoring the Khan's warnings, the Porte insisted that the Khan should immediately leave the Crimea to join the Sultan's army on the Hungarian front. In July 1695, while the Czar came to besiege the fortress of Azak, the Cossacks under the Russian commander Sheremetiev, attacked the Crimean defenses on the border in the west. After taking Gazi-Kerman, these forces advanced as far as Ferah-Kerman on the Crimean isthmus, thus threatening to invade the Crimea itself. The Crimean troops under Kaplan Giray and Şahin Giray (the Khan Selim Giray was then on the Danube with the Ottoman army) foiled the Russian attacks under a heavy Russian artillery fire against Azak. After a siege of six days, the Czar decided to retreat after building a fortress facing Azak.

The Russian retreat was explained both by the delay in the construction of the river fleet and the Tatar attacks on the supply lines of the Russian army. However, in the meantime Cossacks and Russian troops under Sheremetiev had succeeded in capturing the Crimean fortresses of Nusret-Kerman, Şah-Kerman, and Mubarek-Kerman on the border.

In May 1696, employing engineers from Austria, Holland, Prussia, and Venice, the Czar succeeded in putting a strong fleet on the Don River and now in full trust, marched against Azak. While Sheremetiev and Zaporojian Cossacks advanced in the direction of the lower Dnieper and the Crimea, the Russian army was able to encircle Azak. On the sea side the Cossack fleet had intercepted Ottoman relief convoys to the fortress. Cossacks were also active on the land trying to foil the Crimean attempts to bring aid to Azak. Although the Porte now realized the grave situation in the north, time was overdue for the necessary measures to reinforce the fortress against the powerful Russian army. In an emergency meeting, the Grand Vizier admitted that if Azak fell, not only the Black Sea coasts but Istanbul itself would come under Russian threat. Azak surrendered on August 17,1696. Before he returned home, the Czar converted it into a Russian stronghold on the shores of the Black Sea. Now the Crimea found itself surrounded on two sides since the Dnieper Cossacks from the west continued their raids on the Crimean coasts. After the fall of Azak the Crimeans sent messengers to Istanbul saying that unless a strong Ottoman defense was provided, the Crimea could not resist long in the face of the Russian armies equipped with formidable artillery. In the last years of the war

Crimean attempts to take back the lost fortresses on the Ukrainian border were not successful.

At the peace negotiations in Karlowetz, the Ottoman delegation demanded the surrender of the fortress of Azak, and asserted that the final peace would be considered concluded only after the approval of the Crimean Khan. The Russian delegation not only categorically refused such conditions but demanded the surrender of Kerch, the gate to the Black Sea. Since no progress was possible, only an armistice of two years was agreed between Russia and the Porte at Karlowetz. In the peace treaty concluded with Poland the Porte agreed to the surrender of Kaminiec and Ottoman sovereignty claims over the Ukraine.

Even after Karlowetz, the Crimeans were in fear of a renewed Russian attack. Ignoring the Crimean Khan, the Czar now sent his ambassador for peace negotiations directly to Istanbul on a galleon constructed at Azov.

In the peace treaty concluded in Istanbul in 1700, demilitarized zones were defined around the Crimea for the safety of the Khanate and on the banks of the Dnieper River. Perhaps the most important provisions of the treaty were the abrogation of all kinds of practices reminiscent of the Khan's suzerainty over Russia, that is annual "tribute" and the obligation to obtain the Khan's permission for the Russian ambassadors to go to Istanbul. A separate provision stipulated that a peaceful solution of the disputes arising between the Crimeans and the Cossacks was to be negotiated directly between the Ottoman and Russian governments. Thus, under these provisions the Khan and the Hetman lost their freedom of action in favor of a closer control of the two imperial governments. The Czar's claim to the great power status was also manifest in the provision stipulating that Russian ambassadors to the Sultan should be treated in the same way as those of the other European states. The Sultan also accepted the responsibility of making Tatars apply and respect the provisions regulating Crimean-Russian relations.

Drastically changing the balance of power in East-Europe, the treaty of Istanbul ushered in a new period as far as the Khanate and the Ottoman Empire were concerned. Now the Crimean Khanate was no more in a position to be a threat to the Russian territories including the Ukraine. In fact, weakened and reduced in status, it was itself open to Russian invasions, and the Crimeans were bitterly aware of the drastic change in their position vis-à-vis the Russians. Azak provided the Czar a stronghold to reach the Crimea at any moment and even threaten the Ottoman capital. Perhaps the most important development was Russia's joining the European concert of states which it fully exploited to partition and invade the Ottoman territories in the 18th and 19th centuries. For the following period the Porte, taking advantage of the new conflict in the north between Sweden and Russia, declared war against Russia and recovered Azak in 1711. Then, the Ottoman state and the Crimean Khanate emerged as the staunch defenders of the independence and territorial integrity of Poland against Russia.

To sum up, historically the Muscovite state is to be considered as the heir to the Golden Horde empire. With this historical perspective we can better understand the origin and formation of the Russian empire in East-Europe. Actually, the first step was the Russian invasion of the whole Volga basin down to Astrakhan, including the quasi-sacred region of the two Sarays of the Ulugh-Khans. It was after this development that the Russian state was able to challenge the power of the Commonwealth of Lithuania-Poland in the west and to annex the remaining Russian principalities and Ukraine. Claiming rights as the legitimate heirs to the legacy of the Golden Horde, the Crimean Khans came up against Russian expansion in the east as well as in the Ukraine. They had lost the contention in the east already in mid-16th century. In the following century, Ukraine became the principal scene of rivalry now involving the Ottoman Empire directly. It was to ensure the autonomy of the area that the Ottomans fought their first major war against the Russian Empire in Ukraine in 1678. However, the Long War (1683-1699) against the Holy League which the Czar joined in 1686, gave him the golden opportunity to descend to the Black Sea by capturing Azak as well as to consolidate its grip on the territories taken from Poland, Smolensk, and Ukraine. In the treaty of Istanbul of 1700, both the Khanate and the Ottoman Empire had to recognize the full control of East-Europe by the Czar. At the same time, Russia became a full member of the European state system while the Ottoman Empire was now considered an area for further conquests by Russia and Austria. By capturing Azak, Russia had gained a position to invade the Crimean Khanate, the last remnant of the Golden Horde Empire.

As for the Ottoman-Crimean cooperation in the face of the Russian expansion, throughout their partnership the Crimeans and Ottomans were not always in harmony in their reaction to the developments in East-Europe. While directly under the threat of the Cossacks and then of the Russian armies, the Crimeans wanted the Ottoman Empire to give full support to the Khanate and to mobilize the Ottoman forces against them. The Ottomans themselves, having to concentrate their forces against the more pressing tasks in Hungary or the Mediterranean, always postponed action in the north and what is more they pressed the Crimeans to join the imperial campaigns in the western fronts. This innate conflict not infrequently resulted in alienation of the *mirza*s from the Ottomans, or even to rebel against the Khans who subserviently followed orders from Istanbul. While Ottomans reminded them of Islamic solidarity, and the fact that the ultimate safety and well-being of both countries depended on close cooperation on all fronts, Crimean *mirzas* argued that their own homes and families were in immediate danger when they left Crimea to be defenseless in front of a possible Cossack or Russian invasion.

The danger became imminent when during the Long War Russian armies came to invade the Crimea twice and occupied Azak. In the 18th century the peninsula was, in fact, invaded three times and became the scene of massacres and deliberate destruction by Russian armies. During the disastrous war of 1768-1774, the *mirzas*, seeing the Ottomans totally incapable of defending the Crimea, sought to compromise with the Czar. The Russians first appeared to support Crimean independence against the Ottomans in 1774 which proved to be only a stratagem to invade the Crimea and all the territories belonging to the Khanate from Dniester to Circassia in 1783. The Russian governments adopted a systematic policy to drive out and annihilate the Tatar-Turkish Muslim population in the Crimea in order to transform the peninsula into a Russian base for further expansion in the south. Russian rule over the Crimea saw the shameless plunder of the lands of the Crimean Tatars, a cynical policy to force hundreds of thousands of Tatars to leave their homes to migrate to Turkey, and a systematic policy to eradicate Turkish-Tatar culture in the land.

9

Mutual Influences
Between Europe and the Ottomans

I. Mutual Cultural Influence

Acculturation and cultural borrowings are separate processes.[1] According to one perception, acculturation means a change in the system of basic values determining a culture. Religion determines the system of basic values in traditional societies.[2] Some sociologists and historians claim that the European culture is a synthesis of humanism and the Christian religion. Some historians agree on the point that European civilization with its rational and humanistic character is a common heritage of mankind, and for this reason, it can be the basic culture of every secular society. Naturally, it is impossible for those who claim that culture is a value system to accept this final interpretation. In the end, the question of cultural change depends on how we understand and interpret culture. Muslims in the classical period considered anything coming from the Christian world (from Europe which they called *Kâfiristan* [the country of the infidels]) to be disgusting and the conservative circles regarded the imitation of the *Frenks* (Europeans) to be blasphemy. The first change in attitude towards European civilization was realized after the Treaty of Karlowitz in 1699, which documented the Ottoman defeat against Europe.

As far as the exchange of cultural elements is concerned, this is a continuing process among all cultures.[3] When we speak of cultural elements, we mean all the cultural entities from weapons to fashion and public administration. Although the Ottomans accepted technical elements only up

---

[1] B. Barber, *Science and the Social Order* (Glencoe: Free Press, 1952); R. K. Merton, *Social Theory and Social Structure* (Glencoe: Free Press, 1949), part 4; G. Agoston, "Muslim-Christian Acculturation: Ottomans and Hungarians from Fifteenth to the Seventeenth Centuries", *Chrétiens et Musulmans à la Renaissance*, 293-303.

[2] Ziya Gökalp, *Turkish Nationalism and Western Civilization*, trans, and pub. Niyazi Berkes, New York: Columbia University Press, 1959; C Geertz, *The Interpretation of Cultures* (New York: Basic Books, 1973), 97-125.

[3] M. D. Sahlins, *Evolution and Culture*, Ann Arbor: Univ. of Michigan Press, 1960; E. E. Hagen, *On the Theory of Social Change*, Homewood: Dorsey, 1962.

until the nineteenth century, thereafter they started to borrow from the West for the purpose of administration, laws and even customs. Along with these, there were also close cultural borrowings prior to the nineteenth century.[4]

It is necessary to consider those who separate cultural elements and value systems, in other words, those dependent on religion and those that are neutral.[5] Rejection of the elements that determine the cultural identity of the West is strong, especially in the period of collapse. We can place all of the technical and technological means and positive sciences within the neutral category. The manufacture of weapons, everything from the printing of currency to the customs administration, are included into this category. The Ottomans did not fear the West during their period of expansion and did not hesitate to borrow from the West. Ever since the beginning, they had not hesitated to adopt innovations that would aid in increasing their military efficiency. On the other hand, the techniques which we call neutral, moreover the items of trade, are also a part of a culture and those who use them enter into a process of acculturation.[6] The Ottoman upper class, when adopting cultural trends from the West, at the same time, like it or not, also started to imitate the customs related to life style and for this reason, the reactions of the traditional and conservative masses of people also emerged in the same period.

A cultural element does not spread solely due to its intrinsic value. The prestige of the individual or society that carries it is essential. The Ottomans adopted things related to the Western life style and value system only after the Treaty of Karlowetz in 1699. Prior to Yirmisekiz Mehmed Celebi,[7] no Ottoman felt or expressed admiration for the Western culture and civilization as he did. In other words, in the eighteenth century the West became an admired and imitated prestige-culture. In the homes of the important people at that time, along with roccoco architecture, Ottoman interiors started to be furnished in European styles. Thus, a hierarchy appears in the borrowing of cultural elements. The first and most important borrowings have been in weapons. Instruments for defense have a special importance in cultural exchange. A society, upon seeing that its own existence is under threat beyond its value

---

[4] N. Berkes, *The Development of Secularism in Turkey,* Montreal: McGill University Press, 1964, 23-82. It gives summary on the subject of the cultural elements taken by the Ottomans from the West.

[5] Z. Gökalp (see footnote 2); E. M. Albert, "Value Systems", *International Encyclopedia of Social Sciences.*

[6] A. Appadurai, ed., *Social Life of Things, Commodities in Cultural Perspective,* Cambridge: Cambridge University Press, 1986.

[7] G. Veinstein, *Le Paradis des Infidèls,* Paris: F. Maspero, 1981; F. M. Göçek, *East Encounters West, France and the Ottoman Empire in the Eighteenth Century,* New York and London, 1987.

system alone, does not hesitate to obtain the weapons of the adversary. Here instinct and rational thought supersedes socio-psychological factors and value judgments. Ottoman Turkish history has provided clear examples of these. Actually, Islamic law, at the very beginning, has determined its definite behavior on this point: It is not against religion to imitate the weapons and the tactics of the adversary to defeat them.

The first sciences that were adopted from the West are also those related to defense. The *Mühendishanes* (Schools of Engineering) were opened in the eighteenth century as schools where positive sciences related to military sciences were taught.[8]

Texts in military technology, Western medicine and geography, because of their practical use have been transferred in the seventeenth century in the form of translations into Turkish,[9] but were only put into the school curricula of the vocational schools in the nineteenth century.

The Islamic ulema, who favored reforms, by exceedingly expanding the concept of weapons and instruments, included all kinds of means, science and technique into this concept which provided for the survival and benefit of Islam and the Islamic society. Ever since the birth of the Ottoman State, it entered into a process of acculturation with Europe according to this principle. The retreat in Rumelia against the invasion of Crusaders in 1444 was transformed into panic. The Ottoman rulers at that time did not hesitate to adopt the weapons and tactics of the adversary at that time. The *Wagenburg* war tactic, for example, was adopted at that time[10] and became one of the most important factors of the Ottoman conquests.

However, modern Turkey, which accepted the principles of science and socio-cultural necessities along with Western technology, as a whole, is a natural and final link of this development.[11]

When treating the conditions that played a role in the adoption of cultural elements, we briefly pointed to socio-psychological factors, such as need for defense, imitation, prestige and exoticism, that is, curiosity and admiration for foreign cultures. Besides these conditions, the conditions and factors such as

---

[8] K. Beydilli, *Türk Bilim ve Matbaacılık Tarihinde Mühendishane, Matbaa ve Kütüphane (1776-1826)* (The school of engineering, printing press and library in the history of Turkish science and printing [1776-1826]) (İstanbul: Eren Yayınları, 1995).

[9] A.A. Adıvar, *La Science chez les Turcs Ottomans* (Paris, 1939).

[10] See *Gazavât-i Sultan Murâd b. Mehemmed Hân* (The military expeditions of Sultan Murâd b. Mehemmed Hân), eds. H. İnalcık, and M. Oğuz (Ankara: Türk Tarih Kurumu, 1978).

[11] "Atatürk'ten Düşünceler" (Thoughts from Atatürk), ed. E.Z. Karal (Ankara: Türkiye İş Bankası Yayınları, 1969), 49-51.

trade that provides social contact from the material aspect, port cities which are open to foreign trade,[12] existence of intermediary groups between the two cultures, exile and migration, religious conversion or the employment of foreign experts are also extremely important. Capitulations, settlement of Western merchant communities in port cities such as Galata, İzmir, Thessaloniki and Beirut, the Levantines, the intermediary Greeks, Jews, Armenians and finally converts to Islam have played a definite role in the cultural exchange of the Ottomans.[13] In the classical period in the fifteenth to sixteenth centuries, those who were exiled and converted to Islam were important carriers of culture. The Jewish migration from Spain to Turkey in 1492 paved the way for a significant technology transfer in the textile industries, weapons manufacture and other fields. Accepting exiled groups provides for a forced and rapid culture transfer instead of a long social acculturation (for example, the artists brought from Tabriz and Cairo by Sultan Selim I).

The Ottomans applied this method and also organized artists in groups at the court from various nations. In the art of painting and decoration the Anatolian Turks engaged in activities under the name of *Tâife-i Rûmîyan,* the Persians under the name of *Tâife-i Acemiyân* and the Europeans under the name of *Tâife-i Efrenciyân.* The physicians were also subject to such a differentiation. At the court engineers, artists and other technical persons from among the Europeans were collected in a section under the name of *Efrenciyan.* This system changed in the eighteenth century. The Europeans started to be employed as teachers at the vocational schools.

The socio-psychological and material conditions prepared for the transfer of modern scientific methods as an element of culture. However, it is essential for a certain socio-cultural ambience to have emerged in that society, which would guarantee the establishment and continuation of these methods. A modern observatory was established towards the end of the sixteenth century in Istanbul, but it did not survive. Also, in the eighteenth century, the printing press and the school of engineering was not sustained. Positive sciences had not developed in the Ottoman milieu, and therefore, neither technology transfer nor technological innovations took place.

The bureaucrats played a definite role in acculturation in Ottoman history. While the ulema tried to provide for the definite integrity and control of the religious law, the bureaucrats were subject to pragmatic thoughts such as the

---

[12] Çağlar Keyder, et al. *Doğu Akdeniz'de Liman Kentleri* [The port cities at the Eastern Mediterranean], İstanbul: Tarih Vakfı Yayını, 1993.

[13] See H. D.-Grégoire, *Le Divan Magique,* Paris, 1998; L.T. Fawaz, *Merchants and Migrants in Nineteenth-Century Beirut,* Cambridge: Cambridge University Press, 1983.

imminent needs of the state and society. For the bureaucrats, especially after 1700, to take all kinds of measures to provide security to improve the state was more important than anything else. Until that time, weapons, defense facilities and military tactics were being provided through practical methods through apprenticeship. In the eighteenth century, the reformist bureaucrats observed that this was not sufficient. The French, who were seeking an ally in the East against the Habsburgs and Russians, communicated to the Ottoman high officials at that time, that they were ready to teach Western technology, thus, the political and military interest of the West also played an important role in Ottoman Westernization. The positive sciences developed in Europe were introduced for the first time as a subject of systematic teaching at the schools of engineering.

In summary, it is necessary to study the Ottoman Westernization-modernization movements within the following framework. First was the period when the traditional guild system was dominant in the arts. Besides extensive state military production facilities, cannon factories, shipyards, potassium nitrate factories, steel works, mines and mints were among the most important organizations influenced by Western technology.[14]

In the reform period after 1700, Western methods were borrowed directly and finally positive sciences were employed through the state initiative. However, the need for military defense was always the main reason for the borrowings. After the 1839 Tanzimat period, the administrative methods and regulations also started to be borrowed and a serious dispute with the traditional system of values emerged in this period. At that time, the New Ottomans were saying that we are going to modernize by adopting the technology of the West, but we will reject their value system. Ziya Gökalp tried to incorporate this in a sociological system. Those who asserted that acculturation can be realized as a socio-cultural milieu and those who considered it to be necessary to develop a certain social structure for a complete modernization, merged this cultural policy only in the Republic period.

When it comes to Ottoman influence on the culture of Europe, the borrowings and influences can be treated separately. The borrowings as the result of direct contacts are clearly observed in the use of natural substances and manufactured goods. The influences on Europe are exoticism, romantic visions concerning the East, social customs, fashion, art, literature and forms of behavior. Besides the Turkish Ottoman exoticism accepted by the privileged

---

[14] *Osmanlılar ve Batı Teknolojisi, Yeni Araştırmalar, Yeni Görüşler* [The Ottomans and Western Technology, New Studies, New Views], ed. E. İhsanoğlu, İstanbul: 1992; D. Quataert, *Ottoman Manufacturing in the Age of the Industrial Revolution,* Cambridge: Cambridge University Press, 1993.

class in France, it is necessary to differentiate these types of cultural borrowings of the French people in a more extensive manner. According to D. Gregoire, it is possible to mention the oriental influences, even in village circles.[15]

There was an "Ottoman" colony in France. Besides, a small number of Muslim Turks who went from the Ottoman domains in one way or another to France and settled there, Eastern Christians and Jews, played an intermediary role in cultural value transfers.

Ottoman ambassadors, starting from the fifteenth century and up until the end of the sixteenth century, visited the Italian states and France. As the result of the keen curiosity aroused about the clothing and customs by these visits, a Turkish fashion started among the high classes in these countries. The people would gather in the streets and watch with great interest the ambassador parade at the arrivals and departures of ambassadors. The visit of Yirmisekiz Mehmed Çelebi, the Ottoman ambassador, in Paris in 1720 was a significant stage in the spread of the Turkish fashion. According to what Herbette, the French ambassador, reported about Esseyid Ali Efendi, who lived in Paris as the resident ambassador in France in 1797, "Paris became almost one of the Istanbul districts". Grand visits like these were depicted in the paintings of the French artists. Actually, the French court tried to benefit from these visits in order to show off its prestige to the world and its people.

E. Charrière said that the frequent visits to Istanbul of the French ambassadors in the sixteenth century also paved the way to become acquainted with the life and culture of the Turks. Francis I especially wanted to hear details about Turks. At that time, every European state wanted to learn the secrets of Ottoman military superiority. Important information was provided about the Ottoman State and Turkey in the sixteenth century in the published works of certain ambassadors (J. Maurand, N. de Nicolay, B. de Montluc, Pierre Belon, Monsieur d'Aramon, Charles Du Fresne Du Cange, Jean Chesneau) and were complemented by detailed reports[16] of the Venetian Residents at the Sublime Porte. The reports of the ambassadors, because they used Greek and Armenian translators in Istanbul, also contain a lot of intentionally distorted information against the Turks. On the other hand, because the local non-Muslim dragomans could not always be trusted, by taking the *Giovanni della lingua* in Venice as an example, a school was established in Paris in 1721"during the reign of Louis XIV with the name of *Jeunes de Langues* to teach the French Ottoman Turkish

---

[15] *Le Divan Magique,* see footnote 13.
[16] E. Alberi, *Le relazioni degli ambasciatori Veneti al Senato durante il secolo decimosesto,* Florence, 1839-1863; André Laval, *Voyages en Levant pendant Its XVIe, VIIe et XVllle siècles,* Budapest, 1897.

and the Eastern languages at an early age and the young men taught here would be sent to serve at the embassies and consulates. At the same time, with this school, the foundation was laid for serious scholarship on the Eastern languages and cultures. Concomitantly, translators connected to the Council of State and the Translation Bureau in the nineteenth century became counterparts of this trend..[17]

Besides official visits, the children and servants brought to France with the French ambassadors or consuls when they returned to France, were converted to Christianity by giving them Catholic religious training in Paris. Of course, it is known that female slaves cum servants who had received Turkish-Ottoman training were also brought to France in this manner. Exoticism in the eighteenth century has become more widespread with the influences of the Turkish Fashion *(turquerie)*. We know that in 1700, 12 scholarships were granted to Armenian children to be trained in the Catholic religion in Paris. Even around the beginning of the seventeenth century permission was given for Jesuit and Capuc hin missionaries to engage in activities in Ottoman domains. They spread Catholicism, especially among the Armenians and Greeks. These Greeks and Armenians, because they knew the Turkish language and cultural traits were also used as translators. The following is an interesting incident: In 1743, the King permitted Marechal de Saxe to form a unit composed of Turkish, Tatar, Wallachian and Polish cavalrymen.

We also observe Muslim merchants who went back and forth to Marseilles and Southern France as Turkish-Ottomans or who settled there. In 1728, the Paşa of Crete intervened upon the cheating by the French of some Muslim merchants who imported olive oil to Marseilles. The French authorities were being careful about such incidents, fearing that counter-measures could be taken against their merchants in Ottoman domains. Particularly, the Greeks, Armenians and Jews drew attention as merchants. Armenians formed the most important Eastern Christian colony. We know that in the fifteenth century, Muslim merchants and agents were also settled in Italy and that the famous *Fondaco dei Turchi* palace was allocated for the residence of Muslim merchants.[18]

The following is another interesting incident: It is mentioned that there were women of Turkish origin in the court of the French Queen Marie de Medicis, who were weaving Turkish carpets for her. In this manner, in 1568 in Paris the Muslim carpet makers had formed a corporation of weaving Turkish

---

[17] Frederic Hitzel, *Enfants de langue et drogmans: Dil Oğlanları ve Tercümanlar,* İstanbul 1995; and C. Findley, *Bureaucratic Reform in the Ottoman Empire: The Sublime Porte. 1789-1922,* Princeton, 1980.

[18] Ş. Turan, *Türkiye-İtalya İlişkileri* [Turkey-Italy relations], vol. 1, İstanbul, 1990.

rugs. This production appears to have been completely halted in the seventeenth century.

Especially in the seventeenth and eighteenth century, a rather large Muslim colony in France was formed of Turkish galley slaves. Around the end of the seventeenth century more than one thousand persons were used as galley slaves in the French fleet. Among these, 20 percent were Turks. Turks were particularly preferred as strong oarsmen. Most of these galley slaves were purchased slaves. The galley slaves were able to participate in the social life freely. We see them running coffee shops and as boatmen. Thus, they were in daily contact with the local people in Marseilles. It has been recorded that some of them sent money to their families at home. The Turkish galley slaves wore red fezzes and thus, they were distinguished from the others. Also, an interesting group is composed of Frenchmen who had become prisoners of the Ottomans and lived among the Turks and later were saved by ransom. Moreover, there were French people who had stayed for a long period of time in the service of the consuls and ambassadors at the Ottoman ports and who later returned to France. Naturally, they carried the customs that they have observed there to their own countries. In the meantime, clergymen and missionaries had an important place in cultural exchange. These missionaries, by collecting alms, were carrying out special activities to bring back to their countries the Christians who had been taken prisoner in the Ottoman State.

Besides the French, who obtained free trade privileges in the entire Ottoman Empire with the 1569 capitulations, after Lepanto (1571) the Ottomans, by realizing the importance of the English and Dutch against Spain on the seas, granted capitulations to the English in 1580 and the Dutch in 1612. M. Fontenay[19] examined an important report by the French E. G. d'Ortiers on trade with the Levant in 1686-1687, which determined that in the annual balance sheet Western merchants brought goods worth 3, 735, 000 *gruş* and purchased goods worth 4, 735, 000 gruş in return (1 gruş is about two thirds of a gold coin). The Western merchants were paying for the trade deficit with gold and silver currency. There was a fierce competition among the French, English and Dutch at the Levantine ports and all of them were dependent on the capitulation privileges given by the Ottoman sultan. The sultan, when granting these privileges, primarily took into consideration the political and military usefulness for the Ottomans of that Western state. Towards the end of the

---

[19] For capitulations see "İmtiyāzāt" (privileges) in M. Fontenay. "Le commerce de occidentaux dans les écnelles du Levant vers la fin du XVIIe siècle", *Chrétiens et Musulmans à le Renaissance,* 337-370; for the eighteenth century see E. Eldem, *French Trade in Istanbul in the Eighteenth Century,* Leiden: Brill, 1999.

seventeenth century, the English were ahead in this trade and the French and Dutch were about equal.

Trade relations of the Turkish-Ottoman world, especially with France, were extremely active. The importance of this trade is set forth in research made in the archives of the Chamber of Commerce in Marseilles, which was the center of this trade. In the seventeenth and eighteenth centuries half of the French trade was composed of trade made with the Levant. Especially, the work written by Paul Masson on this trade, by making use of these archives, contains interesting details.[20] We learn from the palace inventories that starting from the fourteenth century, Western Anatolian carpets were imported and used as a luxury item in the palaces in France. The carpets were used not only on the floors, but also on tables and chairs. The carpet trade, starting from the fourteenth century, constituted a significant portion of the trade not only with the French, but also between the European countries and the Ottoman Empire. The valuable Gördes, Uşak and other carpets shipped to Central Europe via *Erdel* (Transylvania) are displayed today in a rich collection at the Braşov Cathedral in Transylvania. The designs and colors of the Turkish carpets were admired by the German, Italian and Dutch master painters (Lotto, Carpaccio, Holbein, etc.) and were copied in their paintings. Today, we learn the characteristics of the old, lost Ottoman art of carpets from these paintings. In the lead of the other articles which had an important place in the trade made with Europe was alum (Kütahya and Şebinkarahisar alum) used in the dyeing of cloth and it brought significant gains to the Ottoman Empire. Besides this, pearls from the Persian Gulf were an important trade item. Animal products, especially wool and leather made up for a significant portion of this trade. Beeswax, vegetable dyes, the coral from Tunisia, and the processed morocco leather were among these. Vegetable products, and up until 1630 Indian spices imported to Europe from the Levantine ports constituted a prosperous trade item. Exports from the Ottoman Empire of items such as saffron, opium, Yemen coffee which was an important trade item, rice, dates, dried fruits, figs, raisins, olive oil and wine, exported in large quantities from Western Anatolia and the Aegean islands were particularly significant. The situation changed considerably in the eighteenth century. This trade lost its former importance with the goods coming from India and Arabia. For instance, sugar, coffee and cotton were now raised in the colonies in America. Moreover, it is known that Brazilian coffee was imported to the Ottoman Empire in the seventeenth and eighteenth centuries. The Yemen coffee was exported to Europe as the best quality coffee.

---

[20] P. Masson, *Histoire du Commerce Français dans le Levant,* vols. 1-2, Paris, 1928; R. Paris, *Histoire du commerce de Marseille,* Paris, 1997.

Besides the wool industry, the history of the European silk and cotton textile industry cannot be comprehended without taking into consideration Levantine influence from the aspect of weaving, dyeing techniques and design.[21] Up until the eighteenth century, Europe imported coarse and fine cotton goods from India and the Ottoman Empire. Cotton goods started to be consumed by the masses of people in Europe after 1700 and when consumption reached great dimensions, each of the mercantilist European states established a cotton industry and started to imitate Oriental products. Europe could not compete in price, because the labor costs were low in this industry in India and Turkey. Then, the Europeans started to think about how to overcome this competition in labor cost and this economic pressure led the inventors to discover the steam engine in the cotton industry. This situation in Europe has been one of the important factors of the industrial revolution. The secrets of the "Turkish crimson" in dyeing, were solved only after extensive efforts and secretly bringing non-Muslim experts from the Ottoman lands to Europe. [22]

Stages in Mutual Cultural Influence

The history of European cultural influences on the Ottomans appears in the early periods and should be discussed in the following stages. The first was in the fourteenth and fifteenth centuries along with Byzantine and Greek influences and especially, when the Italian influence was strong. Extensive conversion to Islam of the Greeks, marriages with Greek women and extensive employment of the Greeks in political, financial and commercial fields by the Conqueror, left unerasable traces in the life and culture of the Ottomans.[23] In the fifteenth century, the strong influence represented by the Italians on

---

[21] *Oriental Carpet and Textile Studies, II, Carpets of the Mediterranean, 1400-1600,* eds. R. Pinner, and W. B. Denny, London, 1986; for information about the items belonging to the Turks in the sixteenth and seventeenth centuries in the valuable collection at the palace of the Nancy Duchy see Paulette Choné, "Le portrait du Turc, les artistes devant le reve héroique de la Maison de Lorraine (XVI-XVIIe siècles) ", *Chrétiens et Musulmans à la Renaissance,* 61-75.

[22] Flachat, *Observations sur le commerce et les arts d'une partie de l'Europe et de l'Asie, de l'Afrique et même de Indes orientales,* Lyon, 1766.

[23] Theodore Spandouynes, *On the Origin of the Ottoman Emperors,* trans. D. M. Nicol, Cambridge, 1997; D.M. Nicol, *The Last Centuries of Byzantium, 1261-1453,* Cambridge, 1993; N. Jorga, *Byzance après Byzance,* Bucharest, 1935; A. Ducellier, "Byzantins et Turcs du XIIe au XVI siècle," *Chrétiens et Musulmans à la Renaissance,* 11-49; H. İnalcık, "The Status of the Greek Orthodox Patriarch under the Ottomans," *Essays in Ottoman History,* İstanbul: Eren Yayınları, 1998, 195-223; F. W. Hasluck, *Christianity and Islam under the Sultans,* vols. 1-2, Oxford, 1929.

Ottoman life and culture, has not yet been the subject of a thorough study.[24] The Conqueror, like the Italian patron princes in art, was protecting the Greek and Italian scholars and artists in his palace. In addition, he established a palace library of the works of the ancient Greek and Latin classics. Even if it were an exaggeration to define (Deismann) the Conqueror as a Renaissance ruler, very important cultural influences of the Italian Renaissance cannot be denied. It is hardly a coincidence that great Italian painters such as Gentile Bellini visited the Ottoman palace and some of them to presented major projects to the Ottoman sultan (Leonardo da Vinci's bridge and other construction projects were found in the Topkapı Palace and were published).[25] The Conqueror had the walls of the palace decorated with the frescoes of the Italian painters. The *alla turca* fashion in Italy can be considered to be the first stage of the *turquerie* (Turkish fashion) in the West. Tursun Bey, who wrote the history of the Conqueror, states that besides the *Rûmî* and *Hatayî* styles in art, there is also the Italian influence known under the name of *tavr-i Frengi* (European style).

The Venetians and Genoese established independent colonies in Constantinople and Galata, in the Crimea, on the Aegean islands and in Greece during the period of collapse of the Byzantine Empire and prohibited the local population from participating in major overseas trading.[26] Mehmed the Conqueror abolished the political control of the Italians in the Levant, but considered it to be necessary to continue economic relations with them. Venice, which had a quasi trade monopoly between the Near East and Europe, thanks to the capitulations providing free trade in the Levant during the fifteenth and sixteenth centuries is indebted to this cooperation for its prosperity and brilliant cultural successes during those centuries.[27]

When the Conqueror entered into war against the Venetians in the period between 1463-1479, he granted the Florentines commercial capitulations and displayed a close interest in them. The Florentines who exchanged the valuable woolen cloth in Bursa with Persian raw silk, owed, to a great extent, their affluence and prosperity to this trade in the fifteenth century. This trade

---

[24] Ş. Turan, *Türkiye-İtalya İlişkileri* [Turkey-Italy relations], vol. 1, İstanbul, 1990; F. Babinger, "Maometto II il Conquistatore e l'Italia," *Revista Storica Italiana* 63, 1951, Turkish translation, "Fatih Sultan Mehmed ve İtalya" [Sultan Mehmed the Conqueror and Italy], trans. B. S. Baykal, *Belleten* 17/65 (1953): 41-82.

[25] F. Babinger, "Vier Bauvorschläge Lenonardo da Vincis an Sultan Bayazid II," *Nachr. Der Akad. Der Vissens. in Göttingen,* Phil. Hist. Kl. No. 1, 1958.

[26] M. Balard, *La Romanie Génoise,* vol. 2 (Paris, 1978), 572.

[27] H. İnalcık, *Osmanlı İmparatorluğunun Ekonomik ve Sosyal Tarihi I, 1300-1600* [The Economic and Social History of the Ottoman Empire, I, 1300-1600] (İstanbul: Eren Yayınları, 2000), 283-296.

developed further after 1463. In the 1500s, Florentine companies which exported woolen cloth, including the Medici family, had trade agencies in Pera, Bursa and Edirne. The Florentines at Galata celebrated the Conqueror's victories against Venice. Moreover, at one stage the Sultan attended a feast given at the mansion of *emino* Carlo Martelli at Pera and displayed a close interest.

In this period, technological exchange between Italy and the Ottomans was at an advanced level. Sultan Bayezid II brought engineers from Genoa to have them build the largest ships which sailed in the Mediterranean. Almost all of the Ottoman maritime expressions are borrowed from Italian.[28] The Italy-Ottoman trade was vital for both sides and the first European communities in the Middle East emerged in this manner.[29] It is mentioned that a total of five thousand families from Venice were settled in the Middle East at the end of the fifteenth century.

As a result of these close relations, it is understood that a type of "Europeanization", even in the life style and customs, was rather widespread among the upper class Ottomans in the fifteenth century. In the Ottoman anonymous history books, reflecting the reactions of the ordinary conservative people, those who had their beards and moustaches cut like the Europeans were strongly chastized. [30]

In later centuries, besides the Italians, other Europeans also came and settled to a great extent in the port cities and these relations reached great dimensions in the nineteenth century when trade relations were intensified. In the nineteenth century in Istanbul, the European banks, insurance, pier, etc. companies increased, especially after the Crimean War (1853-1856). At that time, Galata assumed the appearance of a cosmopolitan European port city, like Marseilles. The first municipal assembly and services were realized at Galata with the initiative and participation of the Europeans.[31] In the period between 1800 and 1912 the Christians and Europeans constituted 20-30 percent of the population in Thessaloniki, another port city.

The Greek, Armenian and Jewish translator families, who had served at the European embassies and consulates in the previous centuries and who had

---

[28] A. Tietze, H. Kahane, and R. Kahane, *Lingua Franca in the Levant,* İstanbul, 1988.

[29] For Italian-Ottoman trade see W. Heyd (1936), Ş. Turan (1990) and H. İnalcık (2000).

[30] *Anonim Tevârîh-i Âl-i Osman* (Anonymous history of the Ottoman Dynasty), ed. F. Giese (Breslau, 1922), reign of Yıldırım Bayezid.

[31] For Galata in the nineteenth century see C. White, *Three Years in Constantinople or Domestic Manners of the Turks in 1844,* vols. 1-3, London, 1845; E. Eldem, D. Goffman, and B. Masters, *The Ottoman City Between East and West: Aleppo, Izmir and Istanbul,* Cambridge: Cambridge University Press, 1999.

obtained a number of exemptions from the Porte, formed a Europeanized domestic community called *Levantin* (Levantine) at Galata in the nineteenth century. Greeks, Armenians and Jews from other districts in Istanbul settled at Galata in the nineteenth century. The schools of the Europeans and Levantines at Galata (Alliance Israelite Universelle, Dames de Sion, etc.) provided European education and also attracted the children of wealthy Muslim families. We also observe developments similar to these in port cities such as Thessaloniki, Beirut and Alexandria. These European and Levantine communities, which were gradually becoming more crowded, brought social services such as churches, schools, theaters, libraries, restaurants and beer halls, that are peculiar to European city life to the districts where they lived and the Ottoman upper classes started to frequent these places and to imitate the customs of "European" life. The Englishman Charles White, who lived in Istanbul in the 1840s, wrote that the members of the Ottoman upper classes no longer shopped at the traditional *Kapalı Çarşı* (Covered Bazaar), but they preferred to shop at Beyoğlu.[32] A common French language at Galata started to be spoken as *lingua franca* and a completely European-like life style started to be imitated. In the Tanzimat Westernization period, the youth in the distant Anatolian cities as well, showed a great desire to go to Europe and to learn French.

Regarding mutual influence, the Italian period was followed by the French period between the sixteenth and eighteenth centuries. Ever since the French-Ottoman alliance against the Habsburgs started around 1525, the Levant trade of France prospered and the cultural mutual influence started, even though limited.

II. The Italian Wars (1494-1559) and the Ottomans, the Balance of Power System in Europe, the Ottoman-French Alliance (1525-1547)[33]

The Italian Wars period (1494-1559), was a time of difficult wars between the Holy Roman-German Emperors and France, aiming at domination in Europe. In 1519, the French Valois and the Habsburgs, which were the two strongest dynasties in Europe confronted each other for the crown of the Empire. Charles V became the inheritor of a world empire as a result of his family connections. In addition to Spain and Austria, the Netherlands and Belgium of today, the

---

[32] Charles White, *Three Years in Constantinople*, vol. 1, see footnote 31.

[33] The following work includes French archival documents on the French-Ottoman relations between 1527-1647: E. Charrière, *Négociations de la France dans le Levant,* vols. 1-4 (Paris, 1848-1860); in general see the section written in volume 1 of this work: "Osmanlı Tarihinin Dönemleri" [The periods of Ottoman history].

Spanish colonies and Burgundy in France, were also united under his crown. In 1519, Charles V and Francis I, the French king, were candidates for the crown of the Empire. Both of them were promising that they would go on a crusade against the Turks. At that time, all of Europe was in fear of an Ottoman onslaught. The German electoral princes elected Charles V as the emperor. As of that moment, to capture the rich, but divided Italy, was the basic objective of both of these rulers. Plans for the Crusades were postponed. Venice, Florence, the Papacy, the Kingdom of Naples and Milan joined either one side or the other in this struggle in Italy. The 1494-1559 Italian wars brought a new concept onto the agenda in the relations between states in the history of Europe. Now, the basic issue was as follows: Emperor Charles V had the ambition of uniting Europe under the sovereignty of a single empire, as it was the case in the Middle Ages. The subject matter of propaganda used the most for this political goal was to protect Europe against the Turks and to start a crusader campaign. Whereas, at that period, national states, such as France and England, had emerged, and each state was determined to defend its own independence against the emperor. The French, English and German princes did not consider it a drawback to engage in relations with any foreign power that would support their independence against the emperor. In other words, at that time, a policy of balance among independent states, a European system of states, had emerged.[34] England was one of the states that closely watched such a balance policy. The English King Henry VIII called this policy the *bascule policy* by siding with the weak against the strong. On the side of the European states, that were seeking balance, the Ottoman State that was arising as a world power in the East, would play an important role as an actual member of this system of states.[35] Every state, which felt itself threatened by the Emperor, would apply to this super power in the east or would threaten to use it. In response to the crusader threat, the Ottoman State would strongly support this balance policy to keep Europe divided. Thus, in this connection, it would become a part of the European states system all on its own. Led by France, the European states would try to guarantee the balance as an ally of the Ottoman Empire in response to the colossal empire of Charles V in the period between 1525-1559. We will discuss below these developments in somewhat further detail.

---

[34] C. Tilly, *The Formation of National States in Western Europe,* Princeton, 1975.

[35] The dramatic meeting between these two "super powers" in Europe led the great German historian L. von Ranke to write a book: *The Ottoman and the Spanish Empires in the Sixteenth and Seventeenth Centuries,* trans. W. R. Kelley, London, 1843; J. Elliott, "Ottoman-Habsburg Rivalry: The European Perspective", *Süleyman the Second and His Time,* İstanbul: ISIS, 1993, 153-162; for details see Kenneth Setton, *The Papacy and the Levant (1204-1571},* vols. 1-4, Philadelphia, 1976-1984; for a good summary see D. Vaughan, *Europe and the Turk,* Liverpool, 1954.

a. The Ottoman State is the Protector of France

Charles V inflicted a terrible defeat on the French army at Pavia in Northern Italy and took the King as prisoner (24 February 1525). The prisoner King was brought to Madrid by Charles V and put in prison. France, like it or not, sought its salvation by applying to the great power in the East, to the Magnificent Sultan Süleyman. The Emperor freed Francis I on 14 January 1526, with the condition that he would abandon his aspirations in Italy. The request for help by the mother of the French King and the response sent by Sultan Süleyman were found in the French archives and published.[36] The text is below.

> Ben ki, Sultanus'selâtîn ve burhânu'l-havâkîn tâc-bahş -i husrevân-i rûy-i zemîn zillulâh fi'l-ardayn Akdeniz'in ve Karadeniz'in ve Rumeli'nin ve Anadolu'nun ve Karaman'ın ve Rum'un ve vilâyet-i Zulkadriyye'nin ve Diyarıbekr'in ve Kurdistan ve Azerbaycan'ın ve Şam'ın ve Haleb'in ve Mısır'ın ve Medine'nin ve Kudüs'ün ve külliyen diyâr-i Arab'ın ve Yemen'in ve dahi nice memleketlerin ki âbây-i kirâm ve ecdâd-i izâmım anârallâhu berâhinehim kuvvet-i kâhireleri ile feth eyledikleri ve cenâb-i celâlet-meâbım dahi tîg-i âteşbâr ve şemşîr-i zafer-nigârım ile feth eyledüğüm nice diyârın sultanı ve pâdişâhı Sultan Bayezid Han oğlu Sultan Selim Han oğlu Sultan Süleyman Han'ım.

You are King Francis of the French province:

> Dergâh-i selâtin-penâhıma yarar adamın Frangipan ile mektup gönderip ve bazi ağız haberi dahi ısmarlayıp memleketinize düşman müstevlî olup, elân habsde idüğünüzü i'lâm edüp halâsınız hususunda bu cânibten inâyet ve meded istid'â eylemişsiz, her ne ki demiş iseniz, benüm pâye-i serîr-i âlem-masîrime arz olunup 'alâ-sebîli't-tafsîl ilm-i şerîfim muhît olup tamam ma'lûmum oldu. İmdî padişâhlar sınmak ve habs olunmak 'aceb değildir, gönlünüzü hoş tutup azürde-hâtır olmayasız. Öyle olsa, bizim âbâ-yi kirâm ve ecdâd-i 'izâmımız nevver-

---

[36] It is known that in a letter written by Ferdinand 18 days after the Pavia battle, Francis I was thinking to request help from the Sultan and that he had established relations with the Bosnian Pasha; see Charrière, 113, note I; this letter has been published in Charrière and in *Paléographie Universelle* (Paris, 1839) and by R. Yinanc, *DTCF Dergisi* 8-12 (1975), 96.

allâhu merâkidehim dâimâ def-i düşmân ve feth-i memâlik için
seferden hâlî olmayup biz dahi anların tarîkine sâlik olup herzamanda
memleketler ve sa'b ve hasîn kaleler feth eyleyüp gece gündüz atımız
eğerlenmiş ve kılıcımız kuşanılmıştır. Hak subhâne ve ta'âlâ hayırlar
müesser eyleyüp meşiyyet ve irâdeti neye müteallik olmuş ise vücûde
gele. Bâkî ahvâl ve ahbâr ne ise mezkûr ademinizden istintâk olunup
ma'lûmunuz ola; şöyle bilesiz. Tahrîren fî evâil-i şehr-i âhiru'l-rebî'ayn
li senet-i isnayn ve salâsîn ve tis'amia. Bi makâm-i dâri's-saltanat-il
'aliyye al-Kostantaniyye el mahmiyye el mahrûse.

The English version of this letter is as follows: "You have sent a letter with
your ambassador Frangipan to the gate where the rulers take shelter and also
sent some verbal news to inform us that your country is under enemy
occupation and at present you are in prison and you are asking help from us for
your release. Whatever you said, is submitted to the feet of our throne holding
the world under his rule. I have been informed about all the details. It is not
something to be amazed about for the rulers to be defeated and taken prisoner.
Keep your spirit up and do not be sad. Under these conditions, our great
ancestors -May God shed light on all of their graves- never refrained from
expeditions to always repulse the enemies and to conquer countries. We are
also on their course and are always conquering countries and precipitous
fortresses. Day and night our horses are always saddled and we carry our
swords at our waists. May the great God give good fortune. Whatever God
wishes, it will happen. Please know that you can ask and learn from the
messenger you sent about all other news and situations other than these.
This correspondence was written in the first days of the fourth month of
the lunar year in AH 932 (January 1526) at the court of the sultan in
Constantinople."

In the introductory section of this letter, Süleyman describes the grandeur
of his sultanate and mentions France as a province compared to his country and
its ruler as an ordinary King without using any title. Only a "verbal news" was
sent by the ambassador about the decisions taken to prevent the enemy from
taking advantage of it.

Süleyman kept his promise. According to Nasûh Matrakî, the court
historian of the period, the Sultan decided on the 1526 Hungarian campaign for
the following reason: The "King of the French province" who was taken
prisoner, "took refuge" in the sultan "to show that he is ready to serve with
respect" and sent an ambassador and wanted the sultan to make a campaign on
the King of Hungary, who was an ally of Charles V. According to Matrakî, the
King said, "we will obey him and be one of his servants". It was known at the

Ottoman palace that Charles V and Francis I had been struggling for the title of emperor of the Holy Roman Empire in Europe.

After conquering Hungary (the battle of Mohács, 29 August 1526), Süleyman found Charles V and his brother Ferdinand against him as rivals and a period of wars that lasted for one and one-half centuries was started for the supremacy in Europe and the Hungarian Kingdom between the Ottomans and the Habsburgs. In Vienna, while Archduke Ferdinand claimed that he was the legal inheritor of the Hungarian King Louis II (1516-1526), who died in the Mohács battle, Sultan Süleyman claimed his sword right, saying that by being defeated in the battle all of the rights of the Hungarian king were removed and that Hungary belonged to him.[37]

In the period between 1526 and 1547, the difficult struggle between the Emperor and the Pope with the Ottoman State continued on two fronts, on the land front in Central Europe and on the sea front in the Mediterranean while a Sacred Alliance would be formed in 1538 against the Ottomans with the efforts of the Pope.

When Ferdinand defeated the newly elected Hungarian King John Zápolya and entered Budin, Zápolya requested help from Süleyman. The Sultan recognized Zápolya as the sole king of Hungary and stated that he would come to help with his army (1527). The Grand Vizier İbrahim Paşa said to Zápolya's ambassador, "We will make Budin a second Istanbul"; he was announcing plans for the future against the Habsburgs. The following spring Sultan Süleyman declared to Ferdinand's ambassadors that besides the Hungarian Kingdom, all the rulers of the Christian world, including France, Poland, Venice and Transylvania, were actually under the protection of the sultan. In 1527, Sultan Süleyman was openly claiming his supremacy over the entire Western Christian world against the emperor and was referring to Emperor Charles V as only the "King of Spain" in diplomatic contacts and correspondence. The Siege of Vienna in 1529 demonstrated the objective of Sultan Süleyman's claims. The European Empire claim of the Ottoman sultan was also proven with the ordering in Venice in 1532 of a magnificent imperial crown and the *regalia,* representing the symbols of the Western rulers (throne with jewels, scepter, gold chain hung on the neck, etc.).[38] All of these were

---

[37] For what İbrahim Pasha said to Ferdinand's ambassador see J. von Hammer, *Devlet-i Osmaniye Tarihi* [History of the Ottoman State], Atâ trans., vol. 5, İstanbul, AH 1330, 77-81.

[38] See Otto Kurz and especially Gülru Necipoğlu, "Süleyman the Magnificent and the Representation of Power in the Context of Ottoman Hapsburg-Papal Rivalry," *Süleyman the Second and His Time,* eds. H. İnalcık, and C. Kafadar, İstanbul: Isis Press, 1993, 163-194.

being realized with the suggestions of Aloisio Gritti,[39] the illegitimate son of the Doge of Venice, who was the Sultan's adviser in European matters and the Grand Vizier İbrahim Paşa, who had the nickname of "Frenk" (European).

Besides the Ottoman symbols of sovereignty following the Central Asian and Persian tradition, such as the horsetail attached to a standard as a sign of rank, horse and flag, military band, plumed ornament attached to the turban, the sun and moon motif on materials and buildings, depiction of the bird of paradise on rugs and baldachins, now the *regalia* of Europe came to express the new concept of empire dreamed of by the sultan. The imperial crown, which was made for Sultan Süleyman who claimed to unite in his person the Eastern and Western Empire, like "Alexander the Great", was made in Venice and was delivered on 12 May 1532 to the Grand Vizier İbrahim Paşa just at the start of Sultan Süleyman's campaign to Vienna.[40]

Charles V had been declared the Holy Roman Emperor in a great ceremony at Bologna in 1529 and after he was coronated in Rome in 1530, his emperorship was celebrated with a magnificent parade in the company of Pope Clement VII. In 1532 during Sultan Süleyman's German campaign, in the brilliant parade made in the presence of the Habsburg ambassadors in Niş, Süleyman was challenging Charles V for the *regnum mundi* (rule of the world).[41] According to the ambassadors at the parade in Niş, Süleyman "was sitting on a golden throne and was wearing a *keyserliche kron* (imperial crown) on his head worth 115 thousand golden ducats". Süleyman, during this fifth campaign in 1532, summoned Charles V to a major battle and said that the emperorship is determined by the sword at the battlefield. The sultan departed from Istanbul on 25 April 1532 with 300 cannons and a 100 thousand strong army. The small (Köszeg) fortress near Vienna detained him between 8-28 August. Charles V was not there. The campaign season had passed. The attack on Vienna was given up. A 16 thousand strong army under the command of Kasım Bey advanced into the interior of Germany and let terror loose. The following year a cease-fire was signed between the Sultan and Charles V and Süleyman went on a campaign to the east to conquer Tabriz and Baghdad.

In 1532, on the sea front, Charles V's fleet struck a surprising blow to the Ottomans and seized Coron, an important port on the southern coast of Morea.

---

[39] For the importance of Aloisio Gritti in the European foreign relations of the sultan see A. Decei, "Aloisio Gritti au service de Soliman Le Magnifique d'après des documents turcs inédits (1533-1534)," with the contributions of C. Feneşan, and J. L Bacqué-Grammont, *Anatolia Moderna-Yeni Anadolu,* vol. 3 (1992), 1-103.

[40] For a comparison of this four layered magnificent crown, for which 115 thousand gold coins was paid, with the crowns made for the emperor and pope see G. Necipoğlu, footnote 38, 163-170.

[41] Ibid., 170-181.

Ferdinand and Charles V used Coron as a trump for peace with Süleyman. Upon the fall of Coron, the Ottoman State Council realized the necessity of making definite decisions for the Mediterranean. The Mediterranean was becoming the main scene of the struggle against Charles V. Barbaros Hayreddin (Barbarossa), the sea wolf, who had terrorized the Christians in the Mediterranean and who captured Algeria, was summoned to Istanbul and received by the sultan. He was appointed as the captain of the entire Ottoman fleet with the title of *Kapudân-i Derya* (Captain of the Seas). Thus, the fleet of the state and the fleet of the pirates were united under a single command. Barbaros recaptured Coron the next year and settled in Tunisia. When Süleyman was on his Persian campaign (1533-1536), Charles V came and occupied Tunisia.[42] During the difficult struggle in the Western Mediterranean against Spain, the Ottoman Council of State considered an alliance with France necessary. Negotiations between the two states started with the ambassadors sent by the Captain of the Seas in July 1533. At that time, Charles V, encouraged by his successes in the Mediterranean, announced that he would capture Istanbul at the head of the Christian Crusader armies.

In 1537 the Ottoman State was in a state of war with Venice. The struggle in the Mediterranean gained prime importance. After the loss of Tunisia, diplomatic relations with France were accelerated and the French ambassador Jean de la Forest came to Istanbul in February 1535. Among the articles of the alliance, it was included that the Ottoman fleet together with the French naval forces would attack Sicily, Sardinia, Naples and Spain, which were held by Charles V and would recapture Tunisia. Francis I would occupy Italy and enter Lombardy, while the Ottomans would occupy Naples. Thus, the Ottoman State assumed an active role in the Italian wars and was determining its own share of the spoils. Ever since the conquest of Otranto by Mehmed the Conqueror in 1480, the Ottomans had always kept the invasion of Italy an option in their plans of conquest. In May 1537 a 160 galley fleet under the command of Lûtfî Paşa weighed anchor and sailed into the Mediterranean. The French and Ottomans would meet in the Adriatic and the Sultan's army would make a landing on Corfu Island and from there would invade southern Italy. It was mentioned in the Venetian senate that Sultan Süleyman showed the target by saying, "to Rome, to Rome'. At this date, there was no doubt that Sultan Süleyman was determined to invade Italy. During this operation, Barbaros attacked Apulia in southern Italy and the French occupied Savoie in October. Money and supplies were sent from Istanbul to the French fleet, which had

---

[42] S. Deswarte-Rosa, "L'expédition de Tunis (1535)," *Chrétiens et Musulmans à la Renaissance,* Actes de 37. Colloque International du CESR (1994), eds. B. Bennassar, and R. Sauzet (Paris, 1998).

come to the Aegean Sea. The Ottoman-French alliance against the Sacred Alliance in 1538, showed that the period of the Crusaders had finally come to an end. The fleet of the Sacred Alliance advanced to the vicinity of Preveza to reach the Aegean Sea and there the great sea victory of Barbaros against Andrea Doria was realized on 27 September 1538. Superiority of the Ottoman navy in the Mediterranean in the period between 1538 and 1571, was an accomplished fact.

b. Ottoman-French Cooperation in the Mediterranean

The Ottoman State finally made peace with Venice in October 1540 and it was invited to join the French-Ottoman alliance against Charles V. When Süleyman set off on a new campaign against Charles V's forces in Hungary in 1541, Barbaros was cooperating with the French fleet at sea. Against the powerful fleet of the Emperor under the command of the Genoese Admiral Doria, the French fleet could only withstand them with the cooperation of Barbaros.

It is worth mentioning that the Emperor and Francis I were engaged at the same time in a war of propaganda against each other for Christian Europe. Accusing Francis I for making an alliance with the great enemy of Christendom and for betraying the religion, Charles V was distributing pamphlets in French for this purpose. Francis I continued to deny the alliance, however secret negotiations with the Ottoman government were being carried out through ambassadors. This war of propaganda between Francis I and Charles V was actually aimed at the German princes in Germany. Charles V was expending great efforts to obtain the military aid of the princes against the Ottomans, while Francis was declaring that he was avoiding activities that might encourage Sultan Süleyman. Francis I, in a letter he sent on a January 1543[43] to the German princes gathered at Nuremberg, emphasizes the unity of the western Christians that he called "the Christian republic", reminded that he had promised to join the Crusader Army against the Turks with an army of 30 thousand persons and declared that he did not make an "alliance and cooperation" with the Ottoman sultan, but only a temporary cease-fire. As for Charles V, he was claiming that he could not continue the war against the Turks because of the attacks of Francis I, who had been incited by the sultan. The French king rejected the accusations and asserted that Charles V with his attacks against the Turks was actually provoking them in order to gain fame in

---

[43] Charrière, vol. 1, 558-559; the letters written by Antoine Arlier between 1527-1547 contain interesting information. It summarized the letter of Sultan Süleyman to Francis I, see J. N. Pendergrass, *Correspondence d'Antoine Arlier humaniste languedocien (1527-1547)* (Geneva, 1990); for a summary see R. Sauzet, "Les relations entre Chrétiens et musulmans du midi de la France," *Chrétiens et Musulmans à la Renaissance.* 263-274.

the Christian world. Francis I made promises to the German princes that he would be siding with Germany against the Turks, as required by his title of Tres *Chretien*. In fact, Francis I, in the peace agreements he made intermittently with Charles V, was promising to join the Crusader campaigns. In spite of all the propaganda, there was no doubt that the fight was actually a struggle for domination and balance in Europe.

Barbaros Hayreddin at Toulon

In the spring of 1543, when Sultan Süleyman departed once again from Istanbul to march to Hungary, the Ottoman fleet under the command of Barbaros Hayreddin sailed and a very interesting and new phase of the Ottoman-French alliance started.

Sultan Süleyman was aware of the duplicities of Francis I and was trying to dissuade the king to abandon this hypocritical stance through his ambassadors, however in the end, he behaved with understanding and refrained from applying too much pressure and in spite of everything, he did not want to lose this valuable alliance, which was keeping the Christian world divided. Barbaros' fleet arrived at the Italian shores that summer. In fear, the Pope in Rome requested intermediation from Francis I. Upon this, Hayreddin was able to purchase the necessary provisions for the fleet and avoided attacking the Papal territories. According to the agreement, from the moment Barbaros entered into French waters, the necessary provisions for the fleet would be provided by the French. The fleet arrived at the port of Marseilles on 20 July 1543. The Ottoman fleet was composed of 110 galley ships, 40 small galley ships and 3 large-sailed ships with high freeboards. Barbaros saluted the city with cannon fire. The Captain of the Seas was met with a splendid ceremony in Marseilles. The people, who heard that he would arrive in the city, came running from distant places and were anxiously waiting to see this legendary pirate close up. At the banquet given by the city dignitaries, Barbaros sat with grandeur in *a* chair like a throne in front of the French, who were watching him with eyes full of curiosity.

While Francis I was fighting against Charles Vs forces in Flanders, he wanted the Ottoman fleet together with the French fleet to go and capture the city of Nice. Doria was waiting for them with 140 ships. Charles V was in Genoa. In the meantime, four French galley ships, which went to Nice, were captured by the enemy. Barbaros informed the sultan that it was necessary to spend the winter in France to continue the operation the following year. Ambassadors traveled between Istanbul and Paris and at the end of the negotiations it was decided to have the Ottoman fleet spend the winter in the

port city of Toulon. Francis I had promised that the supply needs of the
Ottoman fleet and the salaries of the crew would be paid by his government.
The sultan had spent 1,200,000 gold ducats for the building of this fleet (in this
period, the entire budget of the Ottoman State was 9 million ducats).
Preparations were incomplete when Barbaros reached the port of Toulon. The
entire population of the city would be vacated so that the Ottomans could stay
there. It was impossible to bring provisions from Istanbul under the winter
conditions. The feeding and wages problem of the Ottoman fleet, whose per-
sonnel numbered around 30, 000, caused unpleasant disputes with the French
authorities, who claimed that the Turks were trying to wangle money without
reason. Certain French sources even said that the Ottomans pillaged the city,
while other French sources praised the obedience and discipline among the
Turks.[44]

At that time the city of Nice belonged to the dukes of Savoy and was under
the protection of Charles V. The joint Ottoman-French fleet bombarded the
city. Polin, the French ambassador, who was present at the fleet, requested a
guarantee from Hayreddin that the buildings would not be damaged. Barbaros
paid attention to this. The defenders, who were in a difficult position, informed
Polin at one stage, that if the Ottomans soldiers would withdraw, then they
would surrender. The Ottomans withdrew, but the French started to fight again.
Barbaros was furious because the French were slack and not trustworthy. He
took his fleet and withdrew to a nearby island because of a storm. In the
meantime, in September Doria came with his fleet to the aid of the Nice
fortress, however, he was forced to withdraw against Barbaros. The Ottoman
fleet, before withdrawing from the field of operation, secured the surrender of
many fortresses surrounding Nice and delivered them to the French. After the
operation, Barbaros went to Toulon with his fleet to spend the winter (9
October 1543). The city was vacated on 8 September. The value of everything
was recorded and the city council set aside an allocation of only 20, 000 gold
coins to feed the Turks. From the correspondence between Istanbul and
Barbaros, it is understood that the Sultan was worried about the security of the
fleet. It was almost impossible for the fleet to return because winter was
approaching. Generally speaking, feeding the crew was one of the most
difficult tasks during long journeys.

In general, logistical needs were provided for the Ottoman fleet for only a
six-month campaign. The sultan believed that the French would provide the
provisions and wages in Toulon, which had been guaranteed by the agreement.

---

[44] C. Isom-Verhaaren, "Ottoman-French Interact 1480-1580: A Sixteenth Century
     Encounter" (Ph. D. diss., University of Chicago, Department of History, 1997); for the
     Ottoman fleet at Toulon see Charriere, vol. 1, 570 ff.

The Ottoman sailors were settled in the houses in the city and suburbs of Toulon. King Francis I had granted a ten-year tax exemption to the people in the region. Nevertheless, great difficulties were encountered in finding provisions for a crew of 30, 000. Barbaros had to borrow money from the local French merchants. Although the Ottoman fleet could not capture Nice, according to the reports of the French ambassador at that time, Southern France was protected against an attack, thanks to the Ottoman cooperation. The operation resumed in the spring of 1544. Barbaros sent a 22 ship fleet to attack the Spanish coasts. He himself, with a major portion of his fleet, advanced towards Sardinia and Corsica.

The points asserted in a speech made in Venice by Jean de Montluc, who was sent there in 1542 as an ambassador, is noteworthy. According to Montluc, the emperor was responsible for all the destruction and disasters suffered by Christendom. Montluc reminded that the emperor himself and his brother Ferdinand sent ambassadors to Istanbul and held secret talks with Sultan Süleyman, and the Habsburgs paid an annual tribute to the "Grand Turk". Montluc asked, "Does not the 30,000 gold coins given to the Sultan constitute support against Christianity?" and he dwelled on the fact that the alliance with the Sultan was a mandatory action in the political sense. The French ambassador also drew attention to a historical event: Ludovico Sforza, the duke of Milan, used Sultan Bayezid's forces against his rivals in Italy. Also, he added that in the same period, Emperor Maximilian provoked the Turks against France. He says the following after reminding about the cruelties imposed by the emperor's soldiers against the Venetians in 1544: "This great and powerful army, composed of soldiers (Turks) foreign to our religion, were sent to help His Majesty, the French King. There has not been any complaint about the Turks hurting anyone. They have behaved politely. They paid for everything they got for their living". The French ambassador clearly expressed in his speech that a brand new concept prevailed at that time in Europe, which was the concept of balance among states. According to him, the Emperor's men used the alliance of the French King with the Sultan as an excuse to show that the Emperor was right in attacking France. While the Emperor pretended to defend the cause of Christendom, on the other hand, he did not hesitate to make an alliance with the English King Henry VIII, who was a rebel and heretic against the Pope. In addition, the Emperor did not consider that there were any problems in acting together with the Protestant German princes. All these arguments put forward by Polin are interesting from the aspect of showing how the new concept and status in European diplomacy at that time was dominant within the political balance policy. He wanted the alliance with the Muslim sultan to be interpreted by his contemporaries as a requirement of this balance policy in Europe. The Ottoman Council of State also perceived it in this manner. In the work called *Süleymannâme,* written for the Sultan, the Ottoman view about this alliance is very interesting. According to this source, the Emperor forced France into an alliance against the Muslims with the ambition of becoming the "Kaiser", that is, the ruler of all of Europe. For this reason, the alliance of Süleyman, the sultan of Islam and the French King became a necessity. He says that if France would be dissuaded from this alliance, then it would be unavoidable for the entire Christian world to unite as a single front against the Ottomans. For that reason, the view of the Ottoman historian expresses clearly that the Ottomans were also forced to follow a balance of power policy in Europe. It shows that the alliance of the Ottomans with a Christian state was perceived as a requirement of *realpolitik.*

The French palace at that time considered the Ottoman sultan to be the "greatest ruler in the world".[45] King Francis I has confessed to the Venetian ambassador that the Ottoman Sultan was the sole power to guarantee the independence of the European states.

Up until the Cateau-Cambresis Peace Treaty, that ended the Italian Wars in 1559, the French King Henry II (1547-1559) considered the alliance with the Ottomans as the foundation stone of his policy. He obtained a significant amount of financial support along with military support from the Ottomans. The Ottoman alliance against Habsburg superiority continued to be the traditional policy of France that could not be abandoned. Naturally, the Ottomans also obtained great benefits from this alliance. As a contemporary Ottoman historian stated, keeping European Christianity in a divided state and preventing a Crusader assault planned by the Pope and the emperor, were the basic principles of the European policy of the Ottomans.

III. Revolution in War Technology:
Upsetting the Balance Between Europe and the Ottomans

An approach from a broad spectrum in Europe-Ottoman relations in the fields of politics, economy, culture and military showed that the mutual influence between Europe and the Ottomans was actually quite extensive and profound. The Ottoman-French alliance played a definite role in the emergence of the

---

[45] Pierre de Bourdeille, *Oeuvres complètes,* ed. L. Lalande, vol. 11, 179; On the Süleyman's Bender inscription (1538) the awareness of the world state is expressed as follows:

Gemiler yürüden bahr-i Frenk ve Magrib ve Hinde
Şeh-i Bagdad u Kayser-i Rûm Mısr'a Sultanım

(*I am the Sultan who is ruling over Egypt, the Caesar of the lands of the Eastern Roman Empire and the Shah of Baghdad and I am the Sultan who sent fleets to the seas of the Western Mediterranean as well as to the Indian Ocean.*)

European political map in modern times. Also, the influence of the sixteenth century Ottoman-Middle East in the formation of the European capitalist economy is definite. However, the Ottoman State gradually began to decline and started to be considered in the West as a traditional, backward Medieval state against a rapidly rising Europe in every field in respect to the military and technology, in the period following the sixteenth century.[46]

It is a fact that from the beginning the Ottomans were of close interest for Europe in the political as well as in the military field. Starting from the thirteenth century states in Europe began to fight their wars by hiring professional mercenary military companies rather than using feudal armies.[47] First of all, these mercenary companies were operating under the name of *condottieri* in Italy. One of the companies organized by a *condottiere* and providing service for a fee was the Catalan company of the famous Roger de Flor, that was used in the service of Byzantium between 1303-1304 against the Turks who invaded Western Anatolia. On the other hand, because the Frontier Türkmens (Turcomans) were considered to be among the best warriors in this period, the Byzantine and Balkan states hired Türkmen mercenary companies (the most famous of these was the İshak company which cooperated with the Catalans and captured Athens together with them).[48] These mercenary professional Turkish warriors became known as *Turcopouloi* in Byzantium and Rhodes in the fourteenth century. Italian city states competed with each other to use the mercenary Turkmen soldiers.[49] As we have seen above, when the 500 strong Turkish garrison left at Otranto by Gedik Ahmed was forced to surrender to the King of Naples in 1481, they entered into his service and provided effective services against the Papal forces. The Ottomans were the first to establish a standing army that received pay from the treasury of the sultan and were always under his command.

Sultan Orhan (1324-1362) created a *yaya ordusu* (infantry army) among the Türkmens who were his own people in the first period of his *beylik* (beylic).

---

[46] The Venetian documents reflect this change very well, see L Valensi, *Venise et La Sublime Porte* (Paris: Hachette, 1987).

[47] M. E. Mallet, *Mercenaries and their Masters, Warfare in Renaissance Italy* (Totowa: Roman and Littlefield, 1924). "Feudal armies are in principle, 'noble armies'.When, however, a feudal society faces a danger that its traditional army cannot match to enlarge its armed forces... this problem is solved with mercenaries or peasantry"; A. Boros analyzes this situation well for Hungary, "The Militia Portalis in Hungary before 1526." *From Hunyadi to Ràkoczi* (Brooklyn, 1982), 63-80; G. Rázso, "The Mercenary Army of King Matthias Corvinus," ibid., 125-140.

[48] K. M. Setton, *Catalan Domination of Athens, 1311-1388* (London, 1975).

[49] See H. İnalcık, "The Question of the Emergence of the Ottoman State," *International Journal of Turkish Studies,* 2-2 (1981-1982), 71-78.

Sultan Murad I (1362-1389) established a janissary army from the slaves taken prisoner in war. The Infantry and Janissary armies were the first standing armies in Europe. It is known that the janissaries used muskets in the fifteenth century. Their mastery in the use of firearms was given due credit.[50] The Janissary army was one of the important factors in the continuous military successes of the Ottomans. In Europe, it is accepted that the first standing army from the mercenary companies was formed by the Spanish Kings.[51] For the first time in France, Charles VII (1445-1446) created a standing army by using mercenary companies during the Hundred Years War.

It is stated that during the reign of Sultan Süleyman the Lawgiver the Ottomans had an advanced artillery in Europe.[52] The Turks first encountered firearms in 1344 during the attack on İzmir by a Crusader fleet. The Ottomans had learned about firearms through Italy-Dubrovnik (Ragusa) as early as the reign of Murad I (1362-1389). We know definitely that the Ottomans used cannons in the Kosovo Battle (1389) and they claimed technical superiority of their own cannon fire over those of the Serbs. Firearms were mentioned in Europe for the first time in the period between 1304-1331. It was recorded that large cannons were used for the first time in 1388 for sieges in Europe before large bronze cannons were used by Sultan Mehmed the Conqueror in the siege of Constantinople in 1453.[53] The Conqueror had Urban, the Hungarian cannon master, cast cannon of a size heretofore unseen (it could fire 1200 pounds of cannon balls) to hit the Constantinople city walls and the Ottoman army entered the city through the "breach made by the cannon balls". The Conqueror's cannons no doubt introduced a significant new era in artillery. The large cannons definitely played a role in the destruction of the feudal fortresses in Europe and in the establishment of centralist monarchies. The Ottomans learned the *Wagenburg* tactic in the war with the Hungarians during the reign of Murad II. They used wagons and cannons called *darbuzen* that can be easily, carried on these wagons during wars with the Hungarians.[54]

It appears that the Ottomans first used handguns in 1420. The invention of the rifled guns in Europe was one of the factors providing for the superiority of

---

[50] H. Delbrück, *The Dawn of Modern Warfare,* trans. W. J. Rénfroe, Jr. (Lincoln and London: Univ. of Nebraska Press, 1985), 44.

[51] Ibid., 224.

[52] About the Ottoman artillery effectiveness during the reign of the Lawgiver, during the siege of Rhodes in 1522, besides more than 100 cannons, 12 very large cannons were ussed and in 50 days 11, 416 cannon balls wer shot, see J. Von Hammer, *Devlet-i Osmaniye Tarihi* (History of the Ottoman State), Atâ trans., vol. 5 (İstanbul, IH 1330), 278.

[53] Delbrück, 32.

[54] See "II. Murad," *İslam Ansiklopedisi.*

the European armies (the European war technology, especially the rifled guns, was adopted by the Russians before the Ottomans and provided them with superiority on the battlefields). When the French King Charles VIII withdrew from Italy, many of his cannon masters entered into the service of Sultan Bayezid II. Upon the defeat of the Ottomans in the seventeenth century against the Austrian and Russian armies, they were forced to bring masters from Europe for making and using improved types of firearms. Bonneval who later was called Ahmed Paşa was in the Ottoman service in 1729 and Baron de Tott in 1769, and military schools were opened for teaching military technology at the *Mühendishâne-i Berrî-i Hümâyun* (Imperial School of Engineering for Artillery Officers and Army Engineers) and for maritime technology at the *Mühendishâne-i Bahri-i Hümâyun* (Imperial School of Naval Engineering).[55] Borrowing from the European weapons technology continued in the nineteenth century. In 1889 rifled cannons were developed by experts brought from Europe started to be cast at the cannon factory in Istanbul.

As for borrowings of the Europeans from the Ottoman military, perhaps there have been more influences other than the military band, which appears to be an imitation of the Ottoman *mehterhane* in this field. The state band was known as the *növbet-i sultanî* in the Middle East during the Middle Ages.

The victories of the Ottomans at the battlefields in the sixteenth century left deep impressions on the Europeans and information was given in general books and treatises on the Ottoman army and its tactics at that time. The Europeans, however, produced analytical works on the Ottoman army and its tactics only in the seventeenth century (Montecuccoli, Marsigli). A revolution was experienced in the military technology in Europe in the second half of the sixteenth century.[56] The Ottomans were forced to conform more or less to the

---

[55] K. Beydilli, *Türk Bilim ve Matbaacılık Tarihinde Mühendishane, Matbaa ve Kütüphane (1776-1826)* (The school of engineering, printing press and library in the history of Turkish science and printing [1776-1826] (İstanbul: Eren Yayınları, 1995).

[56] C. Cipolla, Guns, *Sails, and Empires: Technological Innovation and Early Phases of European Expansion, 1400-1700* (New York, 1965); J. G. Parker, *The Military Revolution, Military Innovation and the Rise of the West, 1500-1800* (Cambridge, 1988); J. C. Rogers, ed., Debate on *the Military Revolution* (Boulder, 1995); "Ottomans, Hungarians, and Habsburgs in Central Europe: The Military Confines in the Era of Ottoman Conquest," eds. G. Dávid, and P. Fodor, *The Ottoman Empire and Its Heritage* series, eds. S. Faroqhi and H. İnalcık, vol. 20 (Cologne and Leiden: Brill, 2000); this work contains the latest research on the Hungarian-Ottoman Wars, the military "technology, fortress defense system and the 'Military Revolution' during the Ottoman-Habsburg Wars in the sixteenth century; also for the deep influences of the "Military Revolution" on the Ottoman state structure, see H. İnalcık, "Military and Fiscal Transformation in the Ottoman Empire," *Archivum Ottomanicum* 6 (1980): 283-337; J. Kelenik, "The Military Revolution in Hungary," *The Ottoman,* eds. G. Dávid and P.

conditions of this revolution. The situation was not only limited to weapons, the organization of the army and the tactics, but also paved the way for profound changes in the society and state structure.[57] The Habsburg and Ottoman border region in Europe was a continuous battle front. Soldiers from all over Europe, Germans, Walloons, French and Italians, served in the Austrian army. The long war between Austria and the Ottoman Empire in Central Europe between 1593 and 1606, was one of the important causes of the military revolution in Europe, as well as on the Ottoman side. The Ottomans were now confronted with an army composed of infantry and cavalry who used light firearms with a superior fire power. On the Ottoman side, it was observed that the *timarlı* (fief held under condition of military service) cavalry, who fought with conventional weapons, swords and spears, remained ineffective against the European soldiers equipped with improved firearms. In the *telhîsler* (reports) coming from the front it was stated that it would not be possible for Ottoman soldiery to resist if soldiers with muskets were not sent.[58]

It would be appropriate to give some details on these new European soldiers and weapons confronting the Ottomans. J. Kelenik, who used the *Kriegsarchiv* (Military Archive) of Austria and the Austrian-Hungarian war history literature, made it clear that the "Military Revolution" realized in Western Europe was completely put into practice in Hungary against the Ottomans in the period between 1593-1606.[59]

One of the important points set forth by Kelenik is that manual firearms, rifles and pistols took the place of conventional weapons to a great extent in this war period and as a result, it changed the range of fire power and war tactics. Concomitantly, the number of infantry soldiers using pistols in the army increased and the cavalry acquired the skill of using rifles and pistols while riding on horseback.

At the same time, the supportive role of the artillery in battlefield increased and the artillery started to play a more important role in tactics as of the middle of the sixteenth century. These developments mean the revolutionary increase of fire power of the European armies in this period. It is necessary to keep in mind the technological developments in the making of weapons and metallurgy behind this change. Rifles and pistols had become lighter, more effective and

---

Fodor, 117-159; "Oriental Influences on Occidental Military Music," *Islamic Culture* 15 (1941): 235-242.

[57] H. İnalcık, "Military and Fiscal Transformation in the Ottoman Empire," 283-337.

[58] C. Orhonlu, *Telhîsler (1597-1604)* (Reports [1597-1604]) (İstanbul, 1970).

[59] "The Military Revolution in Hungary" in *Ottomans, Hungarians and Habsburgs*, see footnote 56.

less expensive. In this period the following types of rifles were used in the Austrian army: matchlock, wheel lock, hook guns and harquebus (arquebus).

The musket fired with a matchlock appeared around the middle of the fifteenth century and did not change in the sixteenth century. The Ottomans used muskets in 1444.[60] The matchlock was a dangerous and difficult device to use. The wheel lock rifle became widespread after 1580 and this type of rifle, inexpensive, safe and easy to use, remained in use for two hundred years. This rifle, which made it possible to fire under any circumstance, could especially be used with one hand by the cavalrymen. However, the main weapon of the cavalry at this period was the pistol (1. 2-2 kg in weight, 50-60 cm in length). European cavalrymen equipped with firearms obtained a definite superiority against the Ottoman cavalry. The initiative of Rüstem Paşa, an open-minded paşa around the middle of the sixteenth century, to form a cavalry unit with handguns failed.[61] The *falcognette* or harquebus (arquebus), which is used by being mounted on a hook support, was considered to be a type of small cannon whose firing power was strong and was used during sieges. The changes providing superiority to the European soldiers towards the end of the sixteenth century were decreasing the weight of all of these weapons and thus, making them easy to carry, extending their ranges and increasing the piercing effect against armor.[62] Around the middle of the sixteenth century a musket weighed 8-10 kg and at the beginning of the seventeenth century it weighed 4-5 kg. The rifle which was reduced in size could be carried by the cavalry. A well-trained archer could shoot 10 arrows per minute up to 200 meters. The range of the *"katı* (hardened) bow" of the Turks was longer. The musket loaded from the muzzle took 1. 5-2 minutes. Taking the *yaya* units shooting arrows in the Ottoman army from the battlefield and employing them in services such as transportation and opening roads is related to this new situation. We observe that the Janissaries were gradually equipped with more rifles. According to one Austrian source, during the 1532 campaign of Sultan Süleyman, there were 300 cannons and ten thousand Janissaries, and nine thousand of them carried muskets and one thousand carryed halberds.[63] Along with this, we learn from the fortress weapon inventories that the use of arrows had an important place in

---

[60] The musket had been used in the Ottoman army since 1420, see G. Agoston, "Ottoman artillery and European Military Technology in the Fifteenth and Seventeenth Centuries," *AOASH* 47 (1994).

[61] H. İnalcık, "Military and Fiscal Transformation," see footnote 56.

[62] Kelenik, see footnote 56.

[63] J. Von Hammer, *Devlet-i Osmaniye Tarihi* (History of the Ottoman state), trans. M. Atâ, vol. 5 (İstanbul, AH 1330), 312; for an engraving of the Janissaries with muskets and halberds, see H. İnalcık, *The Ottoman Empire: The Classical Age* (London, 1973), illustration numbers 14 and 16.

the defense of fortresses even in the seventeenth century. In 1643, thousands of bows and arrows were recorded (three types of bows mentioned: *İstanbul, Tatar* and *Çağa* Türkmen bows, *Tatar* and *Mısır* [Egyptian] arrows) in the Egri ammunition register.[64] The ammunition registers document that while the Ottomans had firearms, they also continued to use conventional weapons, bows and arrows, swords, spears, maces, halberds and daggers. The *tüfenk-i kâfirî* (rifle of the non-Moslems) recorded among the rifles could be a type of rifle seized from the enemy or imported. Among the armor there were those imported from Europe. The range of the first clumsy muskets was only 100 meters. In the major 1515 Pavia battle, a musket could shoot a 57 gr bullet 300 paces, whereas, towards the end of the sixteenth century, the range of the harquebus was 200-300 m and the range of the rifle was 400 paces (314 m) and it was effective up to 620 paces. The rifle bullets could pierce armor. Thus, the tradition of using armor ended when confronted with firearms.

Other factors which made the firearms in Europe more effective was advanced metallurgy and the manufacture of high quality gunpowder. The Ottomans imported high quality steel and gunpowder from England in the sixteenth century.[65] This Protestant country did not pay attention to the prohibition by the Pope on exports of strategic war materials to the Turks.

The use of pistols was one of the important factors in the "Military Revolution" in the second half of the sixteenth century. In the seventeenth century Ottoman fortress materials inventories (M. Stein) in Hungary, various large and small cannons, muskets and pistols were registered. The rifles were of the old style, long and with small calibers. European sources of the seventeenth century described that as a typical Ottoman tactic, a large number of soldiers were brought together and they made all out attacks in the form of columns against fortresses. In contrast, the Europeans had firearms superiority. One method used by the Ottomans in the siege of fortresses reminds one of the ancient Mongolian tactics. The Ottoman soldiers, just like the Mongols, piled up soil to the level of the city walls and then marched on.

The widespread use of inexpensive and easy to use firearms in the battlefields along with the "Military Revolution" created profound social and military ramifications both in Europe and the Ottoman domains. The population explosion in Europe in the sixteenth century and increase in poverty replenished the demand for mercenary military service to. In the European

---

[64] M. Stein, "Ottoman Fortresses in Hungary" (Ph. D. diss., University of Chicago, Department of History, 2001).

[65] H. İnalcık, "The Socio-political effects of the diffusion of fire-arms in the Middle East," eds. V. J. Parry, and M. E. Yapp; *War, Technology and Society in the Middle East [London,* 1975), 195-217.

armies, infantry soldiers were composed mainly of these peasant soldiers with rifles. Anyone from the public could be a soldier by purchasing a rifle and other materials from recruitment officers. The use of a rifle did not require an extensive training or hand-to-hand fighting.[66] The population explosion in Anatolia and gradually increasing needs of the state for soldiers with muskets also caused a similar development in the Ottoman lands. According to one record, in 1593, 10 thousand Janissaries in the army who were not equipped with firearms were defeated by the Hungarian infantry.[67] In the long period of wars with Iran between 1578-1590 and Austria between 1593-1606, the Ottomans recruited mercenary soldiers with muskets extensively from the Turkish and Kurdish Anatolian villagers. These soldiers were organized in companies of 50-100 soldiers under the flag of a Janissary officer sent by the State, just like in Europe, and formed the most important part of the army under the name of *Sekban* and *Sarıca*.[68] These companies, which resorted to banditry when their fees were cut off, became an anarchistic element that terrorized Anatolia during this war period under the name of *Celali* bandits.[69]

The gradual expansion of the armies, and recruitment of mercenary infantry with rifles from among the people, appears as a result of the "Military Revolution" in Europe and the Ottoman lands. In other words, the revolution that started in Europe paved the way for a similar development in the Ottoman military structuring and the traditional Ottoman military regime based on the Sultan's slaves and *devşirme* (boys recruited for the Janissary corps) was confronted with a profound change. The fundamental reason for the change on both sides was handguns which became prominent,[70] and the fact that feudal soldier types equipped with bows and arrows, spears and armor, lost their function in the battlefields. Towards the end of the sixteenth century, the Ottoman cavalry *(timarlı* cavalry), who still used conventional weapons, were confronted with the European cavalry carrying a heavy sword, long-range rifle and a short-barreled pistol. The "black cavalry" of the Germans were carrying two pistols ready to shoot. The Ottoman soldiers had to fight against these well-equipped European soldiers for thirteen years between 1593-1606. When all of these points are taken into consideration, the 1593-1606 war against the Ottomans has been the real turning point of the "Military Revolution" in Europe.

---

[66] Kelenik: "the infantry was usually recruited from among the poorest strata", 122-123, see footnote 56.

[67] Kelenik, 151.

[68] See H. İnalcık, "Military and Fiscal Transformation".

[69] M. Akdağ, *Celâli İsyanları, (1550-1603)* (Ankara, 1963); H. İnalcık, "Military and fiscal Transformation".

[70] Kelenik, 126-130.

A superior side of the Ottomans was the fact that they had a light cavalry army with advanced maneuver capability, *timarlı* cavalry and a light infantry. The Europeans became aware of this advantage of the Ottomans and decreased the use of armor to a minimum in their infantry (only a breastplate, neckpiece and helmet) and thus the weight carried by the infantry was reduced to 7-7. 5 kg. Artillerymen and those using muskets bore only a sword and a light helmet.[71] The Ottomans had the advantage of having a standing army, the Janissary army and no doubt a better organized logistic system[72] and were able to increase the number of soldiers continuously. However, problems also started to appear in relation to these subjects. Even at this date in the West, many people believed that the military strength of the Ottoman Empire had declined and that it would collapse and disintegrate in the near future.[73]

At the end, the superiority of the German firearms industry and thus to enable Austria to equip its cavalry and infantry soldiers and castles and fortress redoubts fortified with artillery, may be considered to be the main reason for the failures of the Ottomans during the war between 1593-1606. In other words, this war may be taken as a turning point in which the Ottomans lost their military superiority against the Europeans. Europe left the Ottomans behind in economy, technology and the art of war. Developments in mechanical science and technological revolution in the West, just as with firearms, also showed the finest skill in clock works and astronomical instruments. These inventions captured the admiration of the Ottomans. In 1532 Sultan Süleyman the Lawgiver placed an order to the masters in Venice for *automata* such as an alarm clock in a gold ring, a dancing wooden doll and a sailing ship.[74] In 1547 when a peace treaty was signed with the Habsburgs, Rüstem Paşa asked a master watchmaker to be sent to make a wall clock for the Sultan. In 1721 Ibrahim Paşa wanted to have a microscope and binoculars from France. The latest astronomy instruments were imported from Europe for the Observatory built for Murad III (1574-1593). Upon the reaction of the conservatives who

---

[71] Ibid., 135-136.

[72] C. Finkel, *The Administration of Warfare: The Ottoman Military Campaigns in Hungary, 1593-1606* (Vienna, 1987).

[73] J. Deny, *"Les* pseudo-propheties concernant les turcs au XVIe siècle," *Revue des Etudes Islamiques* 10 (1936).

[74] G. Necipoğlu, "Ottoman-Hapsburg-Papal Rivalry," *Süleyman the Second and His Time* (İstanbul: ISIS, 1993). 171, taken from Sanuto, vol. 5, 636; vol. 6, 6-7 for history of Western technology see H. Kellenbenz, *Technology in the Age of the Scientific Revolution, 1500-1700* (London: Fontana/Collins, 1974); K. Arrow, "Classificatory Notes on the Production and Transmission of Technological Knowledge," *American Economic Review,* Papers and Proceedings 59, 29-35; J. Gimpel, *The Medieval Machine* (London, 1977); E. L. Jones, *The European Miracle* (Cambridge, 1982).

said that the work of God in the skies should not be meddled with, the observatory was destroyed in 1580. The Ottoman administration became aware of the technological superiority of Europe and wanted to base its army on rifled soldiers (increasing fourfold the numbers of the rifled Janissary army and the Sekban and Sarıca soldiery), but these efforts were in vain. One of the main reasons of decline was that the Ottoman economy and finances as well were in deep trouble in this period.[75]

Also, the wars in Hungary in the sixteenth and seventeenth centuries were mainly "Fortress Sieges". The most important advancement in fortification and artillery in Europe was the construction of the fortresses with the bastion system. Walls as low as possible, bastions organized in the form of a star all around supported with soil from behind were the principles observed in the construction of new fortresses. The Ottomans were aware of these innovations. The Ottomans captured some fortresses built in the new style and thus they were learning about the construction of the new fortification system. The Ottomans, who were always waiting for a Habsburg invasion, tried to reinforce the old fortresses with bastions for the defense of Hungary. Montecuccoli (1664) pointed out that fortresses in Ottoman Hungary were generally constructed in the old style and were of poor quality. The modern fortresses made it practically impossible for the Ottomans to invade Austrian lands. After Sultan Süleyman's siege of Vienna in 1529, Austria made great expenses (one million gold coins per year) to build modern bastioned fortresses according to the new methods at the border and on the road to Vienna, and thus prevented Ottoman advance. It took 10 weeks to come to the Austrian border from Edirne and much time was wasted to capture the fortresses on the road to Vienna, and when the Ottoman army approached Vienna, the campaign season was over. Besides bad weather conditions, the *timarlı* cavalry had to return to their villages in the autumn. Their logistic supplies, which had been prepared for six months, would be exhausted by that time (400 thousand liters of feed and food were needed per day for an army of 100 thousand persons and 80 thousand animals).[76] Sultan Süleyman's journal of the 1532 campaign describes the story of the arrival of the Ottomans in front of the Hungarian fortresses held by Austria after overcoming unbelievable difficulties.[77] On 28 August when the army captured the Güns (Köszeg) fortress at a distance of one day from Vienna, they were forced to return. The invasion of Austria had become an impossible task for the Ottomans.

---

[75] H. İnalcık, *An Economic and Social History,* vol. 1, 99.

[76] G. Bayerle, "One Hundred Fifty Years of Frontier Life in Hungary," *From Hunyadi to Rákóczi,* 227-231.

[77] Feridun, *Münşeatu's-Selatîn,* vol. 1 (İstanbul AH 1274), 577-584.

IV. The Ottomans and the Protestant World

The Topkapı Palace documents clearly show that when the Ottomans invaded Hungary in 1526 and confronted the Habsburgs in Central Europe, they became active observers closely watching the actions of Charles V and Ferdinand and followed the political developments in Europe. Thus, they were trying to make use of every kind of separatist power or movement emerging in Europe in their competition for supremacy against the Habsburgs. In June 1533 İbrahim Paşa said to the Austrian ambassador, "The Christian world has never been as divided as it is today".[78]

An Ottoman intelligence report (Topkapı Palace Archives, No. E. 7671)[79] presented to Sultan Süleyman the Lawgiver gives information to the sultan about Martin Luther and his struggle against the emperor. According to the report, "A man called Martin Luther created a religion by himself and opposed the invalid belief of the cursed Spanish king, collected thirty thousand soldiers" and fought against the Spanish at "San Borgo near Bazilya". Among the other information given in the report is the news that Andrea Doria sailed from the Genoese port against the fleet of "Hayreddin Reis" near Morocco, 12 French galley ships sailed from the port of Marseilles, "Megali Mastura" (Great Master of the Knights) set sail from Malta with seven galley ships, and an army (two thousand cavalry and ten thousand infantrymen) belonging to the Spanish King (Emperor Charles V) at Lombardia, which belonged to the duchy of Milan. According to the report, this force was standing by to assist if there was an action by the Ottomans on Apulia in Southern Italy. The Spanish King (Emperor) himself was watching the situation in Vienna with eight thousand of his soldiers. Evidently, the Emperor did not have any other soldiers. The Spanish King received one million florins from the duke of Milan and returned to his country. The King also made peace with Venice. Venice paid 200 thousand gold coins to Spain and 100 thousand gold coins to Ferdinand, the archduke of Vienna. The merchant also added the news that the Emperor "made peace with France in appearance, but the hostility in their minds was not lost".

---

[78] Hammer, vol. 5, 138, see footnote 63.

[79] This report was published by Dr. C. Isom-Verhaaren: "An Ottoman Report about Martin Luther and the Emperor: New Evidence of the Ottoman Interest in the Protestant Challenge to the Power of Charles V," *Turcica* 28 (1996): 299-318. The report gives the Sultan information supplied by an Albanian merchant from Ergiri-Kasn named Dhuka through an Ottoman officer at Drac. Merchants were always used as a source of intelligence. Dhuka, who engaged in the trade of Ankara mohair, was in Europe between 1527-1530 or 1527-1531.

In summary, the report enlightens the Ottoman government on the soldiers and fleet of Charles V and that he made peace with Milan, Venice and France (the 1529 Cambrai peace) and reports that Charles V was keeping his soldiers together in Northern Italy against an Ottoman invasion of Apulia or an attack against Vienna.

This information was important for the Sultan, who had returned to Istanbul from the siege of Vienna in 1529. It is understood that Dhuka relayed the information through an Italian and that he received rather accurate information about Italy. However, the information related to Germany and Luther is not valid. The news is that Luther fought against the emperor's forces in a place called "San Borgo near Bazilya". According to Isom-Verhaaren, this news could be related to the peasant rebellions in Germany between 1524-1526. Actually, in 1529 the German Protestant princes initially refused to help Ferdinand against Süleyman, but upon Ottoman siege of Vienna in the summer of 1529, they were forced to promise military aid to Charles V at the Diet of Augsburg.

The next year in 1531 the Protestants formed a hostile front against the emperor with the Schmalkaldic League, but there was no war at that time. The fighting mentioned in the report is related to the incidents at Basel (Bazilya in the document) in Switzerland. There, the proponents of religious reforms destroyed the images in the city and took control of the city. They made alliances in February 1529 with the German Protestant princes and France. In response to this, in 1530 the Swiss Catholic cantons sought alliance with Ferdinand in Vienna.

In 1531 the reformists in Switzerland formed an army led by Ulrich Zwingli and fought against the Catholics. Thus, all of these incidents in the report were attributed to Luther. As Dhuka stayed in Europe for three years, the information of the report must be for the years 1529-1531 and it must have been narrated in a confused manner in the report of the Ottoman State agent at Drac.[80] Naturally, the Ottomans must have followed these movements in Germany and against Ferdinand in Switzerland with close interest. It is noteworthy that the Ottoman palace perceived the importance of the Protestant movements from the aspect of Ottoman strategy, even at those early dates. Even in 1529, the Protestant princes in Germany became aware of the benefits of the Ottoman pressure for themselves in their resistance against the Emperor and Ferdinand.[81] Historians, in general, concur on the fact that the Ottoman pressure on the Habsburgs played a definite role in the spread and

---

[80] Isom-Verhaaren (pp. 301, 310) shows a tendency to accept the date of the report as 1530.

[81] S. A. Fischer-Galati, *Ottoman Imperialism and German Protestantism* (Cambridge, Mass., 1959), 35-37; Isom-Verhaaren, 310.

establishment of Protestantism and that helped the advancement of the Ottomans in Europe.[82]

Towards 1540, John Zápolya in Hungary and Transylvania under the protection of the Ottomans, the French King, and the Protestant princes in Germany were in contact with each other against the superior power of the Habsburgs. These rulers were considering the Ottomans as a counterweight against the Habsburg hegemony.[83] The emperor could not cope with the Ottomans without receiving military assistance from Germany. For that reason, for the first time the emperor was forced to sign an agreement with the Lutherans in Nuremberg in the summer of 1532. After this, under Ottoman pressure, the emperor made concessions to the Protestants eight times. The *Türkenfurcht* (Fear of Turks) in Germany was a reality and an Ottoman invasion was felt to be a close threat. It was such that *Türckenglocken* (Turkish Bell) and a Turkish Tax were established against the threat. In 1502, the first newspaper, *Newe Zeitung,* was published to give news about the Turks. In the anonymous *Türcken pluclein* treatise, the author said the following:[84] "The best course for the Christian World is to bow and pay tribute to the powerful Sultan. We can trust him to govern us with justice and magnanimity."

The influence of Islam on Lutheranism was recognized in the West. Paul Anderbach, due to freedom of worship, individualistic attribute of belief and other similarities, considered Protestantism to be a type of Islam.[85] In the Unitarian belief that spread in Hungary, the thought of a single God as opposed to the doctrine of the Trinity was dominant. Luther in the treatise he wrote in 1530 called *Libellus de ritu* et *moribus Turcorum,* compares the Turks with Christians and accepts them as having virtues such as being humble, living

---

[82] S.A.Fischer-Galati, see footnote 81; C. M Kortepeter, *Ottoman Imperialism during the Reformation,1578-1608* (New York, 1972); K. M. Setton, "Lutheranism and the Turkish Peril," *Balkan Studies,* vol. 3 (1962), 133-168; C. Göllner, "Die Türkenfrage in Spannungsfeld der Reformation," *Südost-Forschungen* 34 (1975), 61-78; K. M. Setton, *The Papacy and the Levant (1204-1571),* vol. 4 (Philadelphia, 1984); J. Pannier, "Calvin et les Turcs," *Revue Historique* 62 (1937); 268-286.

[83] Setton, "Lutheranism," 137.

[84] Ibid., 138; About the anonymous original work called Viaje de Turquia on the threat of the Ottomans for Europe a Turkish image in Spain in the middle of the sixteenth century see J. Perez, "l'affrontement Turcs-Chrétiens vu d'Espagne, Le Voyage en Turquie," *Chrétiens et Musulmans a la Renaissance,* 255-263; about this work see Paulino Toledo, "Türkiye Seyahati" (Trip to Turkey) (Ph. D. diss., Ankara University, Faculty of Language, History and Geography, 1992).

[85] Setton, "Lutheranism," 158; for the views of Solomon Schweigger, a Lutheran pastor, who visited Turkey, on Luther and the Holy Koran see C. Gauthier, "Un allemand à Constantinople, 1571-1581, Critique du Coran par un pasteur Lutheran," *Chrétiens et Musulmans à la Renaissance,* eds. B. Bennassar and R. Sauzet (Paris, 1998), 163-175.

simple lives and being honorable (Luther read the Holy Koran from its translation and tried to prove that Islam is not a true religion). Luther, by stating a point that is accepted by historians today, said that the living conditions of the peasantry in Eastern Europe were so bad that they sometimes welcomed the Turks as saviors. During the rebellions between 1437-1438 of the Transylvanian villagers against their masters, the forces of Sultan Murad II occupied this country and did not encounter serious resistance. It is known that many villagers from Salzburg and Würzburg escaped to the Turkish side and many German soldiers joined the Ottoman army.[86] Sultan Süleyman requested information about Luther from an ambassador and said that he could be a benevolent master for Luther. When this conversation was relayed to Luther, he made the sign of the cross and said, "God save me from such a benevolent master" *(Tischreden,* vol. 2, 508). Another point indicating how much the times had changed is the following: Luther did not approve of the Pope's *Bellum Sanctum* (Sacred War) against the Turks, and he resembled the attacks of the Turks to natural disasters that were God's punishment of the Christians. Earlier, he said that to resist the Turks was to oppose the will of God. Many people in Germany did not approved the fact that the war against the Turks was a religious war. It was said that the Pope provoked Charles V against the Turks in the Crusader campaign to fulfill his own political interests in Italy.[87] Melanchton, Luther's right-hand man, made contacts with the Greek Orthodox Patriarch in Istanbul in 1559 and sought a religious agreement.[88] The Ottomans were following with interest the struggles of Luther and the Lutherans in Germany. It is noteworthy that the spread of Protestantism is the period when the peasant rebellions spread. As Luther had stated, the propaganda that the Ottomans treated the peasants well, must have reached very distant places in the West. Luther treats the Ottoman pressure in Europe in the framework of his own struggle against the Pope. However, as a German and Christian, he actually perceived the struggle against the Turks and the union among Christians as a matter of life and death. Luther wrote three treatises on the resistance against the Turks. According to him, the Turks were the "Servants of the Devil". The Turk in the eschatology of the German monk was depicted as

---

[86] Setton, "Lutheranism," 161; It appears that the propaganda that the Ottomans behaved well towards the peasantry spread as far as Germany. A German writer said, 'a poor man who has to struggle for a morsel of food, rather than living under these types of Christians, prefers the Turks'; for the policy of the Ottomans towards the peasant subjects see H. İnalcık, *An Economic and Social History,* vol. 1, 143-154; G. Veinstein, "Retour sur la question de la tolerance ottomane au XIVe siècle," *Chrétiens et Musulmans à la Renaissance,* 415-426.

[87] Setton, "Lutheranism," 141-146.

[88] S. Runciman, *The Great Church in Captivity* (Cambridge, 1968).

an Antichrist. The 1529 Vienna siege created a deep anxiety in Luther. In the letters he wrote to Erasmus he advised that the European states should put an end to the wars among themselves and unite against the Turks; the Germans should run to the aid of the Emperor.

On the other hand, the Protestant belief was receiving protection and spreading quickly in the regions where the Ottomans were dominant. Even when Luther was still alive, the Lutheran preachers were going in great numbers to Ottoman Hungary and the new sect was rapidly spreading among the villagers. The hatred of the Catholics against the Protestants was so deep that it was being said that they were even worse than the Turks for Christianity. In time, Transylvania became the center of the most radical Unitarian Protestantism and Bethlen Gabor (1613-1629) and I. Rakoczi (1630-1648), the Transylvanian princes, played an important role in the Protestant front against the Catholics during the Thirty Years War (1618-1648). This struggle against the Habsburg dominance by the Protestants, coincided with the period (1617-1656) when Ottoman power was at an ebb, and thus it was a blessing for the Ottoman State.[89]

V. Europe wants to Know the Ottomans

One of the earliest treatises written about the Ottomans in the West is the work of Nicola Sagundino that was written in 1456 for Aeneas Sylvius Piccolomini, later Pope Pius II (1458-1464). In this treatise, Sagundino mentions Sultan Mehmed's plans to conquer Rome with the claim of being the inheritor of the Roman Empire as the conqueror of Constantinople. Pius II, the humanist Pope, in his letter to the Conqueror, which remained as an essay, wrote that if he became a Christian, then, he would acquire the right to this title.[90] For the history of the reigns of the Conqueror and Bayezid II, the work of Gian-Maria Angiolello covering the period up until 1514, is more important because it included the observations of an eye witness. Angiolello served for years as the *içoğlan*, (boy being educated for service at court) in the Ottoman palace. The work of Theodoro Spandugino Cantacusino, who was from an aristocratic Byzantine family and who went and settled in Venice after the

---

[89] For details see, *From Hunyadi to Rákózi: War and Society in Late Medieval and Early Modern Hungary,* eds. J. M. Bak, and B. K. Király (Brooklyn, 1982), 189-508.

[90] J. C. Margolin, "Réflexion sur le commentaire du Père Celestin, Pierre Crespet de la lettre du Pape Pie II au Sultan Mahomet II," *Chrétiens et Musulmans à la Renaissance,* 212-239.

conquest of Constantinople, is also important. He wrote this work[91] to encourage the Christian world for a Crusader campaign and presented it in 1509 to the French King Louis XII, and in 1519 to Pope Leo X. The Spanish version was dedicated to Charles V in 1520. It appears that the author made use of the Ottoman chronicles. In this work, he proposes to the French King that he should consider the Safavids as the strongest rival against the Turks.

The work entitled *Tractatus de moribus condiconibus et nequicia Turcorum* is especially important as a work that is a source of information on making the Ottomans known to the Western world and on Islam. Luther wrote a foreword to its German translation.

Due to the gradually increasing interest in the Ottomans as of 1453, Francesco Sansovino gathered the main works written in Italy on the Ottomans in a collection entitled *Historia universale dell'origine, guerre, et imperio de Turchi* (Venice, 1560). His work was reprinted seven times until 1654.

The Ottoman Political System Discussed by European Political Writers

The advances of the Ottoman Empire, the threat of invasion of Rome and Italy caused profound reverberations in the Western world and especially in Italy, and many books on Ottoman history and organization were published.[92]

---

[91] For the English version with the most recent interpretations see D. M. Nicol, *On the Origin of the Ottoman Emperors* (Cambridge: Cambridge University Press, 1997).

[92] T. Spandugino (Spandouyn), Gian-Maria Angiolello, F. Sansavino, G. A. Menavino, G. Postel, P. Giovio, B. Ramberti, L Bassano, P. Belon, P. C. du Fresne du Cange, S. Schweigger, O. Busbecq, N. de Nicolay, B. Baudier, W. Dillich, J. Chesneau, H. Dernschwam, H. de Beauvau, J. Thévenot and others; for a complete bibliography see C. Göllner, *Turcica, Die Europaischer Türckendrücke des XVI Jahrhundert, 1551-1606,* vols. 1-2 (Bucharest and Berlin, 1961); for the Turkish image in French literature see C. Rouilard, *The Turk in the French History, Thought and Literature, 1520-1660* (Paris, 1938); in Spanish literature see A. Mas, *Les Turcs dans la litérature espagnole,* vols. 1-2 (Paris, 1967); "... La Peau de Mahomet... Images du Maure et de l'oriental dans le spectacle anglais de La Renaissance, " *Chrétiens et Musulmans à la Renaissance,* 189-212; T. Reyhanlı, *İngiliz Gezginlerine göre XVI. yüzyılda İstanbul'da Hayat* (Life in İstanbul in the sixteenth century according to the English travelers) (Ankara, 1983); see Jacques-Auquste de Thou, *Histoire Universelle de Jacques-Auguste de Thou depuis 1543 jusqu'en 1607,* 16 vols. (London. 1734), of the 10 thousand pages in this work, 900 pages are allocated to the Ottoman Empire and the Turks; see C. Michaud, "Les Turcs dans l'Histoire Universelle de Jacques-Auquste de Thou," *Chrétiens et Musulmans à la Renaissance,* 241-253; R. Schwoebel, *The Shadow of Crescent: The Renaissance Image of the Turk, 1453-1517* (New York, 1967); M. Soykut, *Image of the "Turk" in Italy* (Berlin: Klaus Schwarz Verlag, 2001).

N. Machiavelli (1469-1527), the founder of political science, in his advice to the prince in *Principo,*[93] gives examples not only from Alexander the Great and Roman history, but also from the Ottoman State. When he debates how a conquered country can be kept under control, he connects the fact of the Ottomans being able to establish a continuous sovereignty in the Balkans. He says that if a state decides to remain in a country whose language, customs and laws are different, then it should settle there itself, in other words, it should settle colonies of its own people in several locations in that country. Thus, the sovereignty on the territories conquered will be more secure and long-lived, because if a resistance movement starts, then there is the opportunity to intervene immediately. Likewise, the state should treat the people of that place gently, because when people encounter hardships they rebel. Changing the local laws and taxes should a be avoided, the state should not permit its own civil servants to loot the local people, it should be ensured that the complaints of the people can easily be relayed to the ruler. Thus, he says, the annexed country easily becomes a part of the state in a short period of time.

All of these remarks by Machiavelli actually summarize the policy the Ottomans applied in the territories they conquered and explain how the Balkan nations became a part of the Ottoman imperial order. From the beginning, the Ottomans brought colonies *(Yörükler* [nomadic tribes]) and settled them on the strategic places in the territories they conquered, they guaranteed the life and property of the local people, kept their promises and thus gained the goodwill of the people. In case the officials applied unlawful pressure on the people, they had the right of complaint directly to the sultan, or his Council of State and the culprits were severely punished without delay.[94] Machiavelli must have obtained good information about the Ottoman administrative principles.

On the other hand, Machiavelli[95] dwelled upon the following points among the reasons why the Ottomans were able to soundly establish their sovereignty in the country: The entire country was subject to one master; the sultan is the master and everyone else is his servant. He has the authority to change at any time the governors he sent to the provinces. Every one of the officials is the servant of the sultan and because the officials owe their existence only to the sultan, they only obey him. It is not easy to deceive them with bribes or by other means. Even if he is deceived, he cannot find anyone in his environment to go along with him. Thus, Machiavelli says any foreign power that would attack the Ottomans cannot find collaborators from within.

---

[93] *The Prince,* trans, and ed. Robert M. Adams (New York: Norton. 1992), 6.

[94] H. İnalcık, "Ottoman Methods of Conquest," *Studia Islamica* 2 (1954): 103-129.

[95] *The Prince,* 12-13.

However, if you completely defeat the Ottomans, then you will only be confronted with the ruler (there are no local points of resistance, as is the case in a feudal state). The people do not show resistance, they come and become a subject of the new ruler. The Ottoman regime resembles the regime of Darius in Ancient Persia. When Alexander the Great defeated Darius, his entire country became subject to Alexander. According to Machiavelli, the French King is another prince who established a strong authority in his country, like the Ottomans. However, this situation stems from completely different conditions. While the Ottomans represented a regime that held absolute sovereignty without partners and administered the country with servants, the French King kept his Kingdom under his control through the local feudals and barons who had hereditary rights from father to son and consequently, it was not easy for a foreigner to conquer his country. Machiavelli finds continuous sovereignty in these two separate regimes. Invading France is comparatively easier than invading the Ottoman territories. If you subvert one of the barons, then he will become subject to you together with his people, because the people follow him. Thus, it is easy to invade this type of a country, but it is difficult to hold on to it. Likewise, the other barons can oppose the victor and the people subject to them also resist the invader. Additionally, the barons can start a rebellion anytime with a small excuse. In summary, to establish sovereignty and to maintain it in a country like France is not easy. Whereas, in the East, when a ruler is defeated, then the people are deprived of a leader who can resist.

The frequently observed rebellions in the French and Spanish Kingdoms were because of the excessive number of barons, who had hereditary rights to the Kingdom and had taken the local people under their control. There was not such a situation in the Ottoman country.

Machiavelli, when speaking about the other factors threatening the sovereignty of the prince, discusses the dangers of requesting auxiliary forces from a neighboring state or the use of mercenary soldier companies. In the first case, you accept the sovereignty of the ruler who is providing the assistance. As an example of this, Machiavelli reminds that the Byzantine emperor requested auxiliary forces from the Turks and when the war was over, these auxiliary forces stayed in the country and became dominant. Here, Machiavelli indicates the fact that against the Serbians in 1352, Emperor John VI Cantacuzenus repelled the enemy thanks to an Ottoman auxiliary force under the command of Süleyman, but that this force did not vacate the Tsympe (Cinbi) fortress in Thrace and the invasion of the country started. This is another point proving that Machiavelli knew Ottoman history rather well. Instead of foreign auxiliaries, Machiavelli says that using mercenary soldiers is less dangerous, because there is no state behind the mercenary soldiers. In conclusion, he arrives at the opinion that the best is to use soldiers from the local people.[96]

The Ottoman army, as in the advice given by Machiavelli, was composed essentially from the servant soldiers directly under the command of the ruler (Janissary soldiers, cavalry, etc.) and from the *timarlı* cavalry, whose *timar* did not pass from father to son hereditarily, a majority of them were the descendants of servants and who had no right over the land. The auxiliary soldiers recruited from the subjects and villagers *(yaya* [infantry], *azeb,* nomads, *cerâhor, eflak, martolos,* etc.) would go to war under the commanders appointed by the ruler. The Turkish mercenary soldiers were the most sought after soldiers in the Balkans and Italy as of the thirteenth and fourteenth centuries. Many of these Turkish mercenary soldiers settled in the Byzantine Empire, in the Aegean and in the Italian colonies, converted to Christianity and joined the local forces under the name of *Turkopouloi.*

In the sixteenth century, along with the rise of the national monarchies in the West, absolutism was accepted to be the ideal form of administration and the Ottoman State was considered to be an advanced example of this.[97] Jean Bodin (1530-1596), in his famous influential work,[98] allocated a special place to the Ottoman State.

Bodin, the foremost French political theoretician on the subject of absolutist government and natural rights, defined the Ottoman regime, comparing it with the Western monarchic regimes. When disussing the French monarchy, he says, "the subjects there obey the laws of the ruler; the ruler obeys the laws of nature". This type of monarchy, he argues, is different from the monarchy of the Ottomans where the ruler controls the goods and persons of the subjects. According to Bodin, "The state of the Turks represents an archaic stage of monarchy... Süleyman represents a type of tyrant sovereign".

According to Bodin, Süleyman remained bound to the primitive rule of the "monarchie seigneuriale" (lordship monarchy), considering himself above the civil laws determined by nature and claiming to be the single and sole interpreter of the laws (True, the Ottomans were foreign to the theory of "natural law". The sultan, who made the law, believed that he also had the authority to abolish it whenever he wanted.)

The Europeans, particularly the Venetians, closely watched to see what type of sultan came to the Ottoman throne. A. Teneti, by taking the records in the *Diarii* by Sanudo, (who was a contemporary of Süleyman), as the basis, indicates that the Venetians had a determining influence on the image of

---

[96] Ibid., 32-39.
[97] P. Anderson, *Lineages of the Absolutist State* (London, 1974).
[98] J. Bodin, *Les Six livres de La République* (Paris, 1583).

Süleyman in the West. The Venetian ambassadors, P. Bragadin, M, Minio, P. Zen and the French G. Postel praise Süleyman's justice, magnanimity and his humanitarian attitude towards Christians.

It is noteworthy that the difference in religion was not influential in such judgments. Initially, Süleyman was perceived as a peace-loving sultan, unlike his father. However, his conquest of Belgrade in 1521 destroyed the hopes in the West. Belgrade was considered to be the gate of Europe. The developments after the fall of Belgrade, Mohacs (1526) and the invasion of Hungary, were a turning point in the history of Ottoman-European relations. Now the strength and fear of the Ottomans became a determining factor in European politics. Up until that time, the strong Hungarian Kingdom was believed to be the shield of Europe. Moreover, the Hungarians had even been able to threaten the Ottoman sovereignty in the heart of the Balkans. Then, Austria and the Germanies were seriously worried about an Ottoman invasion after Mohacs.

Sultan Süleyman (1520-1566), is the Ottoman sultan who is talked about the most in the West due his long sultanate and the determining role he played in European politics. François de Bellefort advises the French kings to take the justice of Süleyman as an example. However, upon Süleyman's execution of Mustafa (1553), his son, this positive image changed. It was asserted that he was a cruel tyrant under the influence of his wife Hürrem (Roxelana). Moreover, this incident became the subject of theatrical plays *(La Soltane de Gabriel Bounin,* 1561; A. Thevet, *Vie de Sultan Mustapha, fils* de *sultan Solyman).* Upon this crime of murder, it was claimed that Süleyman violated "natural law". In other words, the new ideologies developed on the basic principles of law in the West were taken as the basis in the interpretation of the Ottoman politics.

The sixteenth and seventeenth century Western writers attempted to determine the basic structure of the Ottoman regime. Paul Rycaut, who had lived in the Ottoman Empire for a long time and who is the author of the detailed work on the Ottoman political regime *(The Present State of the Ottoman Empire,* London, 1668), when trying to determine the basic political concepts *(maxims)* of the Ottomans, first of all, he "admire[s] the long continuance of this great and vast empire and attribute[s] the stability thereof without change within itself, and the increase of dominions and constant progress of its arms" as the basic success of the regime. However, at the same time he observes that it represents a despotic and cruel government without an aristocratic class, and justice is implemented with complete harshness and the sultan expects the blind obedience of the subjects.

The sixteenth and seventeenth century political writers in Europe, when describing the Ottoman regime, follow basically the ideas of Aristotle on tyranny and make their interpretations from that aspect. According to Aristotle,

"Tyranny is of three kinds: 1. The Barbarian despotism and 2. The elective dictatorship but in 3. The strict form of tyranny, there is the lawless rule of one man over unwilling subjects".[99] Basically, the sixteenth century European political writers fashioned after Aristotle, have perceived the Ottoman ruler as a despotic tyrant who does not have a legal foundation, remote from justice, cruel, and who does not recognize laws and rules. However, these writers are completely unaware of the ancient Indian-Persian state theory, followed by the Ottoman regime.[100] In this practical state theory, the authority of the ruler is the state itself; the other elements, country-territory, subjects-producer classes are only means for maintaining this authority. The ruler is above the law, customs and practices; however, since his authority is dependent on the material strength provided by the productive classes; he must rule the subjects with justice and forbearance. Thanks to this, the country and consequently the ruler, becomes prosperous and his power increases. Absolute authority is a necessary condition for justice, namely, for the protection of those ruled against the oppression of those in a position of authority. In conclusion, the foundation of the state is justice (the Indian-Persian Circle of Justice theory).

As opposed to the measured observations and interpretations of those who closely followed the operation of the Ottoman regime for many years such as P. Rycaut, S. Gerlach, Chevalier d'Arvieux, Baron de Tott and J. Porter, the travelers and ambassadors left either with incomplete knowledge picked up here and there or misleading portrayals and interpretations, or they recorded some of the striking incidents of the Ottoman regime as its general character. As an example of this final one, we can recall Nicolas de Nicolay,[101] who stated with horror that the *devşirme* (recruiting of Christian boys for the Janissary corps) and the state *kul* institution to be a tyranny in complete violation of humanity. In contrast to this, 0. Busbecq, an ambassador and a humanist with profound perceptions, who came during the reign of Sultan Süleyman the

[99] *The Basic Works of Aristotle,* edition with an introduction by Richard McKeon (New York: Random House, 1941), 1119.

[100] See H. İnalcık, *Osmanlı'da Devlet, Hukuk, Adâlet* (State, Law, Justice in the Ottomans) (İstanbul: Eren Yayınları, 2000).

[101] A. Çırakman, "From Tyranny to Despotism: The Enlightenment's Unenlightened Image of the Turks," *International Journal of Middle Eastern Studies* (2000): 53; see M. Hossain, "l'Empire Ottoman dans les 'Memoires$ et dans les lettres manuscrites du Chevalier d'Arvieux," *Chretiens et Musulmans à la Renaissance,* 177-188; Chevalier d'Arvieux gives detailed information on the Ottoman social life; O. Burian, "Türkiye hakkında dört İngiliz Seyahatnamesi" (Four English travel books about Turkey), *Belleten* 15/58 (1951).

Lawgiver, was able to perceive that the *kul* system was actually a basic institution of the Ottoman autocratic regime.[102]

The eighteenth century Enlightenment Age philosophers, led by Montesquieu, who considered the state to be basically responsible for protecting the individual and his natural rights, would judge the Ottoman regime with this perception. On the other hand, it should be kept in mind that the Ottoman State in the eighteenth century functioned under quite different conditions from those in the sixteenth century.

In the eighteenth century, Western political theoreticians perceived the Ottoman regime, as the result of a rationalist analysis, as an abstract Oriental Despotism type. The most important characteristic of this type of political structure is stated to be the absence of freedom. Montesquieu emphasizes that this type of despotism is unique to Asia, and claims that it is the unavoidable result of climatic conditions and religious beliefs. According to him, the people in these regions, under the backward and immoral administration, are like an obedient and timid herd in the hands of despotic and merciless despots. The geographical conditions and religion have brought the people to this condition.[103] According to Montesquieu, the people from cold climates, the Europeans, are free and enterprising. The political structure in Asia is based on fear, while in Europe it is based on human self-respect, intelligence and virtue. The Asian society has adopted a servile attitude, and is composed of persons who are without security regarding their wealth and property and who idolize their despotic ruler.

With the portrayal of the oriental regimes as despotic, backward and tyrannical regimes that do not recognize the individual and his natural rights, the Enlightenment Age philosophers were in fact trying to criticize their own societies and administrations.[104]

It is noteworthy that recently in his *Oriental Despotism,* K. Wittfogel developed the same theory that despotic regimes in history are a type of government determined by geographical conditions. According to Wittfogel, in Egypt, Mesopotamia and China it was necessary to establish and maintain a huge irrigation system to take under control flooding rivers. In these regions, it became necessary to put the entire population under the command of an absolute power, because any neglect in the canal system results in disaster for everyone. Thus, in these empires, the hydraulic facilities determined the

---

[102] Çırakman, 52; for the *devşirme* and *kul* system see article, "Ghulām" *Encyclopaedia of Islam,* 2d ed., (H. İnalcık); *kuls* (sultan's slaves) formed, in fact, a privileged group instrumental in the ruler's authority.

[103] Çırakman, 56-57.

[104] Ibid., 59.

political regime (hydraulic empires). The bureaucratic (managerial) system created for maintaining the system could only be the work of a despotic will. This despotic administration that can mobilize the labor of the entire population, also found fields of application in other major initiatives, such as the construction of the pyramids. Wittfogel puts other "despotic" empires, including the Ottoman Empire, next to the "hydraulic" empires, but he cannot explain why these despotic empires, which are not "hydraulic" had a despotic character. However, Wittfogel's basic theory on despotism can explain the situation: A vital danger or challenge confronted by the entire society, leads men to enter the command of an absolute authority. We observe this in the creation of all dictatorships. For the Ottomans, from the very beginning, the major challenge that had to be withstood, was the danger of the Crusader campaign coming from Europe. The Ottomans, in their own history starting from 1359, were confronted several times with the danger of being driven from the Balkans to Anatolia. In the period of regression between 1440-1444, the Rumelian Turks were escaping to Anatolia in panic.[105]

The Ottomans, in the life and death struggle against Europe did not only take the weapons and skills of the West without hesitation, but also had to establish an autocratic empire never seen in the Islamic Middle East before them. In the period between 1300-1600 the Ottoman Empire was confronted several times with the threat of division. It is sufficient to remember the Cem Sultan incident (1481-1495). Organizing the Ottoman State on military principles taking the resources of the Empire under the control of an iron hand for the objective of building and defending a vast empire in Anatolia and the Balkans, necessitated state control of the agricultural lands to maintain an extensive *timar* (cavalry) army. Everything should be put under the absolute will of a single authority and all feudal lords in the provinces should be eliminated and the principle of hereditary rights denied.

The Ottomans made their struggle that had the attribute of a *gaza,* holy war that is an overall holy war for Islam and entered into a continuous fight against Christian Europe in the Mediterranean, the Indian Ocean and on the Volga River. Step by step, this fight made the Ottomans gradually more active and they acquired a gradually more expansionist condition and finally brought it to the level of a world empire. In other words, the growth tempo of the Empire was carried out in parallel with the tempo of the life and death struggle with Europe. The history of Europe and the history of the Ottomans are two parallel histories, at least until 1699. For this reason, the history of the two worlds should be studied comparatively. Sultan Mehmed the Conqueror, prior to attacking Constantinople in April 1453, emphasized that the conquest was a

---

[105] H. İnalcık, *Fatih Devri Üzerinde Tetkikler ve Vesikalar* (Ankara, 1954), Chapter 1.

necessity for survival. In the personality of the Conqueror, the typical despotic sultan acquired its final attribute. At the end, in the Ottoman case, the oriental despotism was not the result of geographical conditions or a tradition coming from the Middle Eastern "hydraulic" empires. The 1571 Lepanto naval confrontation is a notable historical event that symbolizes this confrontation in the most dramatic manner.[106]

An explanation of the Ottoman political regime, within the framework of the deterministic view, which has continued since Montesquieu, is also observed in Max Weber. He describes the Ottoman regime as a special form of the patrimonial type of state called autocratic sultanism.[107] According to Weber, an essential difference of the Ottoman sultan from the European patrimonial rulers, as was observed by Machiavelli at one time, is the lack of a class of feudal lords who could put limits on the authority of the ruler, and not having a basic permanent law. The authority of the Ottoman sultan is so absolute that Max Weber ascribes to it the degree of arbitrariness. At the end, he defines sultanism as a form of state in which a hereditary ruler having unlimited, absolute authority is dominant. However, actually the ulema, representing the Islamic Shariah, the hereditary bey families in the frontier regions in the fourteenth and fifteenth centuries, a law regime based on customs and the established bureaucratic rules limited the despotic authority of the sultan. On the other hand, K. Marx and F. Engels, try to explain the Ottoman absolutist regime within the framework of the Asian Mode of Production (AMP) theory. This regime is interpreted as a despotic form of government "confiscating" by force the "surplus product" of the peasantry by the military class. After the Second World War, this method of explanation was accepted by the Balkan, Russian and Hungarian historians, and became the view of an official history.

In particular, ever since the French *Annales* school[108] opened to study the history of society in the light of various objective determinants such as conditions of human geography, economy and mentality, we have started to better understand and interpret Ottoman reality.[109] Even today, when discussing Ottoman realities, most of the modern European historians do not have a different approach most of the time from the writers from the sixteenth to

---

[106] See especially, F. Braudel, *The Mediterranean and the Mediterranean World in the Age of Philip II*, trans. S. Reynolds, vol. 1-2 (New York, 1972-1973).

[107] See H. İnalcık, "Comments on Sultanism: Max Weber's Typification of the Ottoman Polity," *Princeton Papers*, vol. 1.

[108] See the works of T. Stojanovich, P. Burke and I. Wallerstein on the French *Annales* school.

[109] For the influence of the *Annales* school in Turkey see, the publications by Ö. L Barkan and H. İnalcık.

eighteenth centuries. In the past, European thinkers evaluated the Ottoman regime according to Aristotle's tyranny concept or to their own cultural values, in religion, ethics or legal theories. Similarly, the modem historians are also trying to formulate their interpretations according to some sociological theories (Max Weber, K. Wittfogel) or a certain doctrine (Marxism). Today, we are also encountering ethical evaluations of the realistic rules and institutions of the Ottomans, which provided the unity and success of the Ottoman Empire and the dynasty. Each of the particular Ottoman institutions and rules had vital functions in the state. The analytical studies working with the Ottoman archival materials and studying the Ottoman regime, within its own system, have only appeared recently.

The Ottoman State should be considered to be a "European" state at least from the aspect of its territories. A state which was established in Southeastern and Central Europe from Slovakia to Morea, from the Crimea to Buda for five hundred years, has no doubt made not only political, but also cultural influences. In the Balkan countries, the influences of the Ottoman culture have been profound in every field. These influences could not be obliterated up until the present, in spite of all the efforts of the new nation states to erase them. It is sufficient to record only the following. The Turkish words and the Arabic and Persian words through Turkish used today in the Balkan languages vary between 2, 000 to 8, 000 words, depending on the country.[110] Moreover, a major portion of the architectural structures such as mosques, bridges, markets, *bedestans* (vaulted and fireproof part of bazaar where valuable goods are kept), inns, schools and libraries remaining from the Ottoman period in the Balkans and the northern Black Sea region have been destroyed (ninety percent according to M. Kiel) due to lack of maintenance or intentional destruction. We have witnessed in Bosnia-Herzegovina at the present the most recent intentional destruction.

VI. The Ottomans Want to Know the West[111]

Until the appointment of the high-ranking Yirmisekiz Mehmed Çelebi as the ambassador, the Ottoman ambassadors were known at the French court as vulgar, conceited persons. Paris during the reign of Louis XIV (1643-1715) was a center that was an example to the world of French civilization. The ambassadorship of Mehmed Efendi, who visited France's magnificent capital

---

[110] M. Mladenović, "Die Herrschaft der Osmanen in Serbien im Licht der Sprache," *Südost-Forschungen* 20 (1961), 159-203.

[111] B. Lewis, *The Muslim Discovery of Europe* (New York, 1982).

city in 1721, was lived in a completely different atmosphere. It started an intensive mutual cultural influence between France and the Ottoman Empire.

The ambassador, with his large entourage and exotic apparel and lifestyle, attracted intense attention in France. This visit has really become an event in Paris, and the city was busy for months with this unusual delegation and "Excellence Mehmed Efendi" became a general center of attention. In the monthly *Le Nouveau Mercure,* published with the approval of the King, all of the ceremonies and processions in which "Celeby Mehemet effendy, ambassadeur extraordinaire de l'empereur des Turcs auprès de Louis XV, empereur des Français" participated, were described in the finest detail. On 8 March, the ambassador, his entourage and 20 Turkish cavalry settled at the palace at Clarenton where they would stay. Invitations and balls were organized in his honor for days by the King and the high officials. The Paris high society visited him "day and night" and the people of Paris filled the streets during his comings and goings with his large entourage.

As for the political goal of the embassy, in the instructions given to the ambassador by Grand Vizier Damad İbrahim Paşa, it was stated, "to strengthen the former close relations between the two empires". In opposition to the maneuvers initiated by Austria to establish a protectorate over Poland, a joint action was being proposed between France and the Ottomans, just as in the past. The Ottoman government had been closely interested in the Polish problem since 1573. At that time, the Sultan placed Henry from the French Valois dynasty on the Polish throne and always remained alert against the submission of this country under the influence of the Habsburgs or the czars. However, France was not considering action against Austria at that time.[112] At the same time, the ambassador also requested the King to use his influence against the piracies of the knights of Malta who were enslaving Muslims.

Another subject given in the instructions to Mehmed Efendi that is extremely important was coming onto the agenda for the first time. Mehmed Efendi was requested "to investigate thoroughly the instruments of civilization and education and would submit those that could be implemented" to the Sultan Damad İbrahim, who was an open-minded, liberal reformist, wanted to obtain information on the government affairs in France, the wealth of which he admired, and wanted to obtain information on Law's paper currency system, particularly for eliminating state debts (the Law system in France collapsed in 1720 and paved the way for social turmoil). (The Ottomans had tried to use paper currency once in the years after the defeat in Vienna in 1683). For that reason, the French government did not see any use politically for the Ottoman ambassador's visit. Nevertheless, the French palace was pleased with the visit

---

[112] G. Veinstein, *Le paradis des infidèles* (Paris, 1981), 26-27.

of an ambassador holding the same rank and level of the ambassadors sent by the Ottoman sultan to the emperor, so a more pompous reception than usual was given for Mehmed Efendi.

The reception ceremony of the King at the Tuileries Palace on 21 March 1721 was described in all of its details. In the ceremony, the King came with the princes and sat on the throne. The ambassador presented the sultan's letter with a short speech. He started his speech by saying, "what a great honor it is to be appointed for this high duty granting the honor of seeing the face of a great emperor, like a bright sun".

In the letter presented to Le Duc d'Orléans, the regent of the Kingdom, which is considered to be at the same level as the Grand Vizier, "the sincere and continuous friendship that has continued between the two empires from time immemorial" was being expressed. In April, Mehmed Efendi gave permission for his portrait to be painted and accepted M. Bignon, a scientist. Mehmed Efendi obtained information from him about the most noteworthy sciences and arts in France. When the subject came to eastern and western music, Mehmed Efendi showed that he had extensive knowledge on the subject with the indication that the French method of musical notation appeared to be simpler. Later, he listened to a concert from selected symphonies at the palace of Maréchal Villeroi.

In the years of disaster and defeat between 1683 and 1699, a revolution occurred in the mentality of the Ottomans. The Ottomans, who had belittled everything about Europe until that time, accepted the superiority of the West in that period. Thus, the first psychological condition for westernization, the revolution in mentality and behavior, was realized. In the Istanbul high society, Dimitrie Cantemir, a Romanian intellectual, was someone who was familiar with Western humanism and was the close friend of Rami Mehmed Efendi, the Ottoman Minister of Foreign Affairs. After he signed the peace agreement with the title of chief delegate at Karlowitz in 1699, he became the Grand Vizier and adopted for the first time a westernization policy for development.[113] However, as the result of the interferences in state affairs by Sheikh ul-lslam Feyzullah Efendi, the 1703 uprising and the change in the sultanate deprived Rami Paşa of implementing reform. The reformist bureaucracy, that perceived the necessity of adopting the sciences and technology of the West and advances in education, once again came to office in 1718 together with Grand Vizier Damad İbrahim Paşa. The appointment in 1721 of Yirmisekiz Mehmed Efendi as an ambassador to France was directly related to this interest in Western civilization.

---

[113] H. İnalcık, "Eastern and Western Cultures in Dimitrie Cantemir's Work," *Revue Roumaine d'Histoire,* 13 (1974), 27-29.

Upon Mehmed Efendi's return, Sultan Ahmed, the Grand Vizier ibrahim Paşa and the high officials, who particularly wanted to learn about European advancements in technology and science, bombarded him with questions and asked him to write down what he had seen. The Grand Vizier was so pleased about the unbelievable, marvelous things he was told, he said that if it were possible he would also like to go to France. The idea of paper currency as an instrument to save the treasury from debts was believed to be an excellent idea. The detailed information Mehmed Efendi gave on the river canal at Languedoc was the subject of intense curiosity. Mehmed Efendi attracted the interest of the palace, besides technology, especially on the luxurious French palaces and gardens. In his *Sefaretname* (a report of his observations in France) he added quite extensive information about the free and luxurious lives of the French women. Among the things that İbrahim Paşa requested from Marquis de Bonnac, the French ambassador to Istanbul, binoculars, microscope, engravings of chateaus and gardens, French cloth materials and a parrot are noteworthy. Thus, an *alafranga* (European) fashion was started in the court circles in Istanbul.

Mehmed Efendi, in his *Sefaretname,* by reminding about the hadith that this world is the "heaven of non-Muslims", but the hereafter is the "heaven of Muslim believers", tried to console his readers. When Damad Paşa wanted to bring the "heaven of non-Muslims" by making French style villas and gardens at the Kâğıthane district in Istanbul, a great commotion occurred. The reaction of the people in 1730 erupted with the Patrona Halil rebellion. Sultan Ahmed III and his son-in-law ibrahim were eliminated. This closed the "Europeanization" period for a long time. The luxurious life and wasteful practices of the palace in contrast to the increasing poverty of the common people caused the reaction against "Europeanization". Mehmed Efendi was exiled to Cyprus. In the past, the idea of a clock tower during the reign of the Lawgiver was not accepted because it was perceived as an interference with the job of the *muezzins*.

Mehmed Efendi's son Said Efendi, who had the opportunity to mingle with the people in Paris, was roaming freely in the city. He had even learned a bit of French and he was particularly interested in the printing press. Later, Said Efendi found İbrahim Muteferrika, who was of Hungarian origin, and thanks to his knowledge, he established the first printing press in Istanbul (permission was obtained in 1727 and the book, *Vankulu Lûgatı* (Dictionary) was printed in 1729).[114] The *Sheikh ul-Islam*, in the *fetva* (fatwa) giving permission for the

---

[114] G. Káldy- Nagy, "Beginning of the Arabic-letter Printing in the Muslim World," *The Muslim East Studies,* ed. G. Káldy-Nagy, (Budapest, 1974); Erhan Afyoncu, "İbrahim Müteferrika," *TDVİA,* vol. 21; O. Keskioğlu, "Türkiye'de Matbaa Tesisi ve Mushaf

printing press, gave further allowance for the printing of books other than religious works. Müteferrika, when publishing Kâtib Çelebi's *Cihannümâ,* for the first time described the astronomy of Copernicus and the system of the universe in the introduction. This printing house was closed in 1742. It was reactivated in 1784 during the period when reformist bureaucrats came to power.

VII. The Coffee and Coffeehouse of the Ottomans in Europe

Here let us discuss coffee and the coffeehouse as an example of the Ottoman cultural influence that spread in the West. R. Hattox and Desmet-Grégoire[115] tried to explain why and how coffee and coffeehouses became widespread in the Ottoman lands and France. Coffeehouses were first widespread at the Levant trade center of Marseilles in the 1660s. In 1669 Süleyman Ağa, the Ottoman ambassador, introduced the custom of drinking coffee in Paris, and the custom became fashionable among the aristocrats. An Armenian named Pascal opened the first coffee shop in Paris.

Coffee that originated in Ethiopia spread first in Yemen. The custom of drinking coffee, like opium, was widespread among the sufis. Around the middle of the fifteenth century, it spread to the other Islamic countries, starting in Hejaz and Egypt. Then, the pilgrims from Turkey must have been familiar with coffee in Hejaz. Because it was "intoxicating" and made one feel dizzy, coffee, like wine, was initially considered by the ulemas to be against the Islamic religion. We come across the first record about the prohibition of coffee in Mecca in 1511. According to rumor, Sultan Selim had the coffee drinkers in Cairo executed in 1517. Besides the stimulating effects of coffee, its medicinal benefits were recognized and this led to its spread in the Ottoman lands and

---

Basımı" (Printing facility in Turkey and printing of the Holy Koran), *İlâhiyat Fakültesi Dergisi* 15 (1967): 121-139; Peçuyî (Peçevî) (I, 106-107) made an extensive description, according to the Hungarian sources, of the printing press and stated its benefit in the spreading of science; in general, for the westernization in the Ottomans in this period see Niyazi Berkes, *The Development of Secularism in Turkey* (Montreal, 1964); Bernard Lewis, *The Muslim Discovery of Europe* (New York, 1982); B. Lewis, *Istanbul and the Civilization of the Ottoman Empire* (Norman: University of Oklahoma Press, 1963).

[115] R. Hattox, *Coffee and Coffee houses* (Seattle: University of Washington Press, 1995); E. Birnbaum, "Vice Triumphant: the Spread of Coffee and Tobacco in Turkey," *Durham University Journal* (December 1956): 11-17; As for the *Karagöz* entertainment spread in Europe, see W. Puchner, "Das osmanische Schattentheater auf der balkan Halbinsel," *Südost-Forschungen* 19 (1960): 151-188.

France.[116] In the portrayals of the coffeehouse in the sixteenth century Turkish miniatures show that the custom had become rather widespread at that time. In 1585, Morosini, the Venetian Ambassador at the Sublime Porte in Istanbul portrayed a coffeehouse. The coffeehouse, as a social meeting place, seems to have replaced the former *bozahanes* (place where *boza,* beverage made of fermented millet, is drunk). The places and number of bozahanes, which met the social communication needs and where public opinion against the administrators was formed, were limited by the state and kept under control. Later on, these prohibitions were applied to the coffeehouses. In other words, the meeting places where boza or coffee was drunk paved the way for the formation of an important social institution, so that the spread of the Ottoman coffeehouses in Europe is important. This expresses the borrowing of a social institution rather than the borrowing of a substance. Prior to the coffeehouse the boza-*hane* in the Ottoman society fulfilled the function of a social gathering place equivalent to the bar or pub of the Christians. The coffeehouses spread rapidly throughout the Ottoman Empire. Thirteen coffeehouses were counted in Kameniçe, a city in Poland distant from Istanbul, in the 1670s. In the second half of the seventeenth century, *şerbet* (sherbet, sweet fruit drink) and coffee were served to the ambassadors who came to the Ottoman Empire. The Yemen coffee became a major article of trade centered in Cairo. Even though the Europeans took coffee to Brazil and grew it there, the best quality coffee was always grown in Yemen. In 1640, Brazilian coffee is mentioned in the Ottoman official price list register. However, the quality and price of the Yemen coffee was always higher. In the Turkish daily life, drinking coffee after each meal or after the drinking feast was a custom.

> Ba'de mestî ehl-i keyfin keyfini kim tâzeler,
> Tâze elden tâze pişmiş tâze kahve tâzeler.

(Who refreshes the pleasure of a pleasure-seeking person who became drunk with drinking,
Fresh coffee, freshly prepared and served by fresh [young] hands, refreshes him).

According to the historian Peçuyî (d. 1649?) there was no coffee or coffeehouse in Istanbul and Rumelia until 1554. That year, two persons, Hakem from Aleppo and Şems from Damascus, came to Istanbul and each opened a

---

[116] H. Desmet-Grégoire, *Le Divan Magique, l'Orient turc en France au XVIIIe siècle* (Paris, 1996), 64-71; Hattox, 69.

large shop in the Tahtakale district and started to sell coffee. "Some pleasure-seeking people who are addicted to pleasures, especially many refined people from the literate category gathered and started to form groups in twenty to thirty places. Some of them read books and entertaining pamphlets, some played backgammon and chess, some recited their original *gazels* (lyric poetry) with new images, talked about literary styles, gathered by giving one or two akçes to someone who organized feasts to form friendship gatherings and then spending their money generously they enjoyed the pleasure of gathering. The Coffeehouse became so popular that the dismissed officials and cadis staying in Istanbul and *medrese* (madrasa) teachers and the idle people without any earnings, by saying that there is no place like this to entertain oneself and comfort one's heart, filled these places such that there was no more room to sit or stand and all of these places became so famous, besides those high dignitaries, distinguished people started to come involuntarily. The imams and the muezzins and the deceitful Sufis and the people became addicted to the coffeehouse. They said that no one went to the masjids anymore. As for the ulemas, they said it is a house of evil [coffeehouse], it is better to go to a bar rather than to that place and the preachers tried very hard to ban it and the muftis gave fatwas saying that when a thing reaches the state of carbon, that is becomes coal, is forbidden by religion." "The coffeehouses were forbidden by Sultan Murad III (1574-1595). However, the coffeehouses appeared in dead-end streets and at the back of shops. But after that century, the coffeehouses became so popular that they could not be closed. The preachers and muftis started to say, 'Evidently, it does not reach the state of coal and it is religiously permissible to drink it'. There was no one left from among the ulemas and sheikhs and viziers and the distinguished who did not drink it; moreover, it came to such a point that the grand viziers established coffeehouses for profit and started to receive two gold coins per day in rent."[117]

The Greeks and Armenians who settled in France taught the French how to make Ottoman coffee and the custom of the coffeehouse. The coffeehouse became a part of the social life in the European cities in the eighteenth century that remained as an attractive part of European culture to this day.

---

[117] *Tarîh-i Peçuyî* (İstanbul: Enderun, 1980), 363-365.

Bibliography

A. Cevdet Paşa: *Tezâkir*, ed. C. Baysun, vols. I-IV, Ankara: Türk Tarih Kurumu, 1986.

Adıvar, A.A.: *La Science chez les Turcs Ottomans*, Paris, 1939.

Afyoncu, Erhan: "İbrahim Müteferrika, *TDVİA*, vol. 21;

Agoston, G.: "Muslim-Christian Acculturation: Ottomans and Hungarians from Fifteenth to the Seventeenth Centuries," *Chrétiens et Musulmans a la Renaissance*, 293-303.

Agoston, G.: "Ottoman artillery and European Military Technology in the Fifteenth and Seventeenth Centuries," *AOASH* 47, 1994.

Ahmet Cevdet Paşa, *Tarih-i Cevdet*, 2nd edition İstanbul, vol. XI, 1309 H., pp. 156-161, 181.

Akdağ, M.: *Celâli İsyanları, (1550-1603)*. Ankara, 1963.

Alberi, E.: *Le relazioni degli ambasciatori Veneti al Senato durante il secolo decimosesto*, Florence, 1839-1863.

Albert, E. M.: "Value Systems," *International Encyclopedia of Social Sciences*.

al-Fuwāṭī, Ibn: *Al-Ḥawādith al-Jāmi'a*, ed. M. Jawād, Baghdad, 1951.

al-Khoyī, Hasan *Gunyet'ul-Kātib ve Munyet'I-Ṭālib*, ed. A. Erzi (Ankara, 1963); the work was written in 690/1291, the MS published was copied in 879/1474.

Allen, W.E.D. 1963. *Problems of Turkish Power in the Sixteenth Century*. London.

And, M. 1963-4. *A History of Theatre and Popular Entertainment in Turkey*, Forum. Ankara.

Anderson, P.: *Lineages of the Absolutist State*, London, 1974.

Anderson, *The Eastern Question*, pp. 47-8.

Appadurai, A. (ed.), *Social Life of Things, Commodities in Cultural Perspective*, Cambridge: Cambridge University Press, 1986.

Arrow, K.: "Classificatory Notes on the Production and Transmission of Technological Knowledge, " *American Economic Review*, Papers and Proceedings 59, 29-35.

Atatürk, Gazi Mustafa Kemal: *Nutuk*, II, İstanbul: Türk Devrim Tarihi Enstitüsü, 1961.

Atatürk, Mustafa Kemal: *A Speech*, Leipzig, 1929.

Atatürk'ün Söylev ve Demeçleri, vol. I-III, İstanbul: Türk Inkilâp Tarihi Enstitüsü Yayımları I, 1945.

Babinger, F.: "Maometto II il Conquistatore e l'Italia," *Revista Storica Italiana* 63 (1951), Turkish translation, "Fatih Sultan Mehmed ve İtalya" (Sultan Mehmed the Conqueror and Italy), trans. B. S. Baykal, *Belleten* 17/65 (1953): 41-82.

Babinger, F.: "Vier Bauvorschläge Lenonardo da Vincis an Sultan Bayazid II," *Nachr. Der Akad. Der Vissens. in Göttingen*, Phil. Hist. Kl. No. 1, 1958.

Bacqué-Grammont, J-L.; Kroell, A. 1988. *Mamlouks, Ottomans et Portugais en Mer Rouge*. Cairo.

Bailey, F.E.: *British Policy and the Turkish Reform Movement*, Cambridge, Mass., 1942.

Bak, J. M. and B. K. Király: (eds.), *From Hunyadi to Rákózi: War and Society in Late Medieval and Early Modern Hungary,* Brooklyn, 1982.

Balard, M.: *La Romanie Génoise,* vol. 2, Paris, 1978.

Barber, B.: *Science and the Social Order,* Glencoe: Free Press, 1952.

Barkan, Ö.L. 1975. The Price Revolution of the Sixteenth Century. *International Journal of Middle East Studies,* vol. VI, no. I.

Bayerle, G.: "One Hundred Fifty Years of Frontier Life in Hungary," *From Hunyadi to Rákóczi,* 227-231. XXX

Bear, G.: *Egyptian Guilds in Modern Times,* Jerusalem, 1964.

Berkes, Niyazi: *The Development of Secularism in Turkey,* Montreal: McGill University Press, 1964.

Beydilli, Kemal: *Türk Bilim ve Matbaacılık Tarihinde Mühendishane, Matbaa ve Kütüphane (1776-1826)* [The school of engineering, printing press and library in the history of Turkish science and printing (1776-1826)]. İstanbul: Eren Yayınları, 1995.

Bilsel, Cemil: *Lozan,* II, İstanbul 1933.

Birge, J.B. 1937. *The Bektashi Order of Dervishes.* London.

Birnbaum, E.: "Vice Triumphant: the Spread of Coffee and Tobacco in Turkey," *Durham University Journal* (December 1956): 11-17.

Bodin, J.: *Les Six livres de La Républigue,* Paris, 1583.

Booth, A.: and R. M. Sundrum, *Labor Absorption in Agriculture,* London, 1985.

Boratav, Korkut: *Tarımsal Yapılar ve Kapitalizm,* Ankara, 1980.

Boros, A.: "The Militia Portalis in Hungary before 1526", *From Hunyadi to Ràkoczi* (Brooklyn, 1982), 63-80.

Bourdeille, Pierre de: *Oeuvres complètes,* ed. L. Lalande, vol. 11, 179.

Braudel, F. 1949. *La Méditerranée et le monde méditerranéen à l'époque de Philippe II.* Paris. [English trans. Reynold, S. 1972. *The Mediterranean and the Mediterranean World in the Age of Philip II.* New York.]

Braudel, F.: *The Mediterranean* or *the Mediterranean World in the Age of Philip II,* trans. S. Reynolds, vol. 1-2, New York, 1972-1973.

Burian, O.: "Türkiye hakkında dört İngiliz Seyahatnamesi" [Four English travel books about Turkey], *Belleten* 15/58, (1951).

C. Gauthier, "Un allemand à Constantinople, 1571-1581, Critique du Coran par un pasteur Lutheran," *Chrétiens et Musulmans à la Renaissance,* eds. B. Bennassar and R. Sauzet (Paris, 1998), 163-175.

Cahen, C.: "Y a-t il eu des Corporations professionnelles dans le monde musulman classique," *The Islamic City,* ed. A. H. Hourani and S. H. Stern (Philadelphia), pp. 51-63.

Cebesoy, A. H Fuat: *Millî Mücadele Hatıraları,* İstanbul 1953.

Cebesoy, A. H Fuat: *Siyasî Hatıralar,* 2 vols, İstanbul 1957, 1960.

Charrière, E.: *Négociations de la France dans le Levant,* vols. 1-4, Paris, 1848-1860.

Charrière, E.: *Paléographie Universelle* (Paris, 1839) and by R. Yinanc, *DTCF Dergisi* 8-12 (1975), 96.

Chayanov, A. V.: *The Theory of Peasant Economy,* eds. D. Thorner, Basile Kerblay, and R. E. F. Smith, with a foreword by Teodor Shanin, Madison, 1986.

Choné, Paulette: "Le portrait du Turc, les artistes devant le reve héroique de la Maison de Lorraine (XVI-XVIIe siècles), " *Chrétiens et Musulmans à la Renaissance,* 61-75.

Cipolla, C.: Guns,: *Sails, and Empires: Technological Innovation and Early Phases of European Expansion, 1400-1700,* New York, 1965.

Çırakman, A.: "From Tyranny to Despotism: The Enlightenment's Unenlightened Image of the Turks," *International Journal of Middle Eastern Studies* (2000): 53.

D'Ohsson, I. M.: *Tableau Général d'Empire Ottoman,* 7 vols. Paris, 1783-1824.

Darling, L.: "The Ottoman Finance Department and the Assessment and Collection of the Cizye and Avariz Taxes, 1560-1660," Ph.D. diss., University of Chicago, 1989.

Decei, A.: "Aloisio Gritti au service de Soliman Le Magnifique d'après des documents turcs inédits (1533-1534), XXX

Delbrück, H.: *The Dawn of Modern Warfare,* trans. W. J. Rénfroe, Jr., Lincoln and London: Univ. of Nebraska Press, 1985.

Deny, J.: *"Les* pseudo-propheties concernant les turcs au XVIe siècle," *Revue des Etudes Islamiques* 10 (1936).

Desmet-Grégoire, H.: *Le Divan Magique,* Paris, 1998.

Deswarte-Rosa, S.: "L'expédition de Tunis (1535)," Chr*étiens et Musulmans à la Renaissance,* Actes de 37. Colloque International du CESR (1994), eds. B. Bennassar, and R. Sauzet, Paris, 1998.

Dieterici, F.: (ed.), *Al Fārābī's Abhandlung der Musterstaat,* Leiden, 1964, pp. 55, 187.

Ducellier, A.: "Byzantins et Turcs du XIIe au XVI siècle," *Chrétiens et Musulmans à la Renaissance,* 11-49.

Eldem, E., D. Goffman, and B. Masters, *The Ottoman City Between East and West: Aleppo, İzmir and Istanbul,* Cambridge: Cambridge University Press, 1999.

Eldem, E.: *French Trade in Istanbul in the Eighteenth Century,* Leiden: Brill, 1999.

Elliott, J.: "Ottoman-Habsburg Rivalry: The European Perspective, " *Süleyman the Second and His Time,* İstanbul: ISIS, 1993, 153-162.

Evliya Çelebi, Seyāḥatnāme, Vol. 2: İstanbul, 1314-1898, 90-91, 213.

Faroqhi, S. 1984. *Towns and Townsmen of Otoman Anatolia, Crafts and Food Production in the Urban Setting.* Cambridge.

_____. 1987. *Men of Modest Substance: House-Owners and House Property in Seventeenth-Century Ankara and Kayseri.* Cambridge.

Fawaz, L.T.: *Merchants and Migrants in Nineteenth-Century Beirut,* Cambridge: Cambridge University Press, 1983.

Fazlur Rahman: *Islam,* New York: Anchor Books, 1968.

Feneşan, C. and J. L Bacqué-Grammont: *Anatolia Moderna-Yeni Anadolu,* vol. 3 (1992), 1-103.

Ferīdūn, *Munsha'āt al-Salāṭīn,* vol. 1, İstanbul, 1274/1857.

Findley, C.: *Bureaucratic Reform in the Ottoman Empire: The Sublime Porte. 1789-1922,* Princeton, 1980.

Finkel, C.: *The Administration of Warfare: The Ottoman Military Campaigns in Hungary, 1593-1606,* Vienna, 1987.

Fischer-Galati, S. A.: *Ottoman Imperialism and German Protestantism,* Cambridge, Mass., 1959.

Flachat, *Observations sur le commerce et les arts d'une partie de l'Europe et de l'Asie, de l'Afrique et même de Indes orientales.* Lyon, 1766.

Fleischer, C. H.: "Royal Authority, Dynastic Cyclism, and 'Ibn Khaldunism in sixteenth Century Ottoman Letters," *Journal of Asian and African Studies* (1983), pp. 198-220.

Fleischer, C. H.: *Bureaucrat and Intellectual in the Ottoman Empire: The Historian Muṣṭafā 'Ālī (1541-1600),* Princeton: Princeton University Press, 1986.

Fontenay. M.: "Le commerce de occidentaux dans les écnelles du Levant vers la fin du XVIIe siècle, " *Chrétiens et Musulmans à le Renaissance,* 337-370.

Frye, *The Heritage of Persia,* Cleveland and New York, 1963.

Geertz, C.: *The Interpretation of Cultures,* New York: Basic Books, 1973.

Gibb, H. A. R.: *Modern Trends in Islam,* Chicago 1947.

Giese, F.: (ed.), *Anonim Tevârîh-i Âl-i Osman* [Anonymous history of the Ottoman Dynasty], Breslau, 1922.

Gimpel, J.: *The Medieval Machine,* London, 1977.

Göçek, F. M.: *East Encounters West, France and the Ottoman Empire in the Eighteenth Century,* New York and London, 1987.

Gökalp, Ziya: *Turkish Nationalism and Western Civilization,* trans, and pub. Niyazi Berkes (New York: Columbia University Press, 1959);

Göllner, C.: "Die Türkenfrage in Spannungsfeld der Reformation," *Südost-Forschungen* 34 (1975), 61-78.

Göllner, C.: *Turcica, Die Europaischer Türckendrücke des XVI Jahrhundert, 1551-1606,* vols. 1-2, Bucharest and Berlin, 1961.

Goloğlu, Mahmut: *Devrim ve Tepkileri,* 1924-1930, Ankara, 1972.

Hagen, E. E.: *On the Theory of Social Change,* Homewood: Dorsey, 1962.

Hajjī Khalīfe, *Destūr al-'Amel li-Islāḥ al-Khalel,* İstanbul 1280/1863.

Hammer, J. von: *Devlet-i Osmaniye Tarihi,* [History of the Ottoman state], trans. M. Atâ, vol. 5, İstanbul, AH 1330.

Hasluck, F. W.: *Christianity and Islam under the Sultans,* vols. 1-2, Oxford, 1929.

Hattox, R.: *Coffee and Coffee houses,* Seattle: University of Washington Press, 1995.

Heyd, U.: *Studies in Old Ottoman Criminal Law,* ed. V. L. Menage, Oxford, 1973.

Hilâfet ve Milli Hâkimiyet, hilâfet ve millî hakimiyet mesâili hakkında muhtelif zevâtın makâlât ve mütâliâtından mürekkep bir risâledir. Ankara: Matbuât ve istihbârât müdiriyet-i umumiyesi neşriyatından no. 32, 1339/1923.

Hossain, M.: "l'Empire Ottoman dans les 'Memoires' et dans les lettres manuscrites du Chevalier d'Arvieux," *Chretiens et Musulmans à la Renaissance,* 177-188.

İbrahim Peçevi, *Tarîh-i Peçuyî,* I-II, facsimile edition, İstanbul: Enderun, 1980.

İhsanoğlu, E.: (ed.), *Osmanlılar ve Batı Teknolojisi, Yeni Araştırmalar, Yeni Görüşler,* [The Ottomans and Western technology, new studies, new views], İstanbul, 1992.

İnalcık, H. and M. Oğuz (eds.), *Gazavât-i Sultan Murâd b. Mehemmed Hân* [The military expeditions of Sultan Murâd b. Mehemmed Hân], Ankara: Türk Tarih Kurumu, 1978.

İnalcık, H.: "Eastern and Western Cultures in Dimitrie Cantemir's Work," *Revue Roumaine d'Histoire,* 13 (1974), 27-29.

İnalcık, H.: "İmtiyazat" [privileges], in *EI2*, III, 1179-89.

İnalcık, H.: "Military and Fiscal Transformation in the Ottoman Empire", *AO*, VI, (1980), 283-337.

İnalcık, H.: "Ottoman Methods of Conquest," *Studia Islamica, 2* (1954), 103-129.

İnalcık, H.: "Eastern and Western Cultures in Dimitrie Cantemir's Work," H. İnalcık, *The Middle East and the Balkans under the Ottoman Empire*, Bloomington: Indiana University Turkish Studies 1993, 412-416.

İnalcık, H.: "Ghulam" *Encyclopaedia of Islam,* 2d ed.

İnalcık, H.: "Maṭbakh" *Encyclopaedia of Islam,* 2d ed. (*EI²* hereafter), p. 810.

İnalcık, H.: "Military and Fiscal Transformation in the Ottoman Empire, 1600-1700," *Archivum Ottomanicum,* 6 (1980): 283-337.

İnalcık, H.: "Murad, II." *İslam Ansiklopedisi.*

İnalcık, H.: "Pâdişâh" *Islâm Ansiklopedisi,* IX:491-95.

İnalcık, H.: "Rice Cultivation and the çeltükci-Re'âyâ System in the Ottoman Empire," *Turcia* 14 (1982): 69-141.

İnalcık, H.: "State, Lond, and Peasant," in H. Inalcik, et al., *The Ottoman Empire: Economy and Society, 1300-1900* (forthcoming).

İnalcık, H.: "State, Sovereignty and Law During the Reign of Süleyman I," to be published in the Proceedings of the Conferences on Süleyman the Magnificent (Chicago and Princeton, June 1987).

İnalcık, H.: "The Appointment Procedure of a Guild Warden (Ketkhudā)," WZKM, 76 (1986), *Festschrift Andreas Tietze:* 135-142.

İnalcık, H.: "The Question of the Emergence of the Ottoman State," *International Journal of Turkish Studies,* 2/2 (1981-1982), pp. 72-79.

İnalcık, H.: *The Middle East and the Balkans under the Ottoman Empire,* Bloomington, 1993.

İnalcık, H.: *The Ottoman Empire: The Classical Age* (London, 1973), illustration numbers 14 and 16.

İnalcık, H. "Adâletnâmeler," *Belgeler,* II (1965): 49-145.

İnalcık, H. and Quataert, D. (eds.), *An Economic and Social History of the Ottoman Empire,* Cambridge University Press, 1994.

İnalcık, H.: "Comments on Sultanism: Max Weber's Typification of the Ottoman Polity," *Princeton Papers,* vol. 1.

İnalcık, H.: "The Question of the Emergence of the Ottoman State, " *International Journal of Turkish Studies,* 2-2 (1981-1982), 71-78.

İnalcık, H.: "Ḳānūn" *Encyclopaedia of Islam,* 2nd ed. IV, 556-562.

İnalcık, H.: "Ḳānunnâme" (H.I.) *EI²*, IV, 562-566.

İnalcık, H.: "Bursa," *Belleten,* 24 (Ankara, 1960): 45-102.

İnalcık, H.: "Osmanlılar'da Saltanat Verâset Usûlü ve Türk Hakimiyet Telakkisiyle İlgisi," *Siyasal Bilgiler Fk. Dergisi,* XIV (1959): 575-610.

İnalcık, H.: "Osmanlılarda Raiyyet Rüsûmu," *Belleten,* 23, 195, 575-616.

İnalcık, H.: "Reîs-ul-Küttâb," *İA,* 9, 671-83.

İnalcık, H.: "Sened-i Ittifak ve Gülhâne Hatt-i Humâyunu," *Belleten,* 28 (1964): 603-22.

İnalcık, H.: "The Khan and Tribal Aristocracy: The Crimean Khanate under Sahib Giray I," *Harvard Ukrainian Studies,* 3-4 (1979-80): 445-66.

İnalcık, H.: "The Socio-political effects of the diffusion of fire-arms in the Middle East," eds. V. J. Parry, and M. E. Yapp; *War, Technology and Society in the Middle East,* London, 1975, 195-217.

İnalcık, H.: "The Status of the Greek Orthodox Patriarch under the Ottomans," *Essays in Ottoman History* (İstanbul: Eren Yayınları, n.d.), 195-223.

İnalcık, H.: *"The Yürüks, their origins, expansion and economic role",* Oriental Carpet and Textile Studies, II, Carpets of the Mediterranean, 1400-1600, eds. R. Pinner, and W. B. Denny, (London, 1986): pp. 39-65.

İnalcık, H. 1969-89. The Otoman Turks and the Crusades. In: Hazard, H.V.; Zakour, N.P. (eds) *The Impact of the Crusades on Europe.* Setton, K.M. (general ed.). *A History of the Crusades. Vol. VI.* Madison, University of Wisconsin Pres.

İnalcık, H.: *Fatih Devri üzerinde Tetkikler ve Vesikalar,* Ankara, 1954.

İnalcık, H.; Quataert, D. (eds) 1994. *An Economic and Social History of the Ottoman Empire.* Cambridge.

İnalcık, H.: *Osmanlı İmparatorluğunun Ekonomik ve Sosyal Tarihi I, 1300-1600* [The Economic and Social History of the Ottoman Empire, I, 1300-1600], İstanbul: Eren Yayınları, 2000, 283-296.

İnalcık, H.: *Osmanlı'da Devlet, Hukuk, Adâlet* (State, law, justice in the Ottomans) (İstanbul: Eren Yayınları, 2000).

Isom-Verhaaren, C.: "An Ottoman Report about Martin Luther and the Emperor: New Evidence of the Ottoman Interest in the Protestant Challenge to the Power of Charles V, " *Turcica* 28 (1996): 299-318.

Isom-Verhaaren, C.: "Ottoman-French Interact 1480-1580: A Sixteenth Century Encounter" (Ph. D. diss., University of Chicago, Department of History, 1997).

Jones, E. L.: *The European Miracle,* Cambridge, 1982.

Jorga, N.: *Byzance après Byzance,* Bucharest, 1935.

Káldy-Nagy, G.: "Beginning of the Arabic-letter Printing in the Muslim World," *The Muslim East Studies,* ed. G. Káldy-Nagy, (Budapest, 1974);

Karal E.Z.: (ed.) *Atatürk'ten Düşünceler,* [Thoughts from Atatürk], Ankara: Türkiye İş Bankası Yayınları, 1969.

Kelenik, J.: "The Military Revolution in Hungary," *The Ottoman,* eds. G. Dávid and P. Fodor, 117-159; "Oriental Influences on Occidental Military Music," *Islamic Culture* 15 (1941): 235-242.

Kellenbenz, H.: *Technology in the Age of the Scientific Revolution, 1500-1700,* London: Fontana/Collins, 1974.

Keskioğlu, O.: "Türkiye'de Matbaa Tesisi ve Mushaf Basımı" (Printing facility in Turkey and printing of the Holy Koran), *İlâhiyat Fakültesi Dergisi* 15 (1967): 121-139.

Keyder, Çağlar et al. *Doğu Akdeniz'de Liman Kentleri,* [The port cities at the Eastern Mediterranean], İstanbul: Tarih Vakfı Yayını, 1993.

Kınalı-zāde 'Alā al-Dīn 'Alī: *Akhlāḳ-i 'Alā 'ī,* Bulak, 1248/1832.

Kocatürk, Utkan: *Atatürk ve Türk Devrimi Kronolojisi,* Türk Inkilâp Tarihi Enstitüsü Yayımları, Ankara 1973.

Kortepeter, C. M.: *Ottoman Imperialism during the Reformation,1578-1608,* New York, 1972.

Kremer, A. von: *Kulturgeschichte des Orients unter den Chalifen,* Vienna, 1875 and 1877.

Laval, André: *Voyages en Levant pendant Its XVIe, VIIe et XVIIIe siècles,* Budapest, 1897.

Lewis, Bernard: *Istanbul and the Civilization of the Ottoman Empire,* Norman: University of Oklahoma Press, 1963.

Lewis, Bernard: *The Muslim Discovery of Europe,* New York, 1982.

Lewis, Bernard: *The Political Language of Islam,* Chicago and London, 1988.

Lewis, B. 1953. The Impact of the French Revolution on Turkey. *Journal of World History,* vol. I, pp. 105-25.

M. 'Ârif, edited by "Kānūnnāme-i Āl-i 'Oṣmān," *TOEM,* Supplement (İstanbul, 1330/1914), p. 27.

Machiavelli, N.: *The Pirince,* trans. T. G. Bergin, Arlington Heights, 1986 reprint of 1947.

Madelung, W.: "The Assumption of the Title Shāhānshāh by the Buyids and The Reign of the Daylam," *Middle Eastern Studies,* pp. 28, 84-108, 169-83.

Mallet, M. E.: *Mercenaries and their Masters, Warfare in Renaissance Italy,* Totowa: Roman and Littlefield, 1924.

Margolin, J. C.: "Réflexion sur le commentaire du Père Celestin, Pierre Crespet de la lettre du Pape Pie II au Sultan Mahomet II," *Chrétiens et Musulmans à la Renaissance,* 212-239.

Mas, A.: *Les Turcs dans la litérature espagnole,* vols. 1-2 (Paris, 1967); "... La Peau de Mahomet... Images du Maure et de l'oriental dans le spectacle anglais de La Renaissance, " *Chrétiens et Musulmans à la Renaissance,* 189-212.

Masson, P.: *Histoire du Commerce Français dans le Levant,* vols. 1-2, Paris, 1928.

McKeon, Richard (edition with an introduction by): *The Basic Works of Aristotle,* New York: Random House, 1941.

Merton, R. K.: *Social Theory and Social Structure,* part 4; Glencoe: Free Press, 1949.

Michaud, C.: "Les Turcs dans I'Histoire Universelle de Jacques-Auquste de Thou," *Chrétiens et Musulmans à la Renaissance,* 241-253.

Miller, B. 1941. *The Palace School of Muhammed the Conqueror.* Cambridge.

Mladenovic, M.: "Die Herrschaft der Osmanen in Serbien im Licht der Sprache," *Südost-Forschungen* 20 (1961), 159-203.

Mottahedeh, R.: *Loyalty and Leadership in an Early Islamic Society,* Princeton, 1980.

Necipoğlu, Gülru: "Süleyman the Magnificent and the Representation of Power in the Context of Ottoman Hapsburg-Papal Rivalry," *Süleyman the Second and His Time,* eds. H. İnalcık, and C. Kafadar, İstanbul: ISIS, 1993, 163-194.

Nicol, D. M.: *On the Origin of the Ottoman Emperors,* Cambridge: Cambridge University Press, 1997.

Nicol, D. M.: *The Last Centuries of Byzantium, 1261-1453,* Cambridge, 1993.

Ocak, A. Yaşar: "XIV-XVI, Yüzyıllarda Kalenderi Dervişleri ve Osmanlı Yönetimi" (paper submitted to the Colloquium on "Saints and Sainthood in Islam,") Berkeley, April 1987.

Oğuz, Burhan: *Türkiye Halkının Kültür Kökenleri,* II-2; *Tarım Hayvancılık-Meteoroloji,* İstanbul, 1988.

Ökçün, A. Gündüz (ed.): *Türkiye Iktisat Kongresi, 1923-İzmir, Haberler—Belgeler-Yorumlar,* Ankara 1968: Atatürk's opening speech, 246, 253

Orhonlu, C.: *Telhîsler (1597-1604)* [Reports (1597-1604)], İstanbul, 1970.

Ostrorog, Count Léon: *The Angora Reform,* London: University of London Press, 1927.

Pannier, J.: "Calvin et les Turcs," *Revue Historique* 62 (1937); 268-286.

Paris, R.: *Histoire du commerce de Marseille,* Paris, 1997.

Parker, J. G.: *The Military Revolution, Military Innovation and the Rise of the West, 1500-1800,* Cambridge, 1988.

Pendergrass, J. N.: *Correspondence d'Antoine Arlier humaniste languedocien (1527-1547),* Geneva, 1990.

Perez, J.: "l'affrontement Turcs-Chrétiens vu d'Espagne, Le Voyage en Turquie," *Chrétiens et Musulmans a la Renaissance,* 255-263.

Petrovich, D.J. 1975. Fire-arms in the Balkans. In: Parry, V.J.; Yapp, M.E (eds). *War, Technology and Society in the Middle East.* London, Oxford University Press.

Puchner, W.: "Das osmanische Schattentheater auf der balkan Halbinsel," *Südost-Forschungen* 19 (1960): 151-188.

Quataert, D.: *Ottoman Manufacturing in the Age of the Industrial Revolution,* Cambridge: Cambridge University Press, 1993.

Ranke, L von: *The Ottoman and t he Spanish Empires in the Sixteenth and Seventeenth Centuries,* trans. W. R. Kelley, London, 1843.

Rázso, G.: "The Mercenary Army of King Matthias Corvinus, " ibid., 125-140. XXX

Reyhanlı, T.: *İngiliz Gezginlerine göre XVI. yüzyılda İstanbul'da Hayat* [Life in İstanbul in the sixteenth century according to the English travelers], Ankara, 1983.

Rogers, J. C.: "Ottomans, Hungarians, and Habsburgs in Central Europe: The Military Confines in the Era of Ottoman Conquest, " eds. G. Dávid, and P. Fodor, *The Ottoman Empire and Its Heritage* series, eds. S. Faroqhi and H. İnalcık, vol. 20, Cologne and Leiden: Brill, 2000. XXX

Rogers, J. C.: ed., Debate on *the Military Revolution,* Boulder, 1995.

Rouilard, C.: *The Turk in the French History, Thought and Literature, 1520-1660,* Paris, 1938.

Runciman, S.: *The Great Church in Captivity,* Cambridge, 1968.

Sahlins, M. D.: *Evolution and Culture,* Ann Arbor: Univ. of Michigan Press, 1960.

Sauzet, R.: "Les relations entre Chrétiens et musulmans du midi de la France, " *Chrétiens et Musulmans à la Renaissance.* 263-274.

Schmals, H.W.: *Versuche einer gesarnteuropalischen Organisation, 1815-1820,* Aarau, 1940.

Schwoebel, R.: *The Shadow of Crescent: The Renaissance Image of the Turk, 1453-1517,* New York, 1967.

Setton, K. M.: "Lutheranism and the Turkish Peril," *Balkan Studies,* vol. 3 (1962), 133-168.

Setton, K. M.: *Catalan Domination of Athens, 1311-1388,* London, 1975.

Setton, K. M.: *The Papacy and the Levant (1204-1571),* vol. 4 (Philadelphia, 1984).

Setton, Kenneth: *The Papacy and the Levant (1204-1571},* vols. 1 -4, Philadelphia, 1976-1984.

Shinder, J.: "Ottoman Bureaucracy in the Second Half of the Seventeenth Century: The Central and Naval Administration," Ph.D. diss., Princeton, 1971.

Soykut, M.: *Image of the "Turk" in Italy,* Berlin: Klaus Schwarz Verlag, 2001.

Spandounes, Theodore: *On the Origin of the Ottoman Emperors,* trans. D. M. Nicol, Cambridge, 1997.

Srbik, H.R. von: 'Metternichs Plan der Neuordnuung Europe 1815/15', *Mitteilungen des österreichischen Instituts für Geschichtsforschung,* 60, (1925), pp. 109-126;

Stein, M.: "Ottoman Fortresses in Hungary", Ph. D. diss., University of Chicago, Department of History, 2001.

Sungu, İhsan: "Yeni Osmanlılar", *Tanzimat,* I, İstanbul 1940.

The Letter of Tansar, trans. M. Boyce, Rome, 1968.

The Nasirean Ethics, trans. G. Wickens (London, 1964), p. 193.

Thou Jacques-Auquste de: *Histoire Universelle de Jacques-Auguste de Thou depuis 1543 jusqu'en 1607,* 16 vols. London. 1734.

Tietze, A., H. Kahane, and R. Kahane, *Lingua Franca in the Levant,* İstanbul, 1988.

Tilly, C.: *The Formation of National States in Western Europe* (Princeton, 1975).

Toledo, Paulino: "Türkiye Seyahati", [Trip to Turkey] (Ph. D. diss., Ankara University, Faculty of Language, History and Geography, 1992).

Tuncer, H.: *Metternich'in Osmanlı Politikası (1815-1848),* Ankara 1996.

Turan, Ş.: *Türkiye-İtalya İlişkileri* [Turkey-Italy relations], vol. 1, İstanbul, 1990.

Ülken, Hilmi Ziya: *Türk Düşünce Tarihi,* İstanbul, 1988.

Uzunçarşılı, İ. H.: *Osmanlı Devletinin Merkez ve Bahriye Teşkilâtı,* Ankara: TTK, 1948.

Valensi, L.: *Venise et La Sublime Porte,* Paris: Hachette, 1987.

Vaughan, D. M.: *Europe and the Turk, A Pattern of Alliances,* Liverpool, 1954.

Veinstein, G.: "Retour sur la question de la tolerance ottomane au XlVe siècle, " *Chrétiens et Musulmans à la Renaissance,* 415-426.

Veinstein, G.: *Le Paradis des Infidels,* Paris: F. Maspero, 1981.

Weber, Max: *Economy and Society: An Outline of Interpretive Sociology,* trans. G. Roth and C. Wittich, Berkeley: UCP, 1978.

Weber, Max: *On Law in Economy and Society,* trans. E. Shils and M. Rheinstein, ed. M. Rheinstein, New York: Clarion, 1954.

White, Charles: *Three Years in Constantinople or Domestic Manners of the Turks in 1844,* vols. 1-3. London, 1845.

Willan, T.S. 1955. Some aspects of Engilsh Trade with the Levant in the Sixteenth Century. *English Historical Review,* LXX.

Wirth, E. 1975. Die Orientalische Stadt. *Saeculum.* 26, pp. 75-94.

Halil İnalcık

Wittfogel, K. A.: *Oriental Despotism: A Comparative Study of Total Power,* New Haven, 1957.

XXX, "Islâh" *Encyclopaedia of Islam,* second edition, vol. IV, 141-71;

XXX, *Orient turc en France au XVIIIe siècle.* Paris, 1996.

Yücel, Y. (ed.), *Kitāb-i Müstetab, Osmanlı Devlet Teşkilâtına Dair Kaynaklar,* Ankara, 1988.

Zabıtlar Ceridesi, Devre II, cilt VIII, 3-6.

- § -